365
SIMPLE SCIENCE
EXPERIMENTS

365 SIMPLE SCIENCE EXPERIMENTS

with everyday materials

By E. Richard Churchill, Louis V. Loeschnig, and Muriel Mandell

Illustrated by Frances Zweifel

Sterling Publishing Co., Inc.
New York

1   3   5   7   9   10   8   6   4   2

Published by Sterling Publishing Company, Inc.
387 Park Avenue South, New York, N.Y. 10016
Compilation © 1997 by Sterling Publishing Company
This edition was originally published in hard cover by
Black Dog & Levanthal Publishers, Inc.
It contains the reorganized and reset texts of the following works:
Simple Science Experiments with Everyday Materials © 1989 by Muriel Mandell;
Simple Weather Experiments with Everyday Materials © 1990 by Muriel Mandell;
Amazing Science Experiments with Everyday Materials © 1991 by E. Richard Churchill;
Simple Chemistry Experiments with Everyday Materials © 1994 by Louis V. Loeschnig, and
Simple Earth Science Experiments with Everyday Materials © 1989 by Louis V. Loeschnig
Distributed in Canada by Sterling Publishing
c/o Canadian Manda Group, One Atlantic Avenue, Suite 105
Toronto, Ontario, Canada M6K 3E7
Distributed in Great Britain and Europe by Chris Lloyd
463 Ashley Road, Parkstone, Poole, Dorset, BH14 0AX, England
Distributed in Australia by Capricorn Link (Australia) Pty Ltd.
P.O. Box 6651, Baulkham Hills, Business Centre, NSW 2153, Australia

Printed in China
All rights reserved

Sterling ISBN 0-8069-1789-X

CONTENTS

Soap Suds *Page 70*

Slow Start—Fast Finish *Page 81*

Keeping Your Balance *Page 89*

How to Have All the Moves *Page 95*

The Sound of Science *Page 103*

Feeling Stressed? Try Some Surface Tension *Page 111*

INTRODUCTION

Science experiments aren't just for scientists and college students. They are fun for everybody—and that includes you. What's even better, all the experiments in this book have a surprise in them. Some of them will surprise you because they work. Others are surprising because of what happens.

You may decide that some of these experiments are really stunts or tricks. That's true. Some of them are, but it is also true that lots of the best stunts and tricks work because they are based on scientific principles. This book just helps you to put science to work in ways that may seem impossible, but which are always fun and entertaining.

The first five chapters show you how the most ordinary materials—drinking straws, paper, lemons, eggs, cooking oil, string, and soap—can be used in extraordinary ways. From these remarkable projects you will learn how to taste electricity with a lemon, make a water trombone with a drinking straw, and use a spot of butter to tell which light bulb is brighter.

The seven chapters that follow include more than seventy easy-to-do experiments that will surprise, astound, startle, and delight you—and your friends. You'll learn how to catch a coin on your elbow, mysteriously balance a dinner fork, amplify sound with a balloon, tune a glass, break up rays of sunlight, and empty a glass by blowing on it. And, best of all, you will learn why each experiment works while you're having a great time!

The next section shows you how, using everyday supplies like bottles, jars, newspaper, magnets, potting soil, clay, and sand, you can explore the mysterious forces that affect the earth. Discover how earthquakes, light, energy, erosion, and other factors change the face of the planet. You'll learn how magnetism and electricity are related earth forces. Make a pin on a thread sway like a dancing cobra and discover how business security people catch fake coins, or slugs, in vending machines—both by using magnetic force. You'll see how earthquakes are produced and tidal waves, too.

The experiments in the next four chapters are related to weather. From these exciting projects you'll find out about many of the mysteries of climate and weather. You'll learn why the North Pole is colder than the equator, why the sun sets, and what causes thunder and lightning. You'll be able to make your own weather station, putting together the instruments you need to keep track of temperature, air pressure, wind direction and speed, humidity and rainfall.

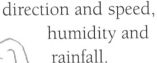

The final three chapters include dozens of sensational experiments and activities that give you a chance to do some real chemistry. A few involve serious chemical changes, like removing salt from water and making your own litmus paper from berries to test for acids and bases. Other experiments may look more like magic tricks, but they all deal with molecules or chemical changes. Try blowing up a rubber glove using a famous gas that chemists study. Pour water into a bottle without actually filling it and make paper worms that really crawl.

You can start with any experiment in any chapter, but you will get the most out of this book if you take one chapter at a time and do most of the experiments in order.

In a few of the projects, you'll need to use a stove, boiling water, or a safety match and these are labelled HOT! You can see them at a glance and get an adult to help you. We'll also let you know when any experiments will involve construction, and alert you to safety concerns.

All the materials needed for the projects are inexpensive and easy to find. You can find most of them around your house. The rest can be found in supermarkets, variety stores, and drugstores. Some materials are used for

many experiments so it might be a good idea for you to begin saving such things as various-size bottles and jars, coffee cans, shoe boxes, small plastic or clay flower pots, plastic spoons, drinking straws, coffee filters, medicine droppers, newspaper, paper clips, quart milk cartons, large plastic soda bottles, a magnifying glass, toy compass, bar and horseshoe magnets, scissors, pencils, paper, protractor, potting soil, gravel, clay, and sand. It is best to check with an adult before using or taking any materials needed for your experiments. You might also want to keep all your science equipment in a special cupboard or box. Besides being safely stored, it will be easy to find and ready for you whenever you want to do some experiments.

All the experiments have been simplified and thoroughly tested—they do work. If one doesn't seem to work for you, just re-read the instructions and try it again. When you get everything just right, the experiment will work. That's a promise! Some of the experiments, however, like those that involve living plants and seeds are long term—take time and patience.

So now the fun will begin and many of the mysteries of science will be revealed to you. We wish you many happy hours and successful experiments! Have fun!

CLUTCHING AT STRAWS

An ordinary drinking straw can become an atomizer, a medicine dropper, an oboe or a trombone, a scale—and more!

About Straws

What is a straw? The dictionary defines it as a stalk or stem of dried, threshed grain, like wheat, rye, oats, and barley. The first drinking straws were cut from stalks of grain. That's how they got their name.

The first paper straw was patented in 1888 by Marvin Chester Stone of Washington D.C. It was rolled by hand from manila paper and coated with paraffin. Drinking straws were handmade until 1905 when Stone's company invented the first successful straw-making machine. Today drinking straws are made of paper or plastic.

1 Make a Paper Straw

Cut out a strip of paper 2 inches x 10 inches (5 cm x 25 cm). Holding the paper at one corner, start rolling it diagonally in a narrow cylinder shape until it is all rolled up. Then fasten the sides with tape.

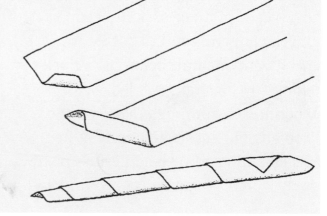

2 How Does a Straw Work?

Do you think you use a straw to pull liquid up into your mouth? Not so!

What to do: Suck a little water into the straw. Then hold your finger across the top of the straw and take the straw out of the water. Place the straw over the empty glass. Then remove your finger from the top of the straw.

What happens: While your finger covers the top of the straw, the water remains in the straw. When you remove your finger, the water flows out.

Why: Your finger on top of the straw lessens the pressure of the air from above the straw. The greater pressure of air under the straw holds the water inside it.

When you suck through the straw, you are not actually pulling the liquid up. What you are really doing is removing some of the air inside the straw. This makes the pressure inside the straw lower than the pressure outside. The greater pressure of the outside air then pushes the water in the glass up through the straw and into your mouth.

A pipette, a tube scientists use to measure and transfer a liquid from one container to another, works the same way.

3 Make a Medicine Dropper

You can make a regular drinking straw into a medicine dropper. Suck up some liquid into the straw. Hold it in the straw by covering the top of the straw with your finger. Then bend your finger slightly and raise and lower your fingertip so that the liquid flows out one drop at a time.

Experiment with the straw until you get the knack of it. It's easy to do.

Make a Straw Atomizer

This is the way window-cleaning sprays and perfume atomizers work.

YOU WILL NEED:
drinking straw
scissors
glass of water

What to do: About one–third of the distance from one end of the straw, cut a horizontal slit. Bend the straw at the slit and slip the short section into a glass of water, keeping the slit about ¼ inch (6 mm) above the surface of the water.

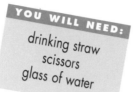

Blow hard through the long section of the straw.

What happens: Water enters the straw from the glass and comes out through the slit as a spray.

Why: As you blow through the long section of the straw, a stream of air flows over the top of the short section, reducing the pressure at that point. As normal pressure underneath forces water up into the straw, the moving air blows it off in drops. In atomizers and spray cans, you use a pump to blow in air.

Make a Straw Oboe

YOU WILL NEED:
drinking straw
scissors

The first wind instruments were probably hollow reeds picked and played by shepherds in the field. You can make music with a straw.

What to do: Pinch flat ½ inch to ¾ inch (12 mm to 19 mm) at one end of the straw. Cut off little triangles from the corners to form wedges, or reeds. Put the straw far enough into your mouth so your lips don't touch the corners. Don't pucker your lips, but blow hard. Cut three small slits along the length of the straw about 1 inch (2.5 cm) apart. Separate the slits so they form small round holes. Cover one of them and blow. Then cover two, then three, blowing each time.

What happens: Each time you blow, you hear a different sound. You can play simple tunes by covering and uncovering the holes.

Why: As in a real oboe, the two wedges, the reeds, opening and closing at high speed, first allow air to flow into the straw and then stop the flow. Vibrating air creates the sound. As you cover and uncover the holes, you regulate the length of the air column and that determines the pitch. The shorter the air column, the faster it vibrates and the higher the note.

Make a Water Trombone

6

With a soda bottle, some water, and a straw you can make a slide trombone.

YOU WILL NEED:
water
empty soda bottle
drinking straw

What to do: Pour water into the bottle until it is about three-quarters full. Put the straw into the bottle. Blow across the top of the straw. Then either lower the bottle or lift the straw and continue to blow.

What happens: As you lower the bottle, the sound gets lower in pitch.

Why: You are lengthening the column of air in the straw. This is how a slide trombone works.

Bend a Straw Without Touching It

7

You can "bend" a straw without touching it!

YOU WILL NEED:
drinking glass
water
drinking straw

What to do: Half fill the glass with water. Put the straw into the glass. Look at it from the top, the bottom, and the sides.

What happens: When you look at the straw from the side of the glass, it appears to be bent or broken at the point where it enters the water.

Why: We see an object because rays of light come to our eyes from it. Light rays travel more slowly through glass and water than through air. Therefore, light from the part of the straw in the water reaches our eyes later than the part that is above the water, and the straw appears bent.

21

Straw Balance Scale

8

This balance can actually be a real scale. All you have to do is "calibrate" it—figure out what its movements mean by checking out items you already know.

YOU WILL NEED:
scissors
small paper cup
drinking straw
pencil eraser cap
large needle
index card
pencil
large spool of thread

What to do: Make two oblong notches on opposite sides of the paper cup. (See A.)

Cut away part of one end of the straw to form a little scoop. (See B.) Fit the eraser cap on the other end of the straw. Pad it with a little paper if it is too large. (See C.)

Push the needle through one side of the cup. Pull out the eraser head a little so the straw slants slightly upward. (See E.)

Tape the index card to the pencil and stand it in the spool. Place the spool so the straw's scoop falls across the index card. (See F.) You can mark the weight of things you weigh on the card.

Your scale is finished: Try it out by placing a few grains of sugar in the scoop, or by hanging a paper clip from it.

What happens: The straw moves down.

Why: Your scale is a lever. It acts like a seesaw. The place at which the lever rests (the needle) is called the fulcrum. When the straw lies flat, the distance and the weight on one side of the needle balance out the distance and the weight on the other side. As you add weight, you change the relationship between the two sides of the needle.

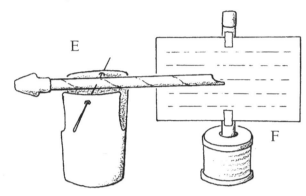

Finding the Center of Gravity

9

Figure out the point at which the straw balances. Do this by hanging the straw on the spine of a book or on the edge of an upright metal ruler. Move the straw about until it doesn't fall off. It will probably be fairly close to the eraser. Mark that point of balance with a pencil.

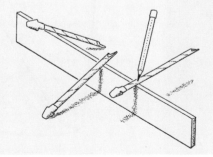

22

Spear a Potato

YOU WILL NEED:
raw baking potato
paper drinking straw

Would you think an ordinary drinking straw could pierce a potato without destroying itself?

What to do: Soak the potato in water for about thirty minutes before trying this experiment. Then, with one fast strong push, thrust the straw straight down into the potato.

What happens: The straw pierces the potato without buckling or bending.

Why: Inertia is the tendency of objects to continue whatever they are doing. An object at rest (the potato) tends to remain at rest while an object that is moving (the straw) tends to keep moving in the same direction.

Straws that grow in fields have been driven into—and through—planks of wooden barns and houses when propelled by tornado-force winds.

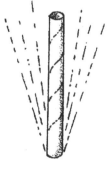

Straw Wheels

Do wheels make work easier? See for yourself.

What to do: Place the book on a table and try to push it. Then place the straws on the table and put the book on top of the straws. Push the book.

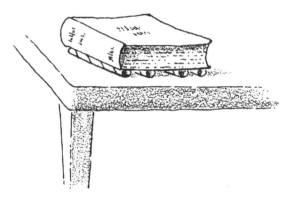

What happens: Without the straws, you have to push hard to move the book. With the straws, the book moves more easily.

Why: When one item rubs against another, it resists moving because both surfaces are not completely smooth. The bumps of one surface (the book) catch against the bumps in the other (the table). The amount of this resistance, known as friction, depends on the kinds of surfaces and the forces pressing them together. The rougher the surfaces, the greater the friction. The greater the weight of the objects, the greater the friction. Rolling results in less friction than sliding.

PAPER CAPERS

Charm a paper snake, electrify
an ordinary newspaper, step
through an index card,
and defy gravity.

About Paper

Paper is believed to
have been invented
by Ts'ai Lung
almost two thousand years ago in China.
Chinese paper was a mixture of rags and
plant fiber.

The craft of papermaking didn't spread
to Europe until twelve hundred years later.
Until 1700, paper was made from cotton
and linen fibers.

Paper was made by hand, one sheet at a
time. In 1798, Nicholas Robert of France
invented the first machine to make paper,
which he sold to Henry and Sealy
Fourdrinier of England. Papermaking
machines are still known as Fourdriniers.

Today paper is thin flat sheets of tissue
made usually from wood pulp.

The many types of paper include stationery, wax paper, cardboard, contact
paper, oaktag, newspaper, wallpaper, index
cards, boxes, and wrapping paper.

Shaping Up

YOU WILL NEED:

4 sheets of
computer paper
transparent tape
can
books

Which of these shapes
do you think is the
strongest? No matter
what materials you are working
with you can make a structure stronger by
simply changing its shape.

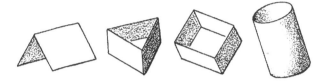

What to do: Fold the sheets of paper into various shapes, such as those shown in the illustrations.

1. Fold a sheet of paper in half and stand it on its edges.

 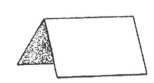

2. Fold a sheet of paper in thirds and tape the ends together.

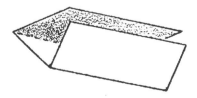

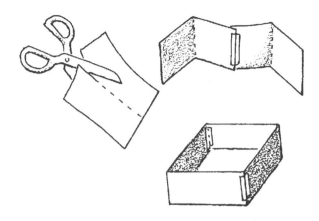

3. Fold a sheet of paper in half lengthwise, cut on the fold, and tape the two halves together at the top and bottom. Then fold the attached halves in half again from top to bottom. Spread the sheets to form the cube.

4. Roll a sheet of paper around the can, secure the paper with tape, then remove the can.

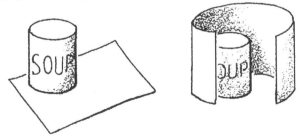

Put a light book on top of each shape. Some will collapse immediately. Keep piling books on the others until they collapse.

What happens: The round paper pillar holds a surprising number of books.

Why: A hollow tube is the strongest because the weight is distributed evenly over it.

Corrugated Paper

What makes a corrugated box strong?

YOU WILL NEED:

3 sheets of computer paper

jar

What to do: Make a crease about ¼ inch (6 mm) from the edge of one sheet of paper. Fold it down and press down on the folds. Using the first fold as a guide, fold a second crease back. Alternate folding back and forth until the entire sheet is pleated, as in the illustration.

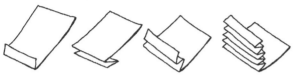

Roll the second sheet of paper around a can and tape the ends together. Remove the can. Do the same thing with the third sheet of paper. Line up the two circles of paper 4 inches (10 cm) from one another on a table. Then place the pleated sheet on them. Rest the jar on top of the pleated sheet.

What happens: The pleated paper holds the jar.

Why: You have added strength by using corrugated paper, which you created by folding the sheet back and forth. An engineer devised this way of making paper stiffer—and stronger.

Powerful Paper

Just how strong can paper get?

YOU WILL NEED:

corrugated carton
scissors
large fruit juice can
rubber bands or masking tape
small board
(a cutting board will do)

What to do: Cut a strip about 4 inches x 12 inches (10 cm x 30 cm) from the corrugated carton. Wrap the strip around the can and secure it with rubber bands or masking tape. Then remove the can.

Place a small board on top of the cardboard circle. Stand on it.

What happens: The cardboard circle will hold your weight.

Why: The strength comes from the combination of the circular shape and the corrugated paper.

Tough Newspaper

15

Your strongest blow cannot budge this fearless newspaper!

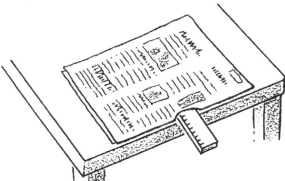

What to do: Place the ruler on the table so that 2 inches (5 cm) projects over the edge. Spread a double sheet of newspaper over the ruler so the paper lies flat along the table edge.

Strike the projecting edge of the ruler as hard as you can.

What happens: The newspaper doesn't budge.

Why: Air pressure on the paper prevents it from moving. Air pushes down with almost 15 pounds of pressure on almost every inch of surface (1 kg per square centimeter). For an average sheet of newspaper, the total resistance is about two tons.

Invisible Shield

16

If you've ever been caught in the rain and tried to keep dry by putting a newspaper over your head, you know that water doesn't treat paper very well. But in the following experiment the paper seems to be protected by an invisible shield.

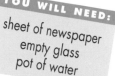

What to do: Crumple the sheet of newspaper and stuff it into the empty glass tightly enough so that it doesn't fall out when you turn the glass upside down. Holding the glass bottom up, sink it deep into the pot filled with water. Hold it there. After a minute or so, pull the glass out of the water and remove the paper.

What happens: The paper is dry.

Why: Water cannot get into the glass because the " empty" glass is already filled with air and the air cannot get out because it is lighter than water.

Why No Flood?

Until you learn how to do this experiment perfectly (and maybe even then), it's best to do it over a sink or basin.

What to do: Place the cardboard over the drinking glass which you have filled to the brim with water.

Make sure no air bubbles enter the glass as you hold the cardboard against it. Then turn the glass upside down over a sink or basin. Take away the hand holding the cardboard.

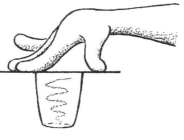

What happens: The cardboard stays in place—and the water stays in the glass.

Why: The pressure of the air outside the glass is greater than the pressure of the water inside. It is the air pressure that keeps the water in the glass.

The Paper Napkin Trick

It's a good idea to practice this trick, too, where spilled water won't do any harm.

What to do: Drape the napkin over the edge of a kitchen counter or table. Place the plastic cup of water on one corner of the napkin about 1 inch (2.5 cm) from the edge.

Pull the napkin quickly away from under the plastic cup.

What happens: The napkin comes out—without any water spilling.

Why: The cup doesn't overturn because of the tendency of things at rest to stay at rest. It's that old law of motion—inertia—at work. If it does spill it's because you're not pulling the napkin fast enough or with enough force.

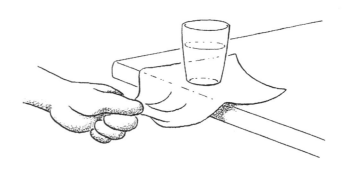

Cantilever Bridge

A cantilever bridge is built with two beams that project toward each other to join and form a span.

What to do: Stack the notebooks on the edge of the table. Slide the top book halfway out from the stack and over the table's edge. When it balances, slide it back a little. Move out the next notebook along with the top one until they balance, and then slide them back a little. Add another notebook and move the top three out and slide them back a little after they balance. Continue in the same way until all six notebooks are staggered.

What happens: The top notebook seems to be suspended in air, but the notebooks do not fall.

Why: You have found the center of gravity, the point at which all the weight of an object seems to be concentrated. Although the top book appears to be suspended in air, more than half the weight of the stack of notebooks is resting on the table.

Flash!

You will need a friend to help you with this experiment.

What to do: Rub the sheet of newspaper vigorously with the plastic wrap for about 30 seconds. Then place the top of the can in the center of the newspaper. Holding the newspaper by its edges, lift it while your friend puts a finger near the metal.

What happens: A spark!

Why: When an electrical charge passes between two objects, the result is a spark. As you rubbed the newspaper, you charged it with static electricity. Your friend's touch made the electrical charge jump from the paper to the uncharged can lid.

You may have seen a similar spark when you've walked on a carpet and then touched a doorknob. Or you may have heard a crackling sound while you combed your hair. These are all examples of static electricity.

Lightning is a huge electric spark that results when charges jump from one cloud to another or from a cloud to the ground.

21

Charming a Paper Snake

It's easier than you think to charm a snake.

YOU WILL NEED:

thin cardboard or heavy
paper
scissors
string
lamp or heated radiator
straight pin
pencil with an eraser
spool of thread

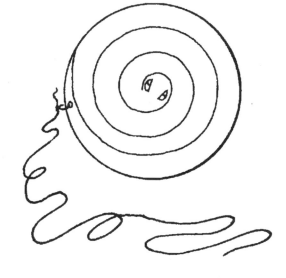

What to do: Draw a spiral snake (as in the illustration) on thin cardboard or any slightly heavy paper, such as oaktag or a large index card.

Cut out the spiral snake and tie a string to its "tail."

Suspend the snake over a lighted bulb or a heated radiator.

What happens: The snake dances.

Why: Hot air is less dense than cold air and therefore it rises. The moving air spins the spiral snake.

To make a stand for your snake: With a pin, attach the head to the eraser end of a pencil, letting the snake curl around the pencil. Stand the pencil in the center hole of the spool of thread.

Dancing Dolls

Did you ever think you'd see paper dolls dance?

YOU WILL NEED:

piece of stiff paper, like oaktag

pencil

scissors

glue or tape

large sheet of cardboard

2 paper clips

magnet

What to do: Fold the stiff paper from top to bottom twice. Draw the right half of a doll along the exposed top fold, extending the doll's arm and leg to the bottom of the exposed fold, as in the illustration.

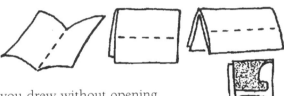

Cut along the lines you drew without opening the folded paper. Form a circle of dolls by gluing or taping the two ends of the group together. Attach the paper clips so that the dolls stand on them.

Balance the large sheet of cardboard so a portion of it hangs over the edge of a table. Stand the circle of paper dolls on top of the cardboard so that one of the clips is on the overhanging portion.

Move your magnet underneath the cardboard—first to the right and then to the left.

What happens: The paper dolls dance.

Why: The paper clips are made of steel. Therefore the magnet attracts them—even through the cardboard.

YOU WILL NEED:
sheet of paper
scissors
glue or tape
pencil

You can cause paper to have only one side! This surprising phenomenon was first discovered by a nineteenth-century German mathematician, August Ferdinand Moebius.

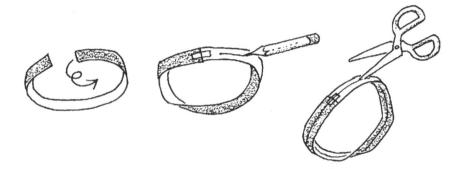

What to do: Cut a strip of paper 1 inch x 10 inches (2.5 cm x 25 cm). Give one end a half twist and tape or glue the ends together to form a loop.

Draw a lengthwise line down the center of the strip until you reach your starting point.

Cut along the line you have drawn.

What happens: There is no side without a line! And you have only one loop, which is twice as long as your original loop.

Why: No one has been able to explain this strange "trick." But it has actually been put to practical use. Ordinarily, the fan belts in cars and factory conveyor belts wear out faster on the inside than the outside. But belts made with a half twist like this wear out more evenly and more slowly.

Through the Index Card

YOU WILL NEED:
large index card
or a piece of
computer paper
scissors

Alice stepped through a magic looking glass—which seemed impossible. You can do the "impossible" too—stretch a very ordinary index card and step through it!

What to do: Fold the card or paper down the middle from top to bottom. Then make seven or nine deep cuts (any odd number will do) alternating with one cut starting at the fold and the other starting at the edge of the card. Unfold the index card and stretch it out.

What happens: You can step through the paper without tearing it.

Why: Because of the way you cut the card, you stretch it first from one side and then from the other. In each case, the opposite side holds firm.

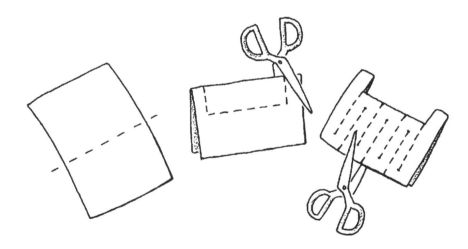

Color Fun

25

Is green really green?

YOU WILL NEED:
strip of paper towel
green felt-tipped pen
or 1 drop of green
food coloring
jar or glass with
1 inch (2.5 cm) of water

What to do: Make a spot of color about 2 inches (5 cm) from one end of the strip of paper towel. Hang the strip in the jar so that the spot is above the water and the end of the strip is in the water. Let it stand for 15 to 20 minutes.

What happen: The green spot is gone, but above the original spot the paper has turned blue, and above that the paper is yellow.

Why: Most dyes and inks are combinations of coloring substances which can be taken apart by adding water or alcohol. Water moves up the paper in the same way as sap rises in trees. As the water moves up, it dissolves the green spot and gradually moves the color up the strip of paper. But since the colors that make up green—blue and yellow—do not move at the same rate, they separate.

Magic Color

26

Mix colors the easy way!

YOU WILL NEED:
small plate
cardboard
pencil
scissors
watercolors or
poster paints
hole punch
string

What to do: Using the plate as a pattern, draw a circle on the cardboard. Cut out the circle. Paint one side red and the other side blue. Punch small holes on the opposite sides of the disk, as in the illustration, and thread short lengths of string through each hole.

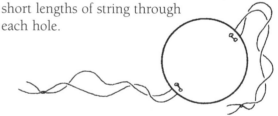

Hold the circle by its strings and twirl it around.

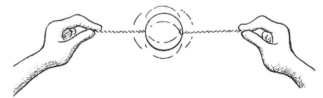

What happens: The color you see is purple.

Why: The eye continues to see each color for a while after it has disappeared, and so your eye and your brain mix the colors of the rapidly whirling disk.

What happens if you make one side red and the other yellow?

Benham Disk

27

The hand is quicker than the eye. Well, is it really? Is it magic, illusion, or trickery?

What to do: Cut a circle 4 inches (10 cm) in diameter out of white paper. Color one half black. Divide the white half into four equal parts. In each segment draw three black arcs about ¾ inch (19 mm) thick, as in the illustration.

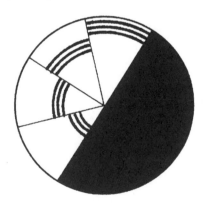

Cut a circle 4 inches (10 cm) in diameter out of the cardboard. Place the paper circle on the cardboard circle.

Mount them together on a pin attached to a pencil eraser.

Spin the disk at various speeds, clockwise and counterclockwise.

What happens:
The arcs seem to close up to form six rings.

At a slow speed, spinning clockwise, the outer rings look blue and the inner rings look red. When you spin them counterclockwise, the colors reverse.

Why: The arcs seem to close to form rings, because the eye continues to see each arc for a short time after it has disappeared.

Why do we see red and blue when the only colors on the disk are black and white? The entire color spectrum is present in white light, but our eyes register the different colors at different lengths of time.

When we spin the disk, light from the colors that make up white reach the eye, but are visible for only an instant before being followed by the black portions of the disk. Our eye is only able to register a part of that color spectrum—the blue, which has the shortest rays, and the red, which has the longest.

Try varying the patterns on the white half of your Benham Disk and see what interesting results you get.

MORE THAN LEMONADE

With a little ingenuity, you can turn an ordinary lemon into invisible ink, cleaning fluid, a rock tester, a rocket launcher, and a wet cell.

About Lemons

The lemon probably came to us from India.

The small thorn-branched lemon tree was first planted in the United States during the California Gold Rush of 1849 to fight scurvy among the prospectors.

Lemon juice will remove rust, ink, and mildew stains. Oil from the lemon skin is used to flavor extracts, perfumes, cosmetics, and furniture polish.

Lemon juice is the main source of citric acid, which is used in textile printing to keep the fabric clear of rust stains from the machinery.

28

Invisible Ink

You can use a lemon to write a secret message.

YOU WILL NEED:

½ lemon
saucer
water
teaspoon
cotton swab
white paper
lamp

What to do: Squeeze the lemon juice into the saucer. Add a few drops of water and mix well with the spoon. Dip the swab into the lemon juice. Then use the swab to write a message on ordinary white paper. When it dries, the writing will be invisible. When you want to read the message, heat the paper by holding it near a light bulb.

What happens: The words appear on the page.

Why: The juice of lemons and other fruits contain compounds of carbon. These compounds are nearly colorless when you dissolve them in water. But, when you heat them, the carbon compounds break down and produce carbon, which is black.

29 Lemon Cleaning Fluid

Don't taste! Iodine is poisonous

Write an invisible message with flour and water and make it appear with iodine. Then use lemon to make it disappear again.

What to do: In the saucer, use the teaspoon to mix the flour and water together. When the mixture is smooth, dip a cotton swab into it. Then use the swab to write a message on the paper towel. When the message dries, it will be invisible.

When you are ready to read the message, use a clean swab to apply a few drops of iodine. Your message will appear in blue-black.

Then dab on a few drops of lemon juice.

What happens: Your message disappears.

Why: The iodine reacts with the flour, a starch, to form a new compound that appears as blue-black.

When you apply the lemon juice, the ascorbic acid (Vitamin C) of the lemon combines with the iodine to make a new colorless compound. So, if you spill iodine on anything, you can use lemon juice to remove it. Lemon juice will also remove ink, mildew, and rust stains from paper and cloth.

30 Bright as a Penny

Soap and water won't clean metals very easily. That takes a special cleaner—or you can try lemon juice!

What to do: Squeeze the lemon juice into the glass. Soak the coin in lemon juice for 5 minutes.

What happens: You fish out a shiny coin!

Why: Oxygen in the air combined with the copper to form the dull copper oxide coating. The acid of the lemon acts chemically to remove the oxide—and the result? A bright copper penny. Vinegar will work the same way.

Nifty Nail

31

Dig out that pile of pennies you've been saving and make yourself a copper-plated nail.

What to do: Squeeze the lemon juice into the glass. Put the pennies into the glass a few at a time. The lemon juice should cover them. Add a pinch of salt. Let the pennies stand for 3 minutes.

Meanwhile, clean the nail with scouring powder and water. Put the nail into the glass.

Wait at least 15 minutes, then fish out the nail.

What happens: The nail is coated with copper.

Why: Copper from the pennies interacts with the acid of the lemon juice to form a new compound (copper citrate). When you put the nail into the solution, the compound plates the nail with a thin layer of copper that cannot be rubbed off.

After you've got your copper nail, you might want to wear it on a string.

Lemon— Save that Apple!

32

Lemon can also keep apples fresh.

What to do: Cut the apple into four parts. Put the apple pieces on the plate then squeeze lemon juice on two of them. Let all the apple pieces stand for 3 hours.

What happens: The pieces of apple that were not treated with lemon turn brown. The apple pieces that were doctored with lemon juice do not.

Why: When exposed to air, certain chemicals in the apple react by destroying cells, which turn brown. But the Vitamin C (ascorbic acid) in the lemon slows down the reaction between the chemicals in the fruit and the oxygen in the air. This preserves the color and the taste of the apple.

Make Red Cabbage "Litmus" Paper

What to do: Strain the liquid from the jar of red cabbage into another wide–mouthed jar. (Or you can make you own with the help of an adult: Grate half a small red cabbage. Put the grated cabbage into a pot with 1 cup of water. Boil for 15 minutes. Let the red cabbage juice cool and then strain it into a wide-mouthed jar.)

Cut 2 inch (5 cm) strips of paper toweling. Soak the paper strips in the cabbage juice for 1 minute, then let them dry. Your "litmus" paper is now ready for testing. It will turn red-pink in acid and green in alkali. You can also experiment and make indicators from fruits, flowers, other vegetables, and even tea. But the color changes will be different.

The litmus paper used in schools and in chemistry labs is colored by lichen plants, a kind of fungus.

Acid or Base

Use your red cabbage indicator to determine which foods are acid and which are alkali.

What to do: Pour 1 tablespoon of red cabbage juice into each glass. Add lemon juice to one; grapefruit juice to the second; tomato or pineapple juice to a third; vinegar to the fourth. Then test baking soda, milk, rubbing alcohol, oil, soap, and other household products.

Those that turn pink are acids. Those that turn green are alkali (bases).

Lemon—Life Saver

35

Poison control centers used to recommend lemon juice or vinegar as an antidote for some poisons. This experiment shows why. You will need "litmus" paper. But that's no problem. You can use the liquid of red cabbage to make your own. (See page 39 for instructions.)

What to do: Apply a few drops of lemon juice to one strip of "litmus" paper. Add a few drops of ammonia to a second strip. Then apply a few drops of lemon juice to the spot made by the ammonia.

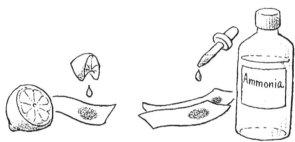

What happens: The strip with the lemon juice on it turns pink. The strip with the ammonia added turns green. When you add lemon to the green ammonia spot, it returns to its original reddish purple color.

Why: The pink color indicates the presence of acid because lemon is a mild acid, a nonmetal combined with hydrogen.

The green color indicates the presence of alkali because ammonia is an alkali (otherwise known as a base), a metal combined with hydroxide. The "litmus" paper returns it to its original color when the ammonia is acted against—neutralized—by the lemon, its chemical opposite.

What does all this have to do with poison? Ammonia is poisonous if someone drinks it. Since lemon neutralizes ammonia, it was once recommended as a temporary antidote, just enough to last until the person could get to a doctor. The current emergency treatment for accidentally drinking a poison, like ammonia, is to dilute it in the stomach by drinking large amounts of water or milk.

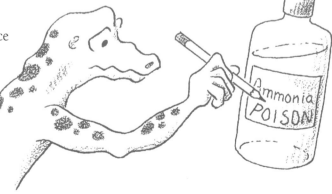

Blowing up a Balloon

Put chemistry to work for you! This experiment will also work if you substitute 2 ounces (60 ml) of vinegar for the lemon juice.

YOU WILL NEED:
balloon
1 ounce (30 ml) of water
empty soda bottle
1 teaspoon of baking soda
drinking straw
juice of 1 lemon

What to do: Stretch the balloon to make it easier to inflate. Pour the water into the clean, empty soda bottle. Add the baking soda and stir with the straw until it has dissolved. Pour in the lemon juice, then quickly fit the stretched balloon over the mouth of the bottle.

What happens: The balloon inflates.

Why: When you mix the base (the baking soda) and the acid (the lemon), you create carbon dioxide, a gas that rises into the balloon and blows it up.

Rock Tester

YOU WILL NEED:
Small sampling of various small rocks, including limestone or marble
2 ounces (60 ml) of lemon juice

37

How do geologists identify their specimens? This is one way. It is best to do this experiment in a sink or basin. Vinegar may be substituted for the lemon juice.

What to do: Pour the lemon juice over the rocks.

What happens: The liquid bubbles on some, but not on others.

Why: When the lemon juice bubbles, the rock sample is either limestone or marble. Limestone, a sedimentary rock formed under water from mud and silt, contains a carbonate form of calcium, an alkaline earth metal. When you add the lemon (an acid) to the alkaline of the limestone, it forms carbon dioxide. That makes the liquid bubble up, just as pancakes and cakes puff up when you add baking soda to the batter. Actually, baking soda can be made from limestone. Marble is a rock formed under great heat and pressure from limestone. It reacts to acid just as limestone does.

You get similar results if you add lemon juice to chalk, because it, too, is made of limestone.

Turn That Lemon On

You can make electricity with your lemon!

38

YOU WILL NEED:

2 stiff copper wires
large paper clip
lemon
scissors
galvanometer (see
page 43 for instructions
to make your own)

What to do: If there is any insulation on the ends of the wire, strip it off. Untwist the paper clip and attach it to an end of one of the wires. Squeeze and roll the lemon to loosen the pulp inside. Make two small cuts in the skin of the lemon about 1 inch (2.5 cm) apart. Insert the bare wire and the paper clip through the skin of the lemon and into the juicy part. The two wires should be close to each other but not touching.

Connect the free ends of the two wires to the terminals of the meter (or to the free ends of the wires of the homemade galvanometer).

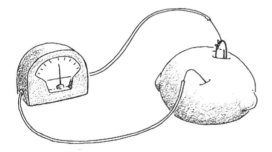

What happens: The meter moves.

Why: Chemical reactions of the two different metals (the copper of the wire and the iron of the clip) in the acid (lemon juice) draw electrons away from one wire toward the other. They flow out of the lemon through one wire, go through the meter, and then enter the lemon by the other wire.

39

Light Up a Bulb

If your hardware or electrical supply store can provide a bulb of less than 1.5 volts, try connecting several lemons and see how many lemon wet cells it will take to light the bulb. Line up the lemons so you can link them to one another with a bare copper wire and a clip in each, as in the illustration. You should end up with two free wire ends, one attached to a clip. Connect these wire ends to the bulb.

42

A Taste of Electricity

40

If you touch the two wires that you've inserted in the lemon to your tongue at the same time, you will taste something metallic and feel a slight tingling sensation. You are tasting and feeling electricity!

YOU WILL NEED:

compass (from a stationery store)

15 feet (4.5 m) of bell wire (from the hardware store)

small rectangular cardboard box

Make a Galvanometer

41

A galvanometer is an instrument designed to detect electric currents. You can make one with a few simple materials.

What to do: Place the compass in the center of the box. Scrape off about ½ inch (6 mm) of insulation from each end of the bell wire. Starting about 6 inches (15 cm) from one end, wind the wire tightly around the box, circling it about twenty-four times. Leave another 6 inches (15 cm) of wire free on the other side of the box.

Rest your galvanometer on the table so it is horizontal and turn it until the compass needle is parallel to the coil of wire.

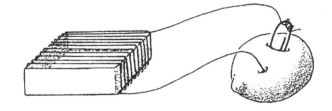

Attach the bell wire ends to the wires of the lemon cell.

42 Shock Them All!

Want to shock your friends? You can do it by repeating an experiment first done two hundred years ago by the Italian physicist Alessandro Volta.

YOU WILL NEED:

lemon
smalll dish
9 1 inch x 2 inch
(2.5 cm x 5 cm) strips of
paper towel
5 pennies or other
copper coins
5 dimes (or any other
coins that are not copper)

What to do: Squeeze the lemon juice into the small dish. Soak the paper towel strips in the lemon juice. Make a pile of coins, alternating the dimes and the pennies and separating each one with a lemon-soaked strip of paper towel.

Moisten one fingertip on each hand and hold the pile between your fingers.

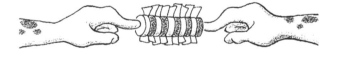

What happens: You get a small shock or tingle.

Why: You have made a wet cell, the forerunner of the battery we buy at the hardware store. The lemon juice, an acid solution, conducts the electricity created by the separated metals of the two coins.

What we call a battery is actually two or more dry cells. In each dry cell, thirty–two metals (a zinc metal container and a carbon rod) are separated by blotting paper soaked in a strong acid.

Make Your Own Lemon Soda

YOU WILL NEED:

lemon
measuring cup
large glass
water
1 teaspoon of baking soda
sugar, to taste

43

You can make a bubbly lemon soda that is tasty enough to drink. You can try this with an orange, too.

What to do: Squeeze the juice from the lemon into the measuring cup. Add an equal amount of water then pour the mixture into the glass. Stir in the teaspoon of baking soda. Taste and add sugar if you like.

What happens: The liquid will be bubbly and taste like lemon soda.

Why: The bubbles are carbon dioxide gas formed when you combine the base (the baking soda) with the acid (the lemon juice).

The bubbles in real soda are also created by carbon dioxide, added under pressure to water and a flavored sweetener.

Lemon Rocket

44

Launch a rocket by following instructions exactly. You don't want the rocket to go off before you're out of the way!

What to do: Fit the cork into the soda bottle, trimming it or padding it with paper toweling, if necessary. Tape the two paper towel streamers to the cork. Put the cork aside; it will be your rocket.

Pour the lemon juice into the soda bottle. Add enough water to fill the bottle halfway. Wrap the baking soda in a little square of paper toweling.

Go outside where your rocket has plenty of space to travel. Drop the wrapped-up baking soda into the bottle and insert the cork loosely. Put the bottle on the ground and stand back.

What happens: The cork will eventually shoot up.

Why: As the water and lemon juice soak through the paper towel, the baking soda reacts to produce carbon dioxide. As more gas forms, pressure builds up inside the bottle and sends the cork flying.

Baby Lemons

45

Don't throw away those lemon seeds. Plant them—and eventually you may even have a lemon tree! At the very least, you can get them to sprout.

What to do: Soak the seeds overnight in water to soften the outside layer.

Wet a piece of blotter or paper towel and line the jar with it. Fill the center of the glass with the bits of paper towel or absorbent cotton. Near the top of the jar, push the seeds between the outside of the jar and the blotter or paper towel,. Pour about 1 inch (2.5 cm) of water into the bottom of the jar. Place the jar in a warm dark place like a closet or cabinet. Check it every day and add more water as it dries up.

What happens: In a week or ten days, the seeds will begin to sprout.

Why: Seeds contain "baby plants" or embryos. The embryos in the seeds may grow into new plants if you give them moisture and warm air. The blotter supplies the moisture without waterlogging them.

Lemon Penicillin

46

Grow your own microbes with a lemon, water, darkness—and patience.

YOU WILL NEED:

lemon

clean, empty jar or can

water

plastic wrap or aluminum foil

magnifying glass

What to do: Place the lemon in the container. Add a few drops of water and cover the container tightly with plastic wrap or aluminum foil. Store it for a week or more in a dark place, like a kitchen cabinet.

Then take out the lemon. Look at it carefully with the magnifying glass.

What happens: You will see soft, green mold growing on the lemon. (Don't touch the mold or breathe on it because you may be allergic to it.)

Why: The green fuzzy mold on the lemons is actually a colony of millions of one-celled plants growing together. They grow on food that is kept too long and make it change color and smell bad.

This particular mold, the same kind that grows on blue cheese, is the one from which scientists make penicillin, the medicine that fights harmful microbes when we're sick.

When you finish examining the moldy lemon (or use it to do the next experiment) place it in the container and replace the wrapping. Dump it in the nearest trash can—and wash your hands.

Ripe Fruit in a Hurry

47

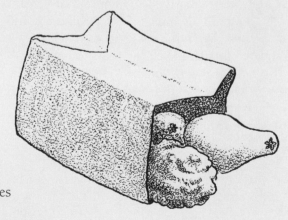

Try putting that moldy lemon in a paper bag with some unripe pears or peaches.

After one day note the results. The green mold on the lemon gives off a gas called ethylene. The mold gives off so much gas that a single moldy lemon can speed up the ripening of hundreds of pieces of unripe fruit.

Be sure to wash the ripe fruit well before eating it and throw the moldy lemon away.

DAIRY DOZEN

The refrigerator can supply the raw materials for a baker's dozen of fascinating—and useful—experiments. You can construct a plastic toy, etch graffiti on an eggshell, and make a "fat" light meter.

About Milk

Mammals, including people, feed their young with milk from the mother's body. Most of our milk comes from cows, but humans also use the milk of the mare, goat, ewe, buffalo, camel, ass, zebra, reindeer, llama, and yak.

About Butter

Butter—probably from buffalo—was known by 2000 B.C. First used as an ointment to beautify hair, it was also used as a medicine to treat burns, and, melted, as oil for lamps.

Butter is made by churning or agitating milk or cream and separating the solid fatty portion.

About Oil

The word "oil" comes from the Greek word for olive, but we use many different kinds of oils from animals and from such plants as cottonseed, palm, corn, peanut, and soybean.

Margarine is made from cottonseed and other vegetable oils.

About Eggs

Various wild birds were first tamed for use as food—flesh and eggs—in India.

Making Muffet Food

Little Miss Muffet was eating her curds and whey when that spider came along.

Just what are curds and whey?

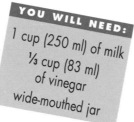

What to do: Mix the milk and the vinegar together in the jar.

What happens: The milk changes. At the bottom there is a thick substance, the curds. On top there is a watery liquid, the whey.

Why: Vinegar turns the milk sour and separates some of its parts. Curds are made up of the fat and minerals and a protein called casein. Cheeses are made from curds. white glue is made from the casein of the curds. To use the curds as glue, just wash away the liquid.

49 Make a Plastic Toy

HOT!

Create your own plastic—and mold it into a tiny toy. But don't expect it to look store-bought. Have an adult help you with this experiment.

What to do: Heat the milk in the pan, stirring frequently, until lumps (curdles) form. Ask an adult to slowly pour off the liquid. Put the lumps into the jar and add the vinegar. Let the lumps stand for about one hour.

What happens: A rubbery blob forms. Again slowly pour off the liquid. The shape the blob into a ball or a face. Leave it to harden for a few hours in the open jar or on a paper towel. If you wish, you can then color it with acrylic paints.

Why: When the vinegar and milk interact, the milk separates into a liquid and a solid made of fat, minerals, and protein casein (made up of very long molecules that bend like rubber until they harden).

At first, plastics were made from milk and plants. Now they are made from petroleum, and this poses a problem because they don't decompose.

50

YOU WILL NEED:
2 raw eggs
1 hard-boiled egg

Detecting the Hard-Boiled Egg

What a dilemma! You've put a cooked egg in the refrigerator and someone stuck it back among the raw eggs. You need the cooked one for a salad. But which one is it?

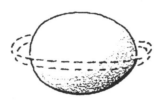 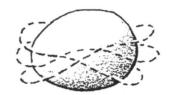

What to do: Spin each egg. Note what happens, Then touch each egg lightly while it is spinning.

What happens: Two of the eggs wobble, but one spins. The spinner is the hard-boiled egg. When you touch the spinning hard-boiled egg lightly, it stops spinning completely. The raw eggs move again after you have tried to stop them.

Why: The loose yolks and whites in the raw eggs revolve slowly because of inertia, the tendency of an object to continue at rest or in motion. This causes the raw eggs to wobble and to continue to move even after you tried to stop them. The solid white and yolk cause the hard-boiled egg to respond more quickly.

How do You Make an Egg Float?

51

YOU WILL NEED:

egg
2 drinking glasses
water
salt

No—this is not a riddle! Find out why it is easier to swim in the ocean than in a freshwater lake or pool.

What to do: Pour water into one glass until it is half full. Put the egg into the water. Notice what happens. Now add 3 tablespoons of salt, stir gently, and observe what happens.

Pour water into the second glass until it is half full. Stir in 10 tablespoons of salt. Slowly add fresh water until the glass is full. Donot stir. Gently lower in the egg.

What happens: In the fresh water the egg sinks. As you add salt, it floats higher and higher.

When you add fresh water to the very salty water, the egg is suspended in the middle.

Why: The denser the liquid the greater its upward life, or buoyancy. Salt makes the water denser.

When you add fresh water to the salty water, it remains on top. The egg sinks through it and floats on the lower, denser salty water.

52 ◆ The Egg in the Bottle Trick

Can you really put an egg into a bottle—if the bottle has a neck that is slightly smaller than the egg—without mashing the egg?

boiling water
small-necked bottle
like a ketchup bottle or
a baby's bottle
pot holder
hard-boiled egg, peeled

HOT!

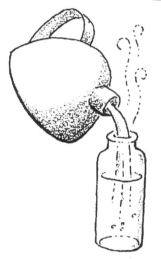

What to do: Pour the boiling water into the bottle. Hold the bottle with a pot holder and shake the water around in it and then pour it out. Quickly place the egg over the mouth of the bottle.

What happens: Although the egg is larger than the opening, the egg drops into the bottle.

Why: The hot water leaves steam in the bottle, which forces out some of the air. As the steam in the bottle cools, it changes into droplets of water and requires less space. This reduces the amount of air pressure in the bottle, and so the pressure of the outside air pushes the egg inside the bottle.

To remove the egg, hold the bottle upside down, place your mouth on the opening of the bottle, and blow into it for 30 seconds. The pressure inside will be greater than the pressure outside—and the egg will be forced out.

Egg Power

Eggshells are fragile, aren't they? Or are they? For this experiment collect the empty eggshells when the family has scrambled eggs or omelets for breakfast.

What to do: Wrap a piece of masking tape around the midsection of each eggshell half. Then, with your scissors, trim off the excess shell so each one has a straight-edged bottom.

Lay out the four eggshells, dome up, so they form a square. Holding a can upright, stand it on the eggshells. Keep on stacking cans on top of that one until the shells crack.

What happens: The "fragile" eggshells can support a surprising amount of weight.

Why: The secret of their strength is their shape. No single point in the dome supports the entire weight of the object on top of it. The weight is carried down along the curved walls to the wide base.

Egg Graffiti

54

Can you etch your initials or a drawing on an ordinary egg—without breaking the shell?

What to do: Carefully draw or write on the eggshell with the crayon. Put the egg into the jar and add enough vinegar to cover it. Let it stand for 2 hours. Then pour out the vinegar. Replace it with fresh vinegar, and allow the egg to stand in it for another 2 hours. Wash the egg and remove the crayon marks.

What happens:
The eggshell may be very fragile, but your drawing or writing remains!

Why: The acid in the vinegar combines with the calcium carbonate of the shell and dissolves much of it—but not the part that you wrote on the crayon. The wax in the crayon protects that part of the shell from the vinegar so the section with your writing or drawing is not dissolved.

Oil and Water

55

"They are like oil and water!" That's how we describe two people who don't get along. Well, how do oil and water get along?

What to do: Pour 2 tablespoons of oil and 2 tablespoons of colored water into the jar or soda bottle. Cover and shake it hard. Now put it down.

What happens: Although the oil and water seem to mix when you shake the container, they separate when you put it down. The oil floats on top.

Why: Many liquids dissolve in water to form a solution, but water and oil do not mix. The oil molecules have a greater attraction for each other than for the molecules of the water. Oil floats on top of the water because it weighs less. That's why it is so easy to remove the fat from chicken soup and from beef gravy. When these liquids stand for a while, and especially after they have cooled, the fats form a solid layer on top of the other liquids.

56 ◆ Liquid Sandwich

Can you make a sandwich with three liquids?

What to do: Into a narrow jar, pour the oil, the water, and the honey or molasses. Cover the jar.

What happens: A liquid sandwich! The honey or molasses sinks to the bottom; the oil floats on top; and the water remains in the middle.

Why: The honey or molasses sinks because it is denser (it weighs more for the same amount) than water. The oil floats because it is less dense than the water.

How Fat is It? ◆ 57

It is surprisingly simple to find out whether a food has fat in it.

What to do: Draw six small circles on the paper. Label each circle with the name of one of the food you will be testing. Rub a tiny bit of each food on its own circle. After 10 minutes, examine both sides of the paper.

What happens: Some of the circles will be dry. Others will be greasy and the spots will be spreading.

Why: Both water and fat produce a spot by filling in the spaces between the fibers of the paper. Spots made by water in the food evaporate in the air and dry. But the fat globules remain. They can only be broken down by soap or a solvent like ether.

A "Fat" Light Meter

Which light bulb is brighter? What flashlight?
You can figure it out scientifically!

YOU WILL NEED:

cooking oil
sheet of white paper
paper towel
2 unshaded lamps
with light bulbs of
different wattage
ruler or tape measure

What to do: Place a few drops of ordinary cooking oil on the sheet of white paper. Let the oil soak in and then, using a paper towel, blot away the excess so that all that remains is an oil spot on the paper.

In a dark room, set up your light bulbs in the unshaded lamps across a table from each other. Hold the paper close to the bulb on the left and gradually move it closer to the bulb on the right. Keep your eyes on the oil spot.

What happens: The spot disappears when the same amount of light falls on both sides of the paper.

Why: How does that help you to find out which bulb is brighter?

If you measure the distance from the spot to each bulb, and the distances are not equal, one of the lights must be brighter than the other.

For example, if Bulb A is 2 feet (60 cm) away from the paper and Bulb B is 3 feet (90 cm) away, Bulb B is brighter. If you want to know how much brighter, multiply A's distance—2 feet—by itself (2 x 2). Then multiply B's distance—3 feet—by itself (3 x 3). Divide the larger number by the smaller (9 divided by 4). Bulb B gives off more than twice as much light as Bulb A.

Magnifying Glass

59

A magnifying glass made of water?
Impossible?

YOU WILL NEED:

paper clip
butter or cooking oil
glass of water
telephone directory,
newspaper, and
postage stamp

What to do: Straighten the paper clip. Form a small loop at one end of the wire and rub a little butter or cooking oil on it. Dip the loop into the glass of water and lift it out. You now have a lens—a kind of frame that holds a layer of water.

Use the lens to read the small print in the telephone directory, the classified ads in the newspaper, and to see the fine details of the postage stamp.

Why: The water lens, just like a glass or plastic lens, has a definite shape. It bends light rays as they pass through it. First, it bends light as the light enters. Then it bends it again as the light leaves. The angle at which the water bends the light depends upon the shape of the lens.

Reflected light spreads out from the object you are look at, hits the lens, and is bent back to your eye. Your eye see the light as though it came on a straight line from the object—and the object seems to be much larger than it actually is.

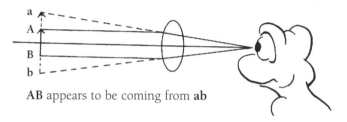

AB appears to be coming from **ab**

60

How Much Bigger?

You can find out just how much larger a lens makes an object by using a piece of graph paper. You can also use an ordinary sheet of paper, but you have to draw graph lines on it.

Look through your magnifying glass at the lined paper. Count the number of lines you see through the "lens" compared to the number you see outside of it.

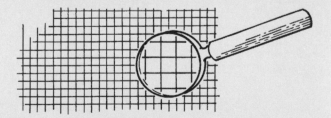

If there are 4 lines outside, compared to 1 line inside, the lens magnifies 4 times.

Adventures with a String

With a piece of string, you can perform all kinds of scientific marvels! You can force water to walk a tightrope, cut a string inside a bottle, lift a heavy weight with a button, make a grandfather clock—and even prove your superior strength!

About String

Through the centuries, string and cord, rope and twine have been made from the fiber of such plants as hemp and flax, jute and sisal. Strands of fiber are twisted or braided together. Today we also use synthetic, or man-made materials, like nylon and polyester to make string and rope.

61 ◆ Cut a String Without Touching It

Can you cut a string without laying a hand on it—when it is inside a covered glass jar? See how easy it is when you "concentrate," but you must do this on a sunny day!

YOU WILL NEED:
small piece of string
jar with a lid
tape
magnifying glass

What to do: Tape one end of the string to the inside of the jar lid. Screw on the jar lid so the string is suspended in the jar.

With the magnifying glass, focus the rays of the sun on the string for a few minutes.

What happens: The string breaks in two.

Why: The magnifying glass concentrates the heat of the sun on the string. The heat becomes intense enough to burn right through the string.

Water Walks a Tightrope

62

Will water travel on a string without falling off? Try this experiment and find out.

YOU WILL NEED:

small nail
plastic cup
12 inch (30 cm) length of string
water
pail

What to do: Using the nail, punch a small hole near the top lip of the plastic cup. Dampen the string and thread it through the hole, tying a knot on the inside. Fill the cup almost to the top with water.

Place the pail on the floor near your left foot. Tie the free end of the string to your left index finger and hold it over the pail.

Then hold the cup up in your right hand. Stretch the string taut and slant it down toward the pail. Tip the cup of water and slowly pour the water onto the string.

What happens: The water travels down the string until it reaches your left index finger and the pail.

Why: The molecules near the surface of the water cling together to form an elastic, tubelike skin through which the water flows along the wet string. This elastic skin is known as surface tension.

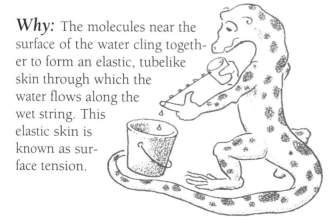

Making a Figure 8 Stopper Knot

63

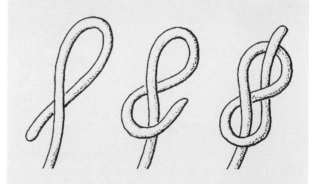

You can secure the string to the inside of the cup in any way that holds. But if you want to do it with a figure 8 stopper, follow the diagram below.

Mining Salt

YOU WILL NEED:
small jar
hot water
tablespoon
salt
nail
small piece of string
pencil

In some tropical areas, salt is not mined from the earth, but is taken from sea water in shallow ponds. You can create your own salt water—and then separate the salt in the form of crystals.

What to do: Fill the jar with hot water and stir in 1 tablespoon of salt at a time until the salt no longer dissolves. It will take about 1 tablespoon of salt for every 1 ounce (30 ml) of water.

Attach the nail to one end of the string. Wrap the other end of the string around the pencil. Rest the pencil on the edge of the jar and suspend the nail in the salted water so it hangs down, but does not touch the bottom of the jar.

Put the jar in a warm place.

What happens: After a few days, the water dries up and crystals form on the string. They taste salty.

Why: Water molecules slowly go into the air as water vapor. As the water evaporates from the salt water, the salt atoms draw close together, forming cube-shaped crystals. When the water is gone, the salt crystals remain.

Make Rock Candy

You can make rock candy, which is really just sugar crystals, the same way you make salt crystals. You will need a jar that is a little larger and a longer piece of string. Add 2 cups of sugar to ¼ cup (125 ml) of hot water and let it stand for a few days.

66 Rescue an Ice Cube

This is a great "icebreaker" for a party! Challenge your guests to use a string to rescue an ice cube from a glass of water without getting their hands wet. Tell them they may use

anything on the party table except the dishes or utensils. After they fail, show them how to do it.

What to do: Float the ice cube in the glass of water. Hang one end of the string over the edge of the glass. Place the other end of it on the ice cube. Then sprinkle a little salt on the ice cube and let it stand for 10 minutes.

What happens: The string freezes onto the ice cube. Then you pull on the string and lift the ice cube out of the water.

Why: When the salt strikes the ice, it lowers the freezing point of the water to a little below 32 degrees F (0 degrees C) and causes the surface of the ice cube to melt a little. As the ice refreezes, it traps the string.

Something Fishy

67

Here is an easy way to spin a sea monster!

What to do: On the cardboard draw and cut out a sea monster, like the one in the illustration. Add three dots, as shown.

Tack up the monster at the top dot and drop the nail from the tack. Draw along the string line. Repeat for the other two dots.

Tack up the monster at the point where the three lines cross. Spin it.

What happens: The cardboard monster spins evenly and stops each time at a different place.

Why: The point where the three lines intersect is the center of gravity. If you hang the shape by any other point, it will be out of balance, spin unevenly, and stop at the same place, where the center of gravity is lowest, every time you spin it.

Lazy Bones

In this experiment you might expect the thin threads that support the stick to break, but instead . . .

What to do: Tie a piece of thread to each end of the stick. Then tie the other end of each thread to the hanger so the stick is suspended underneath. Use clove hitch knots (see instructions below) if you like. Strike the stick with the metal edge of the ruler.

What happens: The threads do not break! If you strike hard enough, the piece of wood will break.

Why: You are applying force not to the threads but to the stick. The stick resists moving—so much that it would rather break than move. It is the law of inertia again: bodies at rest tend to stay at rest.

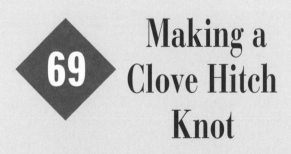

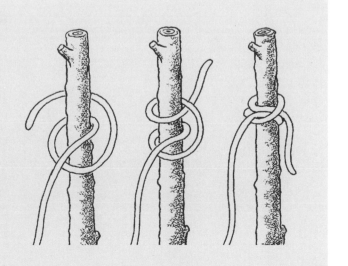

69 Making a Clove Hitch Knot

The clove hitch allows you to join a rope to something else, like a stick or a clothes hanger.

70 Getting It Straight

Bet you can't straighten this string!

What to do: Lay the string out straight on a table or on the floor. Place the book in the middle of the string. Tie the string around the book without making a knot. Lift the book by holding the ends of the string. Then take one end of the string in each hand and pull on it so the two ends of the string form one straight line.

What happens: You cannot pull the string straight—no matter how hard you pull.

Why: You will notice that as you separate the string ends, the book feels heavier and heavier. The greater the angle between the two halves of the string, the greater the force you need to hold the book up. A straight line forms an angle of 180 degrees. You would need an enormous amount of force to hold up the book with the ends of the string at that angle—so much force that the string would break before you got the two ends to form a straight line.

71 Loop-the-Loop

When you are on a loop-the-loop, and it turns upside down, why don't you fall out?

What to do: Tie the rope securely to the handle of the pail. Put the ball into the pail.

Choose a spot where there is no risk of hitting anything—outdoors if possible. Hold the pail by the rope and whirl the pail in circles in the air as fast as you can.

What happens: The ball remains in the pail even when it turns upside down.

Why: Centrifugal force—the force created by that whirling motion—equals the force of gravity and keeps the ball from falling out of the pail. It pulls the object against the sides of the pail rather than down and out of it.

When you get really good at this, you may want to try it with a pail of water—outdoors!

The Talking String

Believe it or not, you can make your string talk!

YOU WILL NEED:
strong, thin string, or thread, 18 inches to 24 inches (45 to 60 cm) long
large two-hole button

What to do:
Thread the string through the holes of the button and knot the ends together. Use a bowline knot (see instructions below), if you like. Center the button.

Loop the string on each side of the button on your index fingers. Swing the button around a number of times, either toward you or away from you, but always in the same direction.

When the string is "wound up," separate your hands, pulling the string taut. Then bring your hands together, releasing it. Alternate pulling and releasing until the string unwinds.

What happens: The button spins very fast until it twists in the opposite direction. If you spin it fast enough, you hear a whirring sound.

Why: The law of inertia is at work again: A body in motion tends to continue in motion. The sound comes from the vibration of the air around the string.

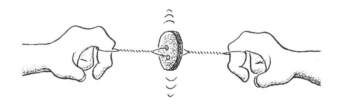

Making a Bowline Knot

You can tie a string to itself with a bowline knot, as shown in the diagram at the right.

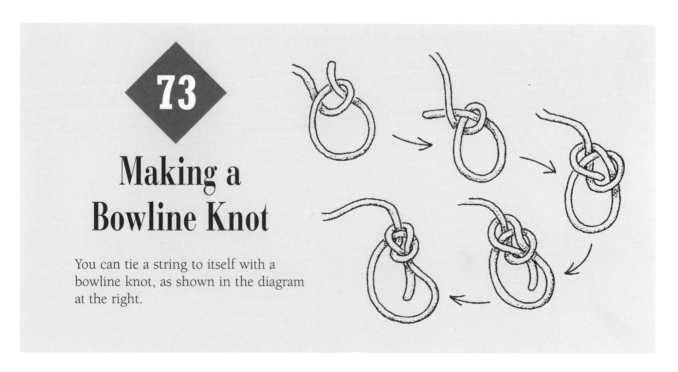

David and
Goliath

Can a button lift
a stone?

74

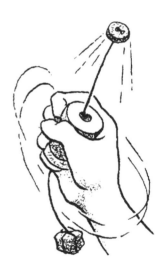

What to do: Thread the string through the spool so about two-thirds of the string is above it. Then tie the button to one end of the string and the stone to the other end. With the button toward the top and the stone toward the bottom, hold the contraption above your head. To do this, hold the spool with one hand and with the other hand hold the string just above the stone. Begin whirling the spool around so both weights move as fast as possible.

Gradually let go of the string below the spool.

What happens: The heavy weight seems to be lifted up by the lighter one.

Why: Of course, the button isn't doing the lifting! When you whirl the weights fast enough, centrifugal force—the force created by the whirling motion—is greater than the force of gravity. and so the stone moves up—against the pull of gravity.

75 Broomstick Block-and-Tackle

YOU WILL NEED:
jump rope or clothesline
2 brooms or long sticks
2 friends

You are amazingly strong! To prove it do this experiment.

What to do: Give a broomstick to each of your friends and ask them to stand a few feet apart. Then tie one end of the rope to one of the sticks and weave the rope in and around the sticks, as in the illustration. You hold on to the other end of the rope. Now ask your friends to pull the broomsticks apart as hard as they can, while you pull on the rope.

What happens: No matter how hard your friends try to keep the broomsticks apart, you can pull them together.

Why: Each time you wrap the rope around the broomsticks, you increase the distance the rope has to be pulled. When you pull on the end of the rope, you exert a small force—but over a long distance. The resulting force is far greater than the force your friends can exert over a shorter distance.

The broomstick block-and-tackle is a form of double pulley. It is used for loading ships, lifting the shovels of cranes, and lowering and lifting lifeboats, pianos, safes, and machinery.

Blow the Book Away

76

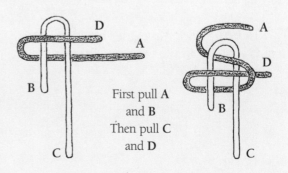

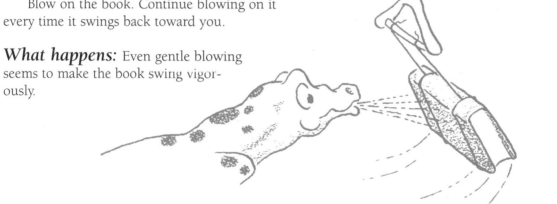

78

Swing Time

Galileo first performed this amazing experiment
with strings in 1583!

YOU WILL NEED:

4 strings of
different lengths
2 strings of the
same length
teaspoon
5 paper clips
clothesline or
clothes hanger

What to do: Tie the teaspoon to one of the strings
that has another string the same length. Tie the paper
clips to the five other strings. Tie each string to the
clothesline or hanger. Swing the teaspoon.

What happens: All the strings with the paper clips
on them start to swing. But the paper clip on that
string that is the same length as the teaspoon's swings
with more energy than the others—and the string
with the teaspoon winds down. Then the teaspoon
strings picks up vigor and the same-length paper
clip slows down.

Why: The swing of the teaspoon moves along the
hanger and gives all the strings and paper clips a push,
starting them all moving. But each string, depending
on its length, swings back and forth at a different time.
Only one paper clip—the one that swings at the same
time as the teaspoon—gets pushed at the right moment
to build up its swing. It swings with more vigor than
the others—until it loses energy to the teaspoon string,
which builds up its swing again. The teaspoon and
the same-length paper clip continue taking turns
speeding up and slowing down.

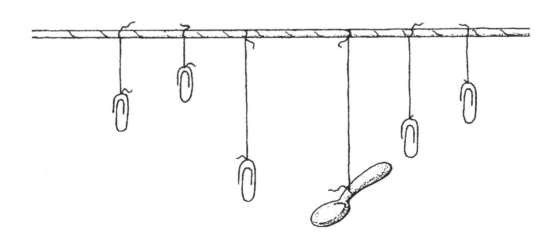

A String Grandfather Clock

79

This experiment will show you how to measure time with a string.

YOU WILL NEED:

4 strings of different lengths: 10 inches (25 cm); 20 inches (50 cm); 39 inches (97.5 cm); and 48 inches (120 cm)

small weight, like a metal washer or a coin

clothes hanger, or a ceiling hook

watch that indicates seconds

pencil

paper

What to do: Tie the weight to the string that is 48 inches (120 cm) long and suspend it from the clothes hanger or ceiling hook. (If you don't have a long enough string, you can use sheet bed knots, see the instructions on page 66, to join strings.)

Pull the string slightly to one side and let it swing. Count the number of swings it makes in 60 seconds. Then pull the string farther over to one side and count the number of swings it makes in 60 seconds. Write down the results.

Now do the same thing with the strings of different lengths: 10 inches; 20 inches; and, finally 39 inches. In each case, count the number of times the weight moves back and forth in 60 seconds and write it down.

What happens: When the string is 39 inches long, the weight moves back and forth 60 times in 60 seconds, or 1 minute.

Why: A pendulum takes the same amount of time to make every swing no matter how far it travels or how heavy the weight at the end of it. But the longer the pendulum, the longer the time it takes to complete its swing, and the shorter the pendulum, the quicker it travels back and forth.

Since a length of string measuring 39 inches swings back and forth 60 times in 1 minute, you know that every complete swing it makes measures one second. You can use that length of string to measure time with great accuracy.

In 1673, Christopher Huygens used this principle in his design for a "grandfather" clock.

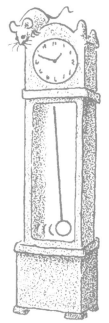

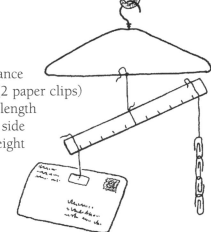

String Balance

You can make your own scale with a few strings and then put it to work weighing small objects.

YOU WILL NEED:

tape
3 strings of different lengths:
4 inches (10 cm);
6 inches (15 cm);
and 8 inches (20 cm)
12 inch (30 cm) ruler
wire clothes hanger
12 small paper clips

What to do: Tape the 6 inch string to the center of the ruler, making sure that it won't come off. Tie the free end of the string to the rod of the hanger, as shown in the illustration.

Attach the other two strings (the 4 inch and the 8 inch strings) so they are the same distance from the ends of the ruler. Knot the free ends of the strings.

Unwind one of the paper clips and bend it so it fits tightly when you hang it over the ruler. Slide it along the ruler until the ruler hangs straight.

Link 2 paper clips and tie them to the 8 inch length of string. Then attach paper clips to the 4 inch length of string until the ruler is balanced again.

What happens: You have to attach 4 paper clips to the 4 inch string to balance 2 paper clips attached to the 8 inch string.

Why: In the balance scale, the weight (2 paper clips) multiplied by the length (8 inches) on one side must equal the weight (4 paper clips) multiplied by the length (4 inches) on the other side.

Using Your Scale

81

You can use your string scale to weigh various objects. It will make a great postage scale.

How many paper clips will you have to add to the 8 inch string if you attach a 1 ounce letter to the 4 inch string?

When you find out, you can tell in a quick glance whether you have put enough postage on a letter.

SOAP SUDS

Make "blood," sink a ship, power a paper boat, move tooth picks at will, put bubbles to work—all with soap.

About Soap

Ancient peoples washed with water and wood ashes and then soothed their clean but irritated bodies with grease or oil from animals or plants.

About two thousand years ago, the Gauls invented a soap that combined wood ashes and animal fat. They used it to make their hair brighter.

A soap factory and bars of scented soap were found in the ruins of Pompeii, the city that was destroyed in the first century A.D.

Today, commercial soap makers combine fat or grease with lye (an alkali made from wood ash) and salt. They add perfumes, coloring, water softeners, and preservatives before they shape or flake the soap.

Although the word "detergent" actually means anything that will clean things, it is usually used today to refer to a cleaner made from a man-made, or synthetic, substance usually derived from petroleum. Detergent was first developed for commercial use in the 1950s.

Dracula's Favorite Soap

Terrify your friends with this amazing soap!

What to do: Pour the rubbing alcohol into a small dish and mash the pills into it. Rub the mixture on your hands and let it dry. Then wash it off with soap.

What happens: The soapy water turns bright red.

Why: The laxative contains a compound known as phenolphthalein. This substance turns a brilliant red when it is mixed with an alkali. Soap is made from fat boiled together with a strong alkali. When you add water, you free some of the alkali. This alkali mixes with the phenolphthalein on your hands—and turns them blood red.

Soapy Shipwreck

What does soap do to water that makes washing easier? Watch!

What to do: Float the pin on the water in the cup. It's easiest if you lower the pin with a pair of tweezers. Then carefully add the liquid soap one drop at a time.

What happens: As you add the soap, the pin sinks.

Why: To start with, the pin is not actually floating. It is resting on the water's invisible elastic skin.

Water molecules are strongly attracted to one another and stick close together, especially on the surface of the water. This creates tension—enough tension to support an object you would think would sink. Surface tension also prevents water from surrounding the particles of dirt, soot, and dust on your skin or clothes.

When dissolved in water, soap separates the water molecules, reducing the surface tension. That's the reason the pin sinks—and the reason soapy water washes dirt away.

Soap Power

Can you use soap to power a boat? Well, maybe, a very small one—in a basin or in the bathtub.

What to do: From the index card, cut out a boat approximately 2 inches x 1 inch (5 cm x 2.5 cm), with a small slot for the "engine" in the rear, as in the illustration.

Float the boat in the pot of water. Pour a few drops of detergent into the engine slot.

What happens: The boat travels through the water.

Why: The soap breaks the water's elastic "skin," the surface tension behind the boat. The boat sails forward—and will stop only when the soap reduces the surface tension of all the water in your "lake."

Picky Toothpicks

You can make a circle of toothpicks come and go at will.

What to do: Arrange the toothpicks in a circle in the bowl of water. Place the cube of sugar in the center of the circle.

Change the water and arrange the toothpicks in a circle again. This time place the piece of soap in the center.

What happens: When you place the sugar in the center, the toothpicks are drawn to it. When you place the soap in the center, the toothpicks are repelled.

Why: The sugar sucks up water, creating a current that carries the toothpicks with it toward the center. The soap, on the other hand, give

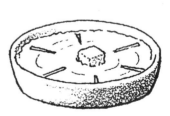

off an oily film that spreads outward. It weakens the surface tension and the film carries the toothpicks away with it.

Polluting the Duck Pond

86

Is anything wrong with washing your clothes with detergent in a lake or a pond? Take a look!

What to do: Stuff the plastic bag with the small pieces of wax paper. Close the bag with its fastener. Draw a duck on the bag with the felt-tipped pen. Float your "duck" in the pan or bowl. Then add a little detergent.

What happens: The duck sinks.

Why: The wax paper and plastic are water-repellent—just the way a live duck is. A duck's feathers are oily. This oil repels water and helps a duck to float. But a detergent enables water to stick to greasy materials. Detergent may be fine for washing dishes and clothes, but it is deadly for the duck.

Handmade Bubbles

87

Bubbles are globs of air or gas inside a hollow liquid ball. Soap bubbles are globs of air enclosed in a film of soapy water. You can make bubbles by blowing through a pipe or a ring dipped in soapsuds. You can do it with just your hand, too.

What to do: Pour the water into the bowl. Gently stir in the dishwashing liquid. Curl your fingers and dip your hand into the soapy mixture. Blow into your curled hand.

What happens: Bubbles form.

Why: When you blow into the mixture of water and detergent on your wet hand, you add the air that forms the center of the bubble.

Bubble Mix Recipes

Recipes for bubble mix differ, partly because soap powders and detergents vary in strength. Experiment and figure out which ones work best for you. Here are some suggestions that may help:

○ Dishwashing detergent usually works well.

○ Use at least 1 part detergent to 8 to 10 parts of warm water for a normal mix. For example, 1 tablespoon (15 ml) of detergent for every ½ cup (125 ml) of water, or ½ cup of soap to 5 cups of water.

○ A larger proportion of soap to water makes larger bubbles.

○ More detergent than water creates giant bubbles.

○ Add sugar or gelatin powder or glycerin to get longer-lasting bubbles. Bubbles burst when they dry out. These substances slow down the evaporation of water that causes the drying out. Try 1 part sugar or gelatin or glycerin to 1 part soap and 6 parts water.

Bubble Tips

○ Save clean jars of different sizes to hold various bubble mixes.

○ Stir gently so as not to whip up soapsuds. (Suds are actually tiny bubbles.)

○ If possible, let the bubble mix stand for a day or two before using it.

○ Put the bubble mix in the refrigerator for a few minutes before using it. Your bubbles will last longer.

○ For best results, blow bubbles on a rainy day. Because there is more moisture in the air, they will last longer.

89 Making a Bubble Blower

You can make a great bubble blower from a wire clothes hanger. Ask an adult to help you.

With the help of an adult, untwist the wire hanger and then wrap a piece of it around the can or thick crayon. Slip the can out. Leave about 4 inches (10 cm) of straight wire for a handle. Then bend the rest of the wire back and forth until it snaps. And now you have your bubble wand.

Dip the wand into the bubble mix and wave it in the air.

What happens: You get a spray of bubbles.

Why: By waving the soapy wand in the air, you add the air that forms the center of each bubble.

90 Other Bubble Blowers

You can make a bubble blower from almost anything: a drinking straw, a clay pipe, a tin horn, a funnel, a paper cup with the end removed, a juice can with both ends removed, even a cutaway plastic bottle.

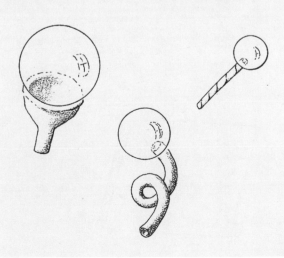

Super Bubble

To create a large bubble, you need a large bubble blower and a strong bubble mix.

What to do: Thread the string through the two drinking straws and tie the ends of the string to one another. Pour the bubble mix into the large baking pan. Wetting your fingers first, hold one straw in each hand and dip the strings and straws into the mixture for a couple of seconds.

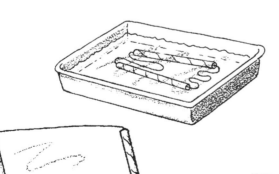

Remove the strings from the mix and pull the straws apart so the strings are taut. Holding the straws as though they were a frame, wave them around several times. Then pull the straws upward and bring them close together.

What happens:
You release an enormous round bubble.

Why: You get a large bubble because you are adding a large amount of air when you wave the straw frame and pull the straws up. As this air pushes out in all directions, you pull apart the molecules of the soapy film. But the molecules are attracted to one another, and the "elastic" skin of the bubble contracts as much as it can to form the smallest surface for the air it contains. The form that has the smallest surface is the sphere. That's why the bubble is round.

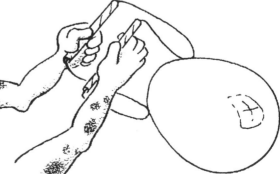

Bubble Duet

Blow two bubbles with one bubble blower— and see how they affect one another.

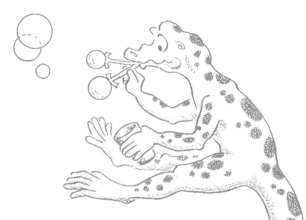

What to do: Cut four slits about ⅔ inch (17 mm) long at both ends of the drinking straw. Bend the cut strips outward, as in the illustration. Make a small slit in the middle of the straw, and bend it at the slit. You have now made a two-ended bubble pipe.

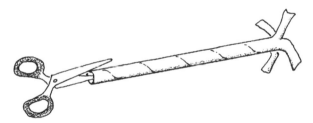

Dip one end of the pipe into the bubble mix. Blow into the middle slit. You'll get a bubble. Blow a second bubble by dipping the other end of your pipe into the mix and blowing the middle slit again. Then seal the slit in the middle of the bubble pipe by covering it with your fingers.

What happens: When you blow the second bubble, the first one gets larger. When the opening is sealed, the smaller second bubble gets ever smaller while the first one gets even larger.

Why: Because a small bubble is more curved than a large bubble, the air pressure exerted by its "elastic" skin is greater than that on a large bubble. Therefore, the small bubble gets smaller. The air from it is forced into the bigger bubble, which then gets even larger.

Make a Bubble Stand

93

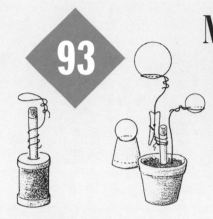

To make a stand for your bubbles, all you have to do is place a plastic cup or container upside down.

Or you can put a pencil in the hole of a wooden spool of thread and wind a wire loop around it, as in the illustration at the left. Transfer a bubble from a bubble blower to the stand by simply shaking it off gently. You can then observe the bubble—and make others.

Rainbow in a Bubble

94

A rainbow in a bubble? Yes!

YOU WILL NEED:
bubble mix
1 tablespoon of sugar
refrigerator
bubble blower, like a
wire ring
bubble stand

What to do: Add the sugar to the bubble mix. Put the bubble mix in the refrigerator for 5 minutes. This will make the bubbles last longer.

Dip the bubble blower into the mix. When you have a film of soap on the ring, blow gently. Attach your bubble to the bubble stand by shaking the bubble blower over the stand.

What happens: After a few minutes, you see different colors.

Why: When light hits a bubble, most of it passes through it because the bubble is transparent. But as the air in the bubble evaporates and the bubble gets even thinner, some of the rays that make up white light do not pass through. Instead, they are reflected back from either the outside or the inside. That's why you see various colors of the spectrum. The colors change and disappear, because the bubble's thickness is not the same all over and is constantly changing.

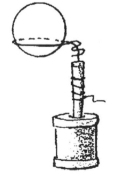

Bubble in a Bubble in a Bubble

Use a bubble stand to put a bubble in your bubble's bubble.

What to do: Turn the plastic cup upside down and wet the bottom of it, which is now on top. Using the wire ring make a large bubble and attach it to the bubble stand.

Wet the plastic straw in the bubble mix and gently push it through the large bubble. Blow a smaller bubble inside the large one. Then carefully push the straw through the smaller bubble, and blow an even smaller one.

What happens: You get a bubble in a bubble in a bubble.

Why: Anything wet can penetrate the bubble without breaking it. The wet surface coming into contact with the soapy film becomes part of it. Do not touch the wet wall with your smaller bubble. If you do you will not get a separate bubble.

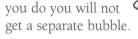

Putting a Bubble to Work

We can make an ordinary soap bubble do work for us!

Carefully stick the needle into the cork with the point out. Put the cork on a table or counter.

Fold the paper diagonally twice. Unfold it. Balance the center of the paper square (where the creases meet) on the point of the needle, as in the illustration.

Dip the spool in the bubble mix and blow a bubble on one end. Hold the other end toward the paper.

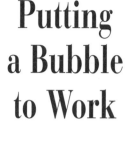
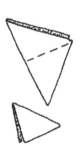

What happens: The paper moves.

Why: Air escaping from the bubble moves the paper.

Take a Bubble Dancing

If you think your bubbles have worked hard enough and need a little recreation, you can take them dancing.

What to do: Rub the comb several times against the piece of flannel or wool. Make a spray of bubbles with the bubble ring and float the bubbles above the fabric so they land on it. Then move the comb close to each of the bubbles in turn.

What happens: Each bubble seems to dance—moving up and then falling down.

Why: You are using static electricity—electricity created by friction—to make your bubbles "dance."

By rubbing the comb on the fabric, you charge it with static electricity. Because charges of electricity that are not alike attract one another, the charged comb attracts the uncharged bubbles. The bubbles then become charged by the comb—and are pushed away because they have the same charge of static electricity as the comb. Charges of electricity that are alike repel one another. Each time the bubbles come up and touch the comb they get charged and each time they go down, they lose their charge and are pulled up again.

SLOW START—FAST FINISH

You know how you feel when you're lying in bed in the morning and you don't want to move? That's inertia.

You're on your bike at the foot of a steep hill and it takes every ounce of strength you have just to get the bike started. That, too, is inertia.

Inertia is a scientific work that says that things that are standing still tend to continue to stand still.

When you are riding your bike along a level road, you don't have to pedal hard every second. You can even stop spinning the pedals and coast a bit. That's inertia.

You see, inertia also means that objects that are moving tend to keep on moving.

These ideas aren't difficult to understand. Of course things stand still until someone or something moves them. What would life be like if you put a pizza on a table and, all by itself, it started to slide to the edge and fall onto the floor?

Engineers found out long ago that an automobile uses only a small part of its power to cruise along the highway. It makes much greater horsepower to get that car moving and up to speed than to keep it going when it is on the open road.

The experiments we are going to do in this chapter show how you can make inertia work for you. Some of the results will amaze you and your friends. If you wish, let them think you are performing a bit of magic.

98 Watching Inertia at Work

Here is a simple experiment that lets you see inertia at work.

What to do: Tie the string around the book. Then tie the free end of the string to the rubber band.

Put the book on the floor. Rough carpet is best. Just don't use a polished floor that might get scratched. Things look like this now:

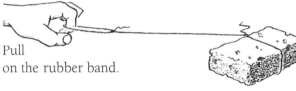

Pull on the rubber band.

What happens: The rubber band will stretch until you get the load moving. Then, as you continue to pull the weight across the floor, the rubber band won't stretch quite so much as when you started pulling.

Why: Inertia tends to keep motionless things where they are. To get things moving, you have to overcome inertia. The greater stretch in the rubber band show you had to pull harder to get the load started than you have to pull to keep it moving after that.

99 The Amazing Bottom Checker

Can you remove the bottom checker in a stack without touching the other checkers in the stack and without having the stack tip over?

What to do: Build a stack of eight or ten checkers. If you use coins, be sure they are all the same size. Medium-sized coins are best.

Place another checker next to the stack. Leave about 1 inch (2.5 cm) between this checker and the stack.

Flip the single checker hard with your forefinger or your middle finger. Give it a really hard snap.

What happens: The bottom checker will fly out from the stack. If all goes well, the rest will stay neatly in place.

Why: Inertia keeps the stack of checkers from moving even when the bottom one is suddenly snapped away. Because the stack was not moving to begin with, it tends to stay that way. Scientists say, "A body at rest tends to remain at rest."

100 The Amazing Middle Checker

To vary this experiment, you need a pencil in addition to the checkers. Use the pencil to hit one of the checkers in the middle of the stack. Hit it sharply and be sure to hit only one. With a little practice you can knock any checker out of the stack without tipping the stack

Catching a Coin on Your Elbow

YOU WILL NEED:
coin

Here is a great trick that is also a neat science experiment.

What to do: Place one coin on your elbow.

Hold your arm parallel to the floor or the coin will fall off.

You are now going to catch the coin that is on your elbow. That wouldn't be much of a trick except for one thing. You are going to catch the coin in the hand of the same arm.

Here's how it works. In one sudden, very quick move you will drop your arm. This will cause your open hand to snap forward. The arrow in the drawing shows the direction your hand will move.

At the same time, your elbow will fall away from under the coin.

What happens: As your elbow moves from under the coin your hand will come down from it. When you get your timing right, you'll catch the coin every time.

Why: Since the coin is still it tends to remain in that position. Good old inertia again! When your elbow moves rapidly it just drops out from under the coin. This leaves the coin hanging in air. Gravity pulls the coin toward the ground, but inertia gives it a slow start. Your hand is faster than the coin because your hand is already moving.

102 Catching More Coins

It's not difficult to flip a lot of coins from you elbow into your hand. After you have the hang of catching one coin, add a second on top of the first, and then three or four or more and catch them all at once.

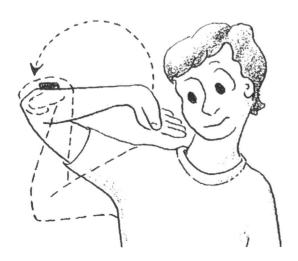

What a Crazy Way to Break Thread

YOU WILL NEED:

hammer or other unbreakable object that weighs about 2 pounds (1 kg)

short piece of string

3 foot (1 m) length of cotton thread

scissors

You can cut thread or even break it between your hands. Her's a way to break a piece of thread you never thought of! It's best to do this experiment outside.

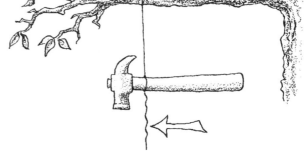

What to do: Choose a hammer or other object that won't break if it is dropped. A heavy wrench or a chunk of wood will work just fine.

Tie a loop of string around the hammer like this:

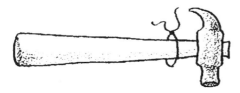

Next, cut the sewing thread in half. Be sure to use cotton thread because the experiment won't work with nylon thread.

Tie the end of one piece of thread to the top of the string loop. Then tie the second piece of thread to the bottom of the loop like this:

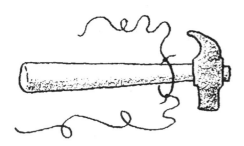

Tie the loose end of the top thread to something solid so the hammer hang below it. A tree branch is great, but any strong support will work fine.

Be sure there is nothing you can break or hurt beneath the hammer.

After you have set up the experiment, get a firm grip on the bottom string. The arrow shows where to grab. Then give a sudden, hard jerk downward.

What happens: You're expecting the hammer to fall on your hand, aren't you? What happens is the thread breaks somewhere between your hand and the hammer. The hammer will continue to hang from the top thread.

Why: Although the hammer doesn't weigh much, it takes a lot of energy to get it moving when it is at rest. The sudden downward pull causes the thread to break because it is not strong enough to overcome the inertia of the hammer.

That's a Lot of Work to Put Soap in a Glass

This experiment in inertia is impressive even if there is no good reason toput a bar of soap in a glass.

What to do: Put the glass on the table with the rim up. Put a plastic plate, like the ones from frozen foods, on top of the glass. (If you don't have a plastic plate use the square piece of cardboard.)

Next, put the outside of a small matchbox on top of the plate. If you don't have a matchbox you can make one. Take a look at the instructions on the right.

Now put the bar of soap on the matchbox. The illustration shows how.

Get a firm grip on the glass with one hand.

Strike the edge of the plate or cardboard with your other hand. Make the blow hard and fast.

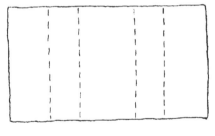

What happens: The plate flies into the air (so be sure there's nothing breakable near it). The soap holder tumbles off and the soap plops into the glass.

Why: Inertia strikes again!

Making a Matchbox

Cut a piece of cardboard 2½ inches by 5 inches (6 cm x 12 cm).

Fold it along each dotted line as shown below. Fasten the overlapping end with tape.

When you finish, your matchbox looks like this:

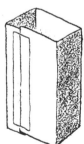

The Strange Case of the Marble in the Bottle

YOU WILL NEED:
empty bottle
piece of cereal box
material
scissors
ruler
marble or coin

Anyone can drop a marble or a coin into a bottle. But can it be done without touching the marble?

What to do: Be sure the open mouth of the bottle is larger than the marble or coin you are going to drop into it.

Cut a piece of cereal box material into a 4 inch (10 cm) square. Place the cardboard square on top of the bottle. Place the marble or coin on the cardboard so it is right over the mouth of the bottle. (It's a good idea to hold off on using a marble until you see how this works. A coin is easier to handle.)

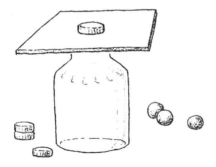

Flip the edge of the card hard and fast with your finger. If you're thinking like a scientist, you'll remember how you flipped one checker into another to move the bottom checker out of the stack.

What happens: The card snaps out from between the marble and the bottle. The marble drops into the bottle without you touching it. Pretty neat!

Why: The marble is standing still. Inertia wants to keep it that way. The card snaps away so quickly that the marble has no chance to follow the card. Gravity pulls it down into the bottle.

If the card moves too slowly, the marble will follow the card instead of falling into the bottle.

What now: If you want to be adventurous, try this with two marbles.

Slow But Steady

Here's an experiment you'll be able to perform only if you're willing to go about it slowly and with a steady hand.

YOU WILL NEED:

scissors
sheet of paper
ruler
pencil
bottle with a small
mouth and neck

What to do: Cut a strip of paper 3 inches (7 cm) wide and 10 inches (25 cm) long.

Place the bottle upside down on the paper near the edge of a table like this:

Your goal is to remove the paper without tipping over the bottle.

Place the pencil on the loose end of the paper and carefully roll it around the pencil. Keep rolling very slowly until the rolled paper touches the mouth of the bottle. Then, with a steady hand, continue rolling the paper.

What happens: As you slowly and steadily keep rolling, the paper gradually creeps out from under the bottle, which won't tip over.

Why: The unmoving bottle tends to say motionless and upright because of inertia. The bottle's mouth can't move because it touches the rolled paper. It doesn't tip over because inertia tends to keep it exactly where it was to begin with—so long as you don't make any sudden moves.

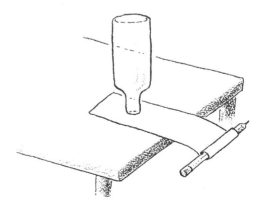

Nail Driving the Hard Way

YOU WILL NEED:
large dictionary and
large books
thick newspaper
wooden board
hammer
several nails

It's one thing to drive a nail into a board. It's another to do it while you hold the board in your lap.

What to do: Stack the dictionary and another large book on your lap. If you don't have a large dictionary use three large books. Place a thick newspaper on top of the books to protect them.

Finish off the stack by placing the board on top of the newspaper. Any scrap of lumber will do, but a piece of 2 x 4 is best. Now you are going to pound a nail into the board. That's right. You'll pound the nail while holding the board in your lap.

What happens: As you pound the nail, you feel the force of the hammer blows on your legs, but it won't hurt. Just be sure you don't pound the nail all the way through the board.

Why: Inertia saves the day.

More Impressive Nail Driving

109

You can experiment with nail driving using fewer books. But if you want to impress you friends, let someone else hammer the nail. Just be sure you always have a thick newspaper pad between the board and the books. Also be sure anyone swinging the hammer holds it so that the hammer head does not come down toward you. The person who is hammering must stand or kneel at your side and aim the hammer away from your face and body.

KEEPING YOUR BALANCE

How many times have you walked along a curb or on top of a stone wall with your arms out at your sides to help keep your balance? Even as a tot you understood that to keep your balance you had to have as much weight on one side of you as on the other. You knew this instinctively.

You also discovered how easy it was to lose your balance when you walked on any wall or narrow line. Instead of stepping off the wall or falling, you bent and twisted and waved your arms a bit. When you did these things your body was regaining its balance by getting its center of gravity right over the curb—or whatever it was you were walking along.

Everyone knows how gravity works. Gravity is that invisible force that keeps us from flying off into space. It's the force that makes your slice of bread fall jelly-side down when you accidentally drop it. Gravity is the pull that turns your home run into a double when the ball falls inside the park. But what is the center of gravity? And what does it have to do with keeping your balance?

The center of gravity is that point in an object where there is as much weight on one side as on the other. When you're walking along a curb or a crack in the concrete, your center of gravity is right on the line where you place your feet. If you stand up straight with your feet spread, your center of gravity is between your feet and straight down in a line from your nose.

When we locate the center of gravity in an object we can get that object to balance. You've balanced a pencil on your finger when things got a little boring in class, haven't you? Its center of gravity is halfway from the eraser to the point— unless you have one of those big erasers. In that case, the center of gravity is closer to the eraser than to the point.

If you want to impress people, you can refer to the center of gravity as the "point of balance." Whichever term you use, there are some really great bits of science that depend on finding where things are in balance.

The Incredible Balancing Hammer

YOU WILL NEED:

hammer
ruler
1½ feet (.5 m) of
strong string

Anyone can stand a hammer on its head and it will balance. But can you tie a hammer to a ruler and balance them both on the edge of a table with only one end of the ruler touching the table?

What to do: Tie one end of the string around the ruler. Tie the other end of the string around the hammer handle. Tie it tightly so it won't slip up and down the handle.

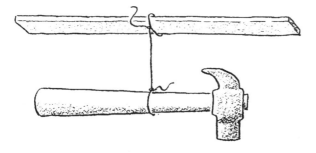

What happens: Now to make things balance. Be sure the end of the hammer handle touches the end of the ruler. Position the ruler so that about 4 inches (10 cm) of it are on top of the table. Carefully test the ruler and hammer to see if they are in balance.

You may have to adjust the string to get the hammer to hang correctly. If you have problems getting things to balance, shorten the string between the hammer and the ruler. Don't give up if things don't balance at first. They will when you adjust the string to the perfect length.

Why: You positioned the hammer and ruler so that the center of gravity is right at the edge of the table. If you look at things from one side, you'll see that the head of the hammer is on one side of the center of gravity and the handle and most of the ruler are on the other.

A hammer with a wooden handle will have a different center of gravity than one with a steel handle because of the heavier weight of the metal handle.

The Amazing Balancing Yardstick

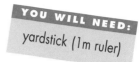

It's not difficult to balance a yardstick on top of your hands when you hold your hands apart. The surprising thing is how difficult it is to make that yardstick lose its balance.

What to do: Hold the yardstick between two outstretched fingers as shown below.

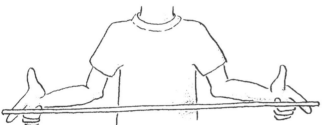

The object of this experiment is to move one finger toward the center of the yardstick until it loses its balance and tips over. Make this move slowly and steadily. It isn't fair to suddenly jerk your finger to the center of the yardstick.

What happens: A strange thing happens as you move your finger toward the center of the yardstick. You only move one finger along the yardstick, but the other finger moves along, too.

Eventually you find yourself with both fingers side by side and the yardstick still balanced.

Try it and see.

Why: The yardstick's center of gravity is right in the middle. When you slowly move one finger toward the center of gravity the yardstick begins to tip toward that finger because that finger is nearer the center of gravity. When it tips, even slightly, it reduces the weight on the finger that isn't moving.

When less weight presses on the unmoving finger, that finger begins to slide along the yardstick. This is because there is less friction on that finger. The finger you moved first has more friction because more weight is on it. Friction slows down movement, so that less friction results in faster movement.

The yardstick keeps rebalancing itself as your fingers slowly move toward one another.

The Rapid Ruler
and the Slowpoke Yardstick

Everyone knows that babies are likely to take a lot of tumbles when they are learning to walk. This is because they are learning how to control their bodies. Did you know that people's height has something to do with how fast they fall?

What to do: Begin by standing a ruler and a yardstick side by side with a few inches between them. Steady each of them with just the tip of your finger as shown in the illustration.

If you don't have a ruler and a yardstick, two dowel rods or other straight pieces of wood will work perfectly.

Lean the ruler and yardstick forward just a tiny bit to make sure both of them will fall in the same direction. Be sure they both have the same amount of forward lean. Now let go.

What happens: The ruler will win the race to the ground every time. Try it and see!

What you've just seen helps to explain why if a child and a taller adult start to fall forward at the same instant, the child will finish falling first. This also helps explain why babies sometimes seem to fall so fast.

Why: The center of the balance for the yardstick is higher than it is for the ruler. The farther that center of balance is from the ground the longer it will take the object to complete its fall.

This does not mean that a high center of gravity makes an object steadier than one with a low center of gravity. Just the opposite! Automobile manufacturers try to keep the center of gravity as low as possible so that cars are less likely to tip over. And that's the reason big trucks and trailers are sometimes required to pull off the highway during high winds. Not only do they have lots of surface to catch the wind, but their center of gravity is high. They are, therefore, more likely to turn over than are cars with a lower center of gravity.

The Mysterious Balancing Dinner Fork

YOU WILL NEED:
long wooden pencil
1 very small
potato or apple
newspaper
table fork

Can you balance a table fork, a potato, and a pencil so only the pencil's tip touches the table?

What to do: Press the pencil through the center of the potato or apple. (If anyone objects to your sticking things into the family's vegetables, a lump of soft modeling clay will do just as well.) Be careful doing this: Place the potato on a thick pad of newspapers. Don't hold the potato in the palm of your hand! If you do, you may run the pencil point into your hand.

Slowly and firmly push the pencil point into the potato. When the point pokes through, pick up the potato and hold it by its sides. Carefully push the pencil on through until about 1½ inches (4 cm) stick out.

When you've gotten the pencil through the potato, press the tines of the dinner fork into one side of the potato so the fork is at about the angle shown here.

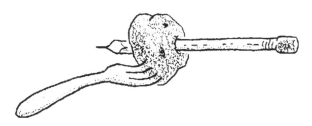

Rest the pointed end of the pencil on the edge of a table as shown below.

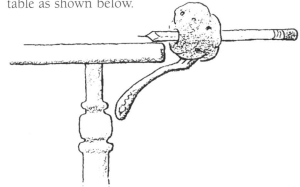

What happens: If you're having a lucky day, the whole thing will balance right away. If it doesn't, try moving the pencil tip farther onto the table or nearer the edge.

You can also slide the potato backward or forward a bit along the pencil. By now this strange combination has probably balanced. If it hasn't, you can begin to feel which direction it is going to move as you steady it with your hands. Don't give up if it doesn't balance the first few times. Keep adjusting it. If necessary, pull the fork out and replace it at a different angle.

When the combination does balance, it looks as if you have found a way to defy the laws of gravity. With a little practice, you can adjust this so the pencil actually slopes downhill and only the point touches the table

Why: This is the same principle as on page 90. You must have as much weight on one side of the center of gravity as on the other.

Twice the Balancing Magic

114

YOU WILL NEED:

very small potato or
apple or a lump of clay
pencil
2 table forks
tall drinking glass

Since you've already messed up a potato or apple, grab another fork and try another impossible feat of balance.

What to do: If you haven't already pulled the pencil out of the potato or the apple from the last experiment, leave it just the way it was. Otherwise, push the pencil through the potato or apple just as carefully as you did before.

You can leave the fork in at the same angle as before if it's still sticking in the potato. Now add a second fork by pushing its tines into the side of the potato opposite the first fork. Try to stick in both forks at the same angle.

Things look pretty much like this:

Turn a tall glass over so you can set the project on top of the glass as seen on the right. (Instead of a glass you can use a soda pop or salad oil bottle or any bottle with a small neck and a wide bottom.)

What happens: By adjusting the angle and location of the forks you can make the pencil stand straight up or lean to one side. Of course, only the point of the pencil touches the glass or the top of the bottle.

It is amazing how far you can get the pencil to lean to one side if you arrange the forks in the right position.

Why: Study the balancing figure and you'll see that there is exactly as much weight on any side of the pencil point as on any other side. The point of the pencil is the center of gravity.

HOW TO HAVE ALL THE MOVES

We already know a lot about motion. We know that many things move. We know that things that are not moving tend to remain still and stay in one place because of inertia. To get something to move that is standing or sitting some kind of force has to be applied to it.

Force can be as simple as giving a toy a push to start it moving. Force can be the wind that fills a sail, carrying a boat across the lake.

Applying force to an object can be complicated, too. It may involve running an engine or motor so that a pulley can turn. That pulley may cause a belt to go around and around, which, in turn, transfers the force to another pulley. This process can go on and become more and more complicated until, finally, a cutting device is put into motion that carefully produces a delicate part for an expensive machine.

We know that when the power of force is applied to an object, that object tends to keep on moving. When the power or force runs out, a moving object begins to slow down and

eventually stops. Gravity pulls on objects and helps to slow them down and use up their force. So does air and wind resistance. If it were not for air and wind resistance, you could hit a home run without having to stop and think about it.

We know that movement and motion can change with the center of gravity. By changing the center of gravity, you can turn an object or tip it over. In the last chapter you learned to create objects that stopped moving after you located their center of gravity. Now let's deal with some other things that affect motion and the way things move.

115 The Turtle and the Hare

Remember the story of the turtle and the hare? When the turtle finally passed the finish line, he said, "Slow and steady wins the race."

YOU WILL NEED:

2 large plastic bottles exactly alike (large soft drink bottles are ideal)

water

2 boards (or a sloping surface)

What to do: Fill one of the plastic bottles half full of water. Screw the lid on good and tight. Leave the second bottle empty.

Place the two bottles side by side at the top of a ramp or slope. A concrete sidewalk or driveway that runs downhill for a few feet and then levels out will be just fine. You can also make a ramp from two boards of the same length. Place one end of each board on a chair and let the lower ends of the boards rest on the floor as shown in the illustration.

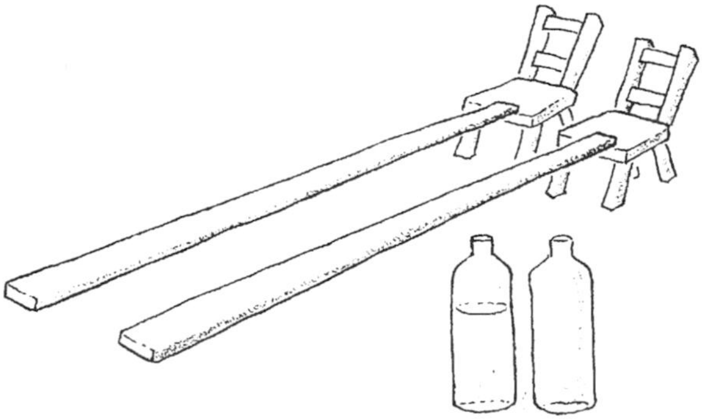

Hold the bottles at the top of the slope and then release them at the same time. Watch carefully as they roll down the slope.

What happens: The two bottles start together. But wait! One bottle starts off faster. That's the hare in this race. When the bottles reach the level floor, however, the slower bottle (that's the turtle) rolls farther than the "hare" that took off faster.

Why: Rub two things together and you create friction. To prove this, just rub your hands together rapidly. Feel the heat that you generate by the rubbing. Heat is created by friction.

The water in the half-filled bottle gives it extra weight. This added weight made it take off faster down the slope. But the water rubbing against the sides of the half-filled bottle created friction. The friction slowed that bottle down.

Friction not only creates heat: it slows movement. Automobile manufacturers use oil in an automobile engine to cut down on friction and heat. They use grease to lubricate other moving parts for the same reason.

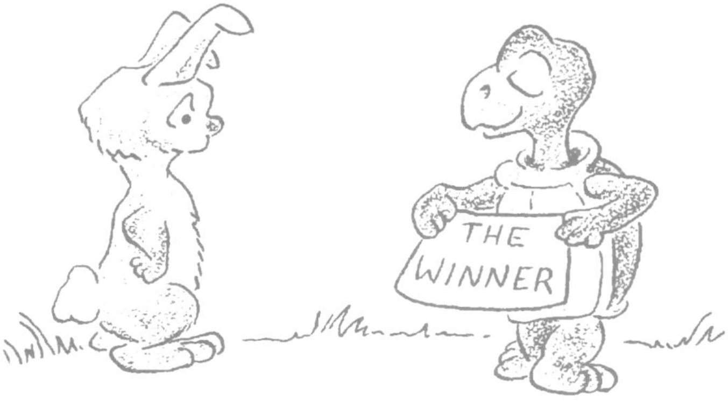

Racing Hoops

YOU WILL NEED:

2 sheets of paper
ruler
scissors
tape
4 paper clips
slope or ramp

You've watched horses and cars race. Perhaps you've even watched roller-skaters race. Well, here's a race the likes of which you've never seen.

What to do: For this experiment you need two paper hoops exactly the same size. (It wouldn't be fair to race hoops of different sizes against each other.)

Cut two strips of notebook paper as long as the sheet of paper and 2½ inches (6 cm) wide. Make each strip into a hoop by taping the narrow ends together. Now tape a paper clip inside one of the two hoops.

Be sure the paper clip is in the exact center of the hoop.

Place the two hoops side by side a few inches apart at the top of a slope or ramp. (The ramp you used for the turtle and hare race is perfect, although if there is much of a breeze blowing you'll need to use an indoor ramp.)

Let go of the hoops at the same time.

What happens: If you look closely, you'll see that the hoop with the paper clip doesn't roll at an even speed. It seems to speed up as the paper clip circles down toward the ramp. Then it slows down when the clip climbs back up away from the ramp. Eventually the hoop with the paper clip loses.

Why: It isn't friction that slows down the hoop with the paper clip. It slows down because it is out of balance. This is the reason the wheels on cars and trucks must be balanced.

Balancing the Hoops

Let's see if we can make the hoop with the paper clip roll at an even speed. Tape a paper clip exactly opposite the first one and repeat the race.

Now add two more paper clips, each one halfway between the clips already in place. The hoop should roll better now.

Why: Objects that turn, like tires and engines, have to be as perfectly balanced as possible. Otherwise, they need more energy to turn and they don't turn easily. This causes extra wear and can even destroy them.

118 The Astounding Balancing Coin

When was the last time you saw someone balance a coin on a spinning clothes hanger? For that matter, did you ever hear of anyone who tried such a stunt?

What to do: If you can't find one of those thick plastic clothes hangers you can try this with a regular wire hanger, but you'll need a great sense of balance.

Now that you have your coat hanger go outside. Don't be tempted to demonstrate this experiment in a room full of breakable things. If you happen to let the hanger slip off your finger, you better be outdoors! Since you're going to be experimenting outdoors, you're better off using a washer instead of a coin. A dropped coin that is easy to find on the living-room floor may be lost outside.

Loop the hanger over you finger. With your other hand balance the washer or coin on the bottom of the hanger so it looks like this:

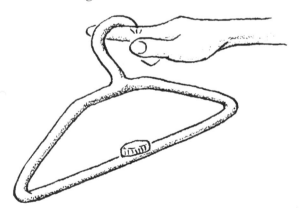

Now you know why it is a good idea to use the thick plastic hanger. It's not hard to balance a washer on a thick hanger, but it's difficult to get it to balance on a thin wire one.

Be absolutely sure to place the coin directly below your finger, which is sticking through the hanger's hook.

When the coin is balanced, begin rocking the hanger gently back and forth on your finger. Speed it up gradually.

When the hanger is swinging well, give it an extra spurt of energy and start it spinning in a circle around your finger.

What happens: The coin will stay in place as long as you keep the hanger spinning and don't jerk it.

Why: Centrifugal force is created when things spin rapidly. It causes spinning things to try to move away from the center around which they are spinning. The coin is pressed against the bottom of the hanger by centrifugal force. It won't slip off unless you slow down or break the smooth spinning motion.

The Spinning Bowl

Scientists demonstrate centrifugal force in huge laboratories. You can do it in your kitchen sink.

YOU WILL NEED:

large mixing bowl or pot
water
dessert bowl
wooden spoon

What to do: Fill the large mixing bowl with about 4 inches (10 cm) of water. If you have a bowl that's about 12 inches (30 cm) across, it will be perfect for this experiment.

Float the dessert bowl inside the large bowl or pot.

Pour enough water into the floating dessert bowl to fill it ¼ inch (1 cm) deep.

Now spin the floating bowl as rapidly as possible using the wooden spoon. Just stick the spoon into the bowl as shown here and begin turning it. If you don't have a wooden spoon, stick your index finger into the bowl to start it spinning. Since the bowl is floating, there is very little friction to slow it down and it will spin easily. Use a little wrist motion and the dessert bowl will pick up speed.

Try to keep it centered in the larger bowl. If the bowls touch, the spinning one will slow down.

What happens: Watch the water inside the floating bowl as you spin it faster and faster. The water will rise along its sides until the bottom of the spinning bowl is completely dry.

Let it slow down and the water will flow down from the sides of the bowl and cover the bottom again.

Why: Centrifugal force works on liquids just as it does on solid things. The faster you spin an object, the more it wants to escape by flying to the outer edge of the circle.

 # Power-Lifting Fingers

YOU WILL NEED:

straight chair
6 people

Your fingers are a lot stronger than you think. This experiment demonstrates that power and it is also a great party stunt.

What to do: One person sits erect in the straight-backed chair with hands clasped, head bent slightly forward, and neck stiff. The sitting person's entire body should be as unbending as possible.

Have each of the other five people extend one index finger. It helps to steady the hand with the other hand like this:

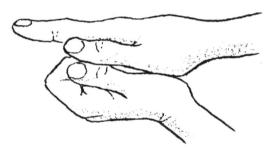

Ask one person to stand beside each of the sitting person's knees. Have them slip their entire index fingers under the sitter's knees.

Two other people will stand behind the chair and place their entire index fingers under the sitter's armpits.

The fifth person may stand beside the sitter or in front, placing an index finger under the sitter's chin.

Tell everyone to take a deep breath and hold it. Count, "One, two, three." All five people lift straight up on "Three." Caution everyone to lift straight up and not to jerk.

What happens: To everyone's surprise the sitting person comes right up out of the chair. Be sure to caution the lifters not to let the person drop when he or she is in the air.

Why: Since the sitter remains stiff, his or her weight is evenly distributed among all five lifters. By having everyone move at the same instant, the weight remains divided evenly, so everyone lifts the same amount So, if the sitter weighs 80 pounds (36 kg) this means each lifter only has to raise about 16 (7 kg) of those pounds.

Pulley Power

YOU WILL NEED:

2 wire clothes hangers
2 empty thread spools
2 chairs
broomstick
scissors
10 foot (3 m) length of strong string
book

If you want to pull a string instead of lifting a weight, a pulley is exactly what you need. You will need an adult's help with this experiment.

What to do: To perform this experiment in motion and movement, you have to build some pulleys. An easy way to do this is to unwind the neck of a wire hanger. Ask an adult to help you do this. Push the end through the center of one thread spool. (If you have to straighten the wire a bit to get it through the spool, that's fine.) Then bend the hanger back into shape.

When you've fastened the hanger back together, your pulley looks like this:

Make another pulley with the other hanger and spool. You will need it for the next experiment.

Now place the two chairs back to back and place the broomstick between them. Then tie a loop of string around the stick to hold the pulley. Cut a piece of string long enough to tie around the book, which is the load you are going to lift.

Cut another piece of string 4 feet (1.2 m) long. Tie it to the string on the book and run it over the pulley.

Now pull down on the string.

What happens: The book rises.

Why: Of course it did! What's so great about that? The great thing is that you changed the direction of motion. You pulled down and the book came up. This ability to change the direction of motion lets us set up factories and do the work needed to construct buildings and bridges.

In this experiment you pulled down just as hard as you would have to pull up to lift the book. You didn't gain any mechanical advantage using just one pulley. The next experiment shows you how to get science to improve your lifting power.

Double Power

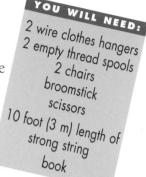

Here's your chance to be twice as strong as you were before.

What to do: Leave the last experiment set up exactly as it was. Hook the second pulley into the string that is tied around the book you plan to lift. Things should be set up like this:

Now pull up on the string that runs around the second pulley. Measure the amount of string you pull up to lift the book 3 inches (7.5 cm).

What happens: You will be using less force to lift the book than you did using only one pulley. You'll also pull 6 inches (15 cm) of string through the pulleys to lift the book 3 inches (7.5 cm)

Why: Using two pulleys gives you what is called a mechanical advantage. This simply means that it is easier to lift the book than it was before. However, you have to pull twice as much string through the pulleys to gain this advantage.

The Mysterious Moving Glass

Can you make a glass of water move without touching the glass?

What to do: Fill both glasses nearly full of water. On a flat surface, like a kitchen counter, place the pencil under the ruler, as shown in the drawing. Put one glass of water at each end of the ruler. Hold onto each glass until it is balanced.

Now move the pencil along under the ruler until the raised end is almost ready to tip downward.

Put two fingers into the water, but don't touch the glass. Push your fingers down into the water.

What happens: As your fingers move down in the water, that glass will move down as shown by the arrow in the drawing. The level of the water will rise in the glass as your fingers push into the water.

Why: As your fingers push into the water they move, or displace, water, which causes the water level to rise. The glass's weight is increased by exactly the amount of water that is displaced.

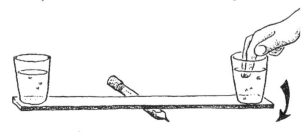

THE SOUND OF SCIENCE

Sounds are all around us. We are used to hearing the sounds of other voices, of a dog's bark, the honking of an automobile horn, or the slamming of a door. Sounds are so much a part of our lives that a sudden, total silence can be frightening. Total silence is so different from what we are used to that some people claim the silence itself creates sound.

Everyone knows how to create sound. Strike one hand against the other and you'll cause sound to be made.

What actually causes the sound of two hands clapping? When two objects come together hard and fast to create a sound, they cause the air to move or vibrate—the result of the force of their coming together. This vibration of the air causes little waves of sound to travel out in all directions.

Some of those sound waves, or vibrations, reach your ear. They cause your eardrum to vibrate, or move back and forth, slightly. This movement causes the tiny bones inside your ear to pick up that vibration and relay it through a tiny tube of liquid to the hearing or auditory nerves. These nerves communicate the sound to your brain and you hear.

When you speak, your vocal cords vibrate in your throats. The force of the air coming out of your lungs and passing the vocal cords creates these vibrations. The moving vocal cords set air in motion and the sound is carried from your mouth.

If you would like to test how this works, try to speak out loud while you are pulling air into your lungs. You can make a sound, but you can't speak when you breathe in. Try it now just to make sure.

In this chapter there are experiments in sound that are fun and offer some surprises. They will also help you understand how you hear.

Noisy Paper

YOU WILL NEED:
2 sheets of notebook
or computer paper

Two sheets of notebook or computer paper
make a great noisemaker.

What to do: Hold the two sheets of paper up
in front of you. The bottom sheet should stick out
toward you about ½ inch (12.5 mm) past the top
paper.

They should look like this:

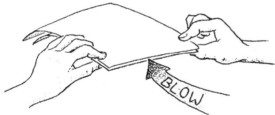

Now blow directly toward the two sheets at
the point shown by the arrow.

What happens: The two papers will make a
strange, noisy sound.

If you don't get some kind of sound from the
papers, move your mouth closer and blow again.
When you blow between the two sheets of paper
they vibrate rapidly back and forth.

If you still haven't created some sound, adjust
the way you hold the papers. Move your fingers closer to your mouth or farther back. Blow harder or less
hard. Eventually you'll find the right combination.

Don't blow until you get dizzy. Blow, then rest
a few seconds.

Why: When the papers flutter back and forth their
vibration creates the sound you hear. Their vibration
creates sound waves that your ear picks up.

104

The Screamer

YOU WILL NEED:
piece of cellophane,
2 inches (5 cm) square

Here's your chance to
make all the noise you want
and do it in the name of science.

What to do: Hold the piece of cellophane
stretched tightly between the thumbs and index
fingers of both hands.

Place your hands directly in front of your face
so the cellophane is right in front of your lips. The
set-up looks like this:

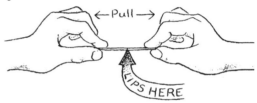

Blow hard and fast right at the edge of the tightly
stretched piece of cellophane. Keep your lips close
together so you send a thin stream of air right at
the cellophane's edge.

What happens: When the jet of air hits the
edge of the cellophane you will create the greatest,
most terrible sound you've ever heard!

If you don't get a
terrible sound, adjust
the distance between
the cellophane and your
lips until the air hits it just
right.

Why: The rapidly moving air
from your lips causes the
edge of the cellophane to vibrate quickly. Because
the cellophane is extremely thin, the jet of air
makes these vibrations extremely fast. The faster
something vibrates the higher the tone it creates.

Balloon Amplifier

YOU WILL NEED:
1 ordinary round balloon

You're used to seeing big sound amplifiers that make sounds louder. These amplifiers are often called "speakers." But did you know a balloon can increase the volume of sound?

What to do: Blow up the balloon. Hold the blown-up balloon right against your ear.

Tap lightly on the side of the balloon away from your face.

Do not do anything that will make the balloon pop while it's next to your ear. The loud noise of an exploding balloon won't do your ear any good at all.

What happens: The sound you hear is lots louder than the light tapping of your finger.

Why: The air inside the balloon is tightly compressed. When you blew up the balloon you actually let your lungs work as an air compressor, forcing the air to expand the rubber balloon. The air molecules are much closer to each other inside the balloon than they are in the air in the rest of the room. When you crowded the molecules closer together inside the balloon, that air became a better conductor of sound waves than ordinary air.

The Spoon That Thinks It's a Bell

YOU WILL NEED:

scissors
4 foot (1 2 m)
length of string
teaspoon
4 feet (12 m) of string

How can a spoon act like a bell? Read on and find out.

What to do: Tie a simple sliding loop in the middle of the string. Do this by simply wrapping one end of the string over the other and pulling the open loop down so that it is halfway between the ends of the string.

Don't tighten the loop into a knot. Leave it open about ½ inch (13 mm) like this:

Slip the handle of the teaspoon through the loop and tighten the loop so the spoon won't slip out. Adjust the spoon so it hangs with the scoop end just a little lower than the handle.

Now press one end of the string against the outside of your right ear and the other string end against the outside of your left ear. Don't put the string into your ear.

Swing the string gently so the scoop of the spoon hits the edge of a table. Listen to the sound you hear.

What happens: By swinging the spoon gently you will hear a sound that is nothing like a spoon striking a table. It's more like a bell, a church bell.

Why: The string conducts the vibration of the spoon. Not only does string carry sound waves better than air, it directs them right into your ear. This accounts for the deep bell-like tone you hear.

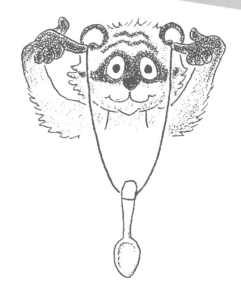

128

Big Bells

Repeat the last experiment using a soup spoon and listen to the deeper tone it creates.

Then, give your ears a treat, and do the experiment with a serving spoon. Because of its greater size its sound is much, much deeper.

The Tapping Finger

Do you know how to make even the lightest taps of your finger sound loud?

What to do: Sit at the table or desk. Place your ear flat on top like this:

Tap with your finger on the surface of the table about 1 foot (30 cm) away from your ear. Tap hard. Then tap softly.

What happens: The sound of your tapping finger is much louder than when you listen to the same tapping with your head not touching the table. Check right now to be sure this is true.

Why: Sound waves don't only travel through air. They also travel through solids, such as a table or desk. Many solids—like wood—carry sound waves much better than air because the molecules in wood are closer together than the molecules in air. This is the reason your tapping finger sounds louder when you hear it through wood than through air.

The Listening Yardstick

Did you ever try to hear through a yardstick? Now's the time!

What to do: A wind-up alarm clock is perfect for this experiment. If you don't have one, then check your electric alarm clock. Does it make a whirring sound? Most of them do if you listen carefully. If it doesn't, find some other appliance in the house that hums or makes a mechanical sound that isn't very loud. If you don't have a yardstick, a ruler will work. So will a wooden dowel rod.

Hold the yardstick so that one end touches the clock and the other end presses against the outside of your ear, like this:

What happens: The sound of the clock is much louder now than when you listen to it without the yardstick. You can check this by using the yardstick to listen to other appliances around the house.

Why: The wooden yardstick carries sound waves better than air. Therefore, you hear the clock's sounds more loudly through the yardstick than when you listen normally.

The Strange Vibrating Bowl

Can you hear the sounds from a vibrating bowl? Let's find out. It is helpful to do this experiment with a friend.

YOU WILL NEED:
large bottle
bowl
dinner fork
pencil with an eraser
3 foot (1 m) length of string

What to do: Set the bottle on the table. An empty, large soft drink bottle is great.

Balance the bowl upside down on top of the bottle like this:

Put your ear close to the bowl and tap the edge of the bowl with the eraser end of the pencil. Better still, have a friend do the tapping.

Then repeat the experiment, but this time have your friend touch the edge of the bowl with his or her finger.

What happens: The first time you'll hear a pleasant sound. The second time, when your friend touches the edge of the bowl, you won't hear it.

Why: The sound is created because the bowl is vibrating. When your friend touches the bowl with a fingertip it causes the vibration to stop and the sound to end.

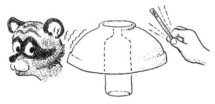

Can You Tune a Fork?

YOU WILL NEED:
3 foot (1 m) length of string
dinner fork
soup bowl
pencil with an eraser

It's sad but true that a piano can be tuned, but no one can tune a fork. However, even an untuned fork is good for a tone, if not a

What to do: Tie one end of the string around the fork, as shown in the illustration. Lift the fork by the string so the tines hang straight down.

Tap the bowl with the pencil and lower the fork so the tines are lightly touching the opposite side of the bowl.

What happens: When the fork touches the bowl its tines begin to vibrate. If you hold your ear close to the tines you can probably hear the tone.

If you're working with a friend, have him or her tap the bowl again. This time press the string holding the fork against the outside of your ear, just as you did with the spoon experiment. Now you can hear the tone more clearly.

Why: The fork tines pick up the vibrations from the bowl. This is called "sympathetic" vibration. The string helps to conduct the sound, just as it did with the spoon that thought it was a bell.

133 Tuning a Glass

YOU WILL NEED:
8 drinking glasses
water
pencil

We said you can't tune a fork, but who said you can't tune a glass?

What to do: Line up the eight drinking glasses in a row on the kitchen counter. (Plastic bottles won't work this time.) It does not matter if the glasses are all the same size or not. If they are, however, it's quicker to tune them.

Fill the glasses part full of water, so that they look pretty much like those in the illustration:

As you can see, each glass has a little less water in it than the one to its left.

Now use the pencil to gently but firmly strike the side of each glass.

What happens: You will hear a different tone from each of the glasses. The more water there is in a glass, the lower the tone that it makes.

Call the first glass on your left "do," which is the first note of the musical scale. Strike the next glass. If its tone is the next step up the scale move on. If not, either add a bit of water or pour some out until the glass's tone is one step up.

Continue in this manner until you have tuned the eight glasses to play a musical scale.

Why: We know that vibrations cause sound. Striking the side of a glass causes it to vibrate. The speed of the vibration depends upon how much glass and water there are to set in motion. The more water, the slower the vibrations and the deeper the tone.

134 Tune More Glasses

Now set up eight glasses that are different in size. The more different, the better.

Keep in mind that it is the total amount of water that determines the tone of the glass.

Tune these eight glasses to play a musical scale by adding or pouring out water until each tone is one step above the one to its left.

Seeing Sound Waves

Now is your chance to see sound waves, but you must do this experiment on a sunny day.

YOU WILL NEED:

empty can
balloon
scissors
rubber band
small mirror
newspaper
hammer
glue

What to do: Remove both ends from a tin food can. Wash the can carefully with warm water and soap. Watch out for sharp edges left from the can opener.

Next you need a piece of balloon to fit over one end of the can. It's a good idea to blow up the balloon and play with it a while before stretching it over the can. This makes the rubber easier to pull. Then let the air out and cut the neck off the balloon with the scissors. Stretch a piece of the main part of the balloon over one end of the can. Hold it in place with the rubber band. You'll probably have to wrap the rubber band around the balloon and can several times.

You need a small piece of mirror. (If you don't have an old mirror, use a piece of aluminum foil.) Wrap the mirror in several sheets of newspaper. Then tap it with a hammer. Unwrap the newspaper and carefully pick out a piece of mirror about ½ inch (12.5 mm) square. Wrap up the other scraps in the paper and throw them away.

Use a drop of glue to fasten the mirror to the balloon as shown here.

Stand so the sunlight from a window hits the reflector. Move the can around until the reflection shows up on a wall, like this:

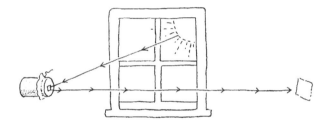

Talk directly into the open end of the can. Shout. Make different sounds. Watch the reflection.

What happens: The sounds you make cause movement of the reflection.

Why: The rubber on the can picks up the vibrations of the sound waves from your voice. As it vibrates, so does the reflector. That's what makes the reflection on the wall move.

FEELING STRESSED?
TRY SOME SURFACE TENSION

Water is an extremely important part of our lives. Without it, human life cannot survive.

Not only do we drink water, but the major part of our bodies is also composed of water.

We bathe in water, we sail across it, we use it as the basis for drinks ranging from sodas and juices to tea and coffee.

Without water we'd have no trees, no grass, no flowers—-no life as we know it. Water is essential to living.

In this chapter you will find out some interesting facts about water. You'll see that it can do some amazing things, and that it's great to experiment with. You'll find out something else about water, too. You've probably heard a lot about tension and stress. Water has tension, too, but of a different type than the one that comes with stress.

Water has surface tension. Surface tension is a scientific term that means that the surface of a bowl of water has the ability to hold itself together. This happens because the molecules that make up a container of water tend to cling to one another.

Normally, we don't think of a lake or ocean as having water molecules clinging together to form a covering for the water. But that is exactly what surface tension does. You don't feel it when you poke your finger into a cup of water or when you dive into a swimming pool. But it exists, even if you are not aware of it.

Let's begin this chapter with some experiments that show some of the surprising things water does because of surface tension.

Then we'll move on to some really interesting things below the surface.

Full to Overflowing

Everyone has filled a glass or a cup until the liquid flows over the top. Here's your chance to fill a glass to overflowing without spilling a drop.

What to do: Put the glass on a kitchen counter or in the sink. Add water until the glass is full to the brim.

Now to answer this question: How many pins can you drop into the glass before it runs over? Ten? Twenty? Fifty?

Carefully hold a pin over the glass so its point just touches the surface of the water.

Let go of the pin so it slides into the water. Add another pin and then another until the water finally runs over.

What happens: You'll add more pins than you believed possible. Look sideways at the glass and you'll see the level of the water is above the edge of the glass.

Why: Surface tension keeps the water from over-flowing long after it seems possible for the glass to hold any more pins.

137 The Strange Expanding Loop of Thread

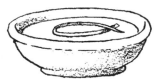

Once something is done to change water's surface tension, strange things happen as you will see.

What to do: Fill the bowl with water nearly to the top.

Form the thread into a loop by lapping one end over the other, but don't make a knot in it. Carefully place the loop on the surface of the water. Keep the loop sort of skinny so it looks like this:

Now touch the corner of the bar of soap to the water inside the loop in the thread.

What happens: The loop will form a circle around the soap.

Why: The soap destroys the surface tension of the water inside the loop. The thread keeps the soap from spreading beyond the loop. Since the water outside the loop still has its surface tension, it pulls away taking the thread with it. This leaves a circular loop around the soap.

138 The Stubborn Cork

YOU WILL NEED:
cork
drinking glass
water
teaspoon

Can a cork be stubborn? Here's how to deal with one that refuses to obey your commands.

What to do: Fill the glass with water almost to the top. Now float the cork in the glass. Within a short time the cork will drift to the side of the glass.

Your challenge is to convince the cork to come to the center of the glass without touching it or taking it out of the water. If you want to blow on it, that's okay, but when it reaches the center of the glass it must stay there after you stop blowing.

Here's how to make the stubborn cork obey. Slowly, one spoonful at a time, begin to add water to the glass. Eventually the water will rise above the top of the glass as surface tension holds it in place.

What happens: The cork drifts to the center of the glass and stays there when the water level rises high enough.

Why: Surface tension lets the water rise above the glass. It causes the water to form a little curved dome whose high point is at its center. The cork seeks the highest point of the water.

A Strainer Full of Water

YOU WILL NEED:
small strainer
cooking oil
empty bowl
glass of water

139

A strainer won't hold water. Or will it?

What to do: Use a small strainer because a large one requires too much cooking oil.

Coat the strainer with cooking oil. A good way to do this is to pour the oil into the bowl and then gently slosh the strainer around in the bowl until it is coated with oil.

Shake the strainer carefully into the bowl so that all the holes are open. (Don't throw away the cooking oil you just used. If you set it aside, you can use it in the experiment on page 120.)

Hold the strainer over the sink. Start pouring water very, very slowly from the glass into the strainer.

What happens: As you carefully pour the water, you'll see the strainer begin to fill with water. Look closely and you'll see tiny beads of water pushing through the wires, but very few of them will leak out.

Why: It is the surface tension of the beads of water that makes this experiment work. The oil helps by giving the wires a smooth coating. It also makes the spaces between the wires a fraction smaller, because, even after you shake the oil off, some of it clings to the wires.

The Incredible Upside-Down Bottle

140

Anyone can turn a bottle upside down. But how many people can do it without having the water spill out? This experiment really needs at least three hands some of the time. Unless you happen to have an extra hand yourself, make sure you have a friend around who can help when needed.

YOU WILL NEED:
bottle with a small mouth and neck
water
small piece of screening or a strainer
6 inches (15 cm) of soft wire or rubber band

What to do: Fill the bottle with water all the way to the top.

Cover the mouth of the bottle with screen wire, if you have a little chunk of screening available. If not, check to see if you have any plastic screen of the type that comes in some frozen dinner cooking pouches. Attach the screen to the top of the bottle with the piece of wire or a rubber band.

If you don't have a piece of screen available, you can hold a strainer tightly against the mouth of the bottle. That's where you need that extra hand your friend will supply.

With the screen in place or the strainer held tightly against the bottle's mouth, quickly turn the bottle upside down.

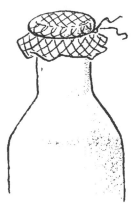

What happens: The water doesn't run out.

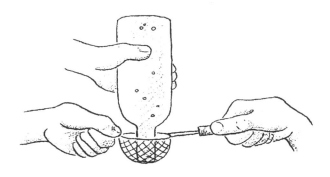

Why: Surface tension is helping. It also helps that the bottle is full so that no air is trapped inside the bottle to push down on the water. The only direction air pressure is pushing is up against the water that might want to run through the screen.

The Hawk and the Sparrows

YOU WILL NEED:
dinner plate
water
talcum powder
bar of soap

Hawks often fly into a flock of sparrows and scatter them. You'll see why this experiment was named for them when you complete it.

What to do: Place the dinner plate on a table and pour water into it until the plate is nearly full. When the water is calm, sprinkle a bit of the powder onto the surface of the water—just a pinch of it between your thumb and finger.

The powder will float on the water like this:

The bits of powder are the "sparrows."

Rub the tip of your finger the soap. Touch the surface of the water with your fingertip. Your finger is the "hawk."

What happens: The instant your soapy finger touches the water the powder the "sparrows" scatter.

Why: The soap breaks the surface tension of the water. The water around the edges of the dish pulls away and carries the powder with it.

A Scale You Never Thought Of

YOU WILL NEED:
large bowl
baking pan
water
apple or orange
measuring cup

Can you use a bowl of water as a scale? Do this experiment and find out.

What to do: Put the bowl in the baking pan. Fill the bowl to the rim with water. Place the apple or the orange in the bowl of water.

What happens: Water will overflow into the baking pan. Carefully lift the bowl of water out of the pan. Pour the water from the pan into the measuring cup. Read the scale on the side of the cup to see how many ounces of water are in it. This reading gives you the weight of the fruit.

Why: The water that overflowed was displaced by the fruit. The amount of water a floating object displaces is the same as the object's weight.

143 Water's Great Escape

YOU WILL NEED:
drinking glass
water
bowl
2 paper towels

You've heard that water doesn't run uphill. Here's an experiment that shows how you can coax water to do it. Just in case there's a leak it's a good idea to do it in the kitchen sink.

What to do: Fill the glass nearly full of water. Put it next to the bowl.

The plan is to have the water move up and over the rim of the glass and down into the bowl. To do this you need a wick through which the water can travel. A wick is a tight roll of paper or cloth that will absorb water. Just as a candle wick carries melted wax up to the flame, your water wick will carry water along its length.

Twist the paper towels together fairly tightly to form the wick. Bend the wick in the middle. Then place one end in the glass. Be sure the other end reaches into the bowl, like this:

What happens: Within just a minute or so you'll see the wick getting wet as water begins to travel along it. After a few minutes some water will appear in the bottom of the bowl.

Water won't flow from the glass into the bowl. Instead of flowing, it sort of oozes. This experiment takes time. Check back once in a while to see how it is coming.

When the water level in the bowl is as high as the level of the water left in the glass, the water stops moving. If you set the glass on something higher than the bowl you get most of the water out of it.

Why: There are thousands and maybe millions of tiny spaces between the fibers of the paper towel. Water moves into these openings and advances along the twisted material. Its movement is known as capillary action. Moisture moves from plant roots into the rest of the plant in this same way.

Slow But Mighty

144

Is it possible for a can full of cardboard squares to lift a heavy board?

YOU WILL NEED:

empty can
2 or 3 empty cereal boxes, or pieces of cardboard
scissors
water
dishwashing detergent
piece of wood about 2 feet (.6 m) long or a stack of old magazines

What to do: Wash out the empty can with soap and water. Watch out for sharp metal around the edge.

Cut enough square pieces of cereal box cardboard to fill the can when you stack the pieces on top of each other. Don't worry about making the pieces of cardboard the exact size of the can. It's better and faster to cut them a bit smaller, like this:

When the stack of cardboard pieces fills the can fill the can with water. Add a squirt of dishwashing detergent or a bit of dishwasher powder. Within a minute or so you'll see that the water level has dropped as much as 1 inch (2.5 cm). This is because the water is seeping into the pieces of cardboard. Add enough water to bring the water level back to the top of the can.

Push down on the cardboard. You can probably add a few more pieces.

Now place the piece of wood on top of the can like this:

What happens: Within a short time the piece of wood will begin to rise. When it stops rising, remove it and try to push the cardboard back into the can. This will be difficult, if not impossible!

Why: Capillary action causes the water to soak into the pieces of cardboard. When each piece of cardboard fills with water it is a fraction thicker than it was without the water. This is what causes the lifting action which raised the piece of wood.

The Case of the Shrinking Tissues

YOU WILL NEED:

drinking glass
water
6 facial tissues
pencil

Facial tissues don't get smaller and smaller—or do they? Here's an experiment that asks the question: What happened to the tissues?

What to do: Fill the glass with water to about ¼ inch (9 mm) below the rim.

Tear each of the facial tissues into strips about 1½ inches (3.75 cm) wide. The dotted lines in the illustration show where to tear the tissues. Don't worry if you don't tear them straight.

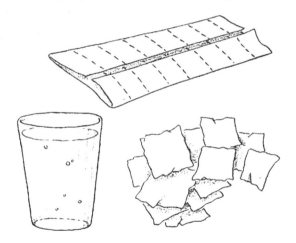

Now, stuff one strip of tissue at a time into the glass of water. Use the pencil to keep pressing the tissues down toward the bottom of the glass.

What happens: You'll see small bubbles rise through the water from time to time. This is because some air was trapped by the tissue when you pushed it into the water.

As you push the tissues down with the pencil you free the trapped air. This makes room for more tissues in the water.

Why: Highly absorbent products like facial tissues have only a bit of solid material in them. They are made up largely of air space. When the air is gone from the tissues there isn't a lot left. This is the reason you can stuff so many into the glass of water. Cotton balls, incidentally, work the same way.

The Moving Mystery Match

YOU WILL NEED:
wooden match
coin
water
spoon

Why does a wooden match suddenly decide to move?

What to do: Bend the wooden match in half. Don't break it in two pieces. Leave several wood fibers holding it together. Place the coin so that just its edges rest on the match.

Run a few drops of water into the spoon. Let a single drop of water fall onto the broken match at the point shown by the arrow.

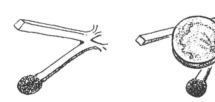

Drop here

What happens: Almost instantly the two halves of the match will move apart slightly and the coin will fall off at least one of the halves.

Why: Water causes wood fibers to expand or swell, which makes the match move slightly.

If you want to use this experiment to impress your friends, set it up so the match rests on the rim of a bottle. Just be sure the neck of the bottle is large enough so the coin falls into the bottle when the match moves.

147 You Can't Keep a Good Button Down

If you've ever wanted to see a button rise and fall in a glass of liquid, now's your chance.

YOU WILL NEED:
shirt button, or one no larger than ¾ inch (18 mm)
drinking glass
carbonated soda

What to do: Fill a glass with carbonated soda to about ½ inch (12.5 mm) of the top. (One of the clear sodas is probably best because you can see through it easily.)

Drop the button into the glass. If it floats on top of the soda, give it a tap with your finger and send it to the bottom of the glass.

What happens: Small bubbles begin to form around the button.

Suddenly the button rises to the top of the glass. Give it a tap to knock the little gas bubbles off and it will sink to the bottom

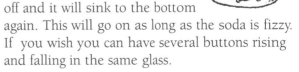

again. This will go on as long as the soda is fizzy. If you wish you can have several buttons rising and falling in the same glass.

Why: The gas bubbles are carbon dioxide, which is what gives soda its "fizz." When the bubbles attach to the button they give it enough lift, or buoyancy, to make it rise.

The Great Cooking Oil Trade Off

YOU WILL NEED:
2 small glasses the same size
cereal box cardboard
scissors
water
cooking oil
baking sheet

Can you trade a glass of cooking oil for one of water without pouring one into the other? Have a friend help you try.

What to do: Begin with two glasses exactly the same size. Juice glasses are perfect.

Cut a piece of cereal box cardboard about 4 inches (10 cm) square, large enough so that when you place it over the mouth of a glass, it sticks out ¾ inch (18 mm) on each side.

Fill one of the glasses to the top with water. Fill the other to the top with cooking oil. For safety's sake, set both on a baking sheet.

Place the cardboard on top of the glass of water. Hold the cardboard firmly in place and turn the glass over so it looks like the illustration above.

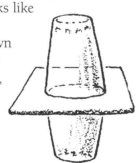

Put the upside-down glass of water, with the cardboard still in place, on top of the glass of cooking oil. Don't let the cardboard slip!

Hold both glasses steady and slowly move the cardboard sideways. Here's where your friend comes in. You need an extra hand to hold things in place. Move the cardboard until its edge is exactly where the rims of the glasses meet, like this:

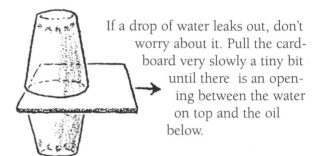

If a drop of water leaks out, don't worry about it. Pull the cardboard very slowly a tiny bit until there is an opening between the water on top and the oil below.

What happens: A few oil bubbles rise into the water glass. They will form a little oil dome on the bottom of the water glass (which is at the top, of course).

Pull the cardboard a bit farther and suddenly you'll see the oil begin to roll upward into the water glass. At the same time, water flows down to replace the oil.

In a minute or less the top glass is full of oil and the water is in the bottom glass.

Why: Because water is heavier than cooking oil, the water flows downward, forcing the lighter weight oil upward. This is why oil and water don't mix and oil floats on water.

Science Can Give You a Warm Feeling

Light is something we take for granted. The sun shines. We turn on an electric light. Light shines through glass. It is light that enables us to see reflections in mirrors.

Light travels in rays that move in a straight line at great speed. When we speak of the speed of light we are talking about a light ray that travels through space at 186,000 miles (297,600 km) per second! To get a good idea of what this speed means, consider that the sun is 93,000,000 miles (148,800,000 km) away from us. Light travels from the sun to the earth in just about eight minutes.

Although light rays travel in straight lines, these rays can be bent, or refracted. When light enters water or passes through glass, the light ray bends at an angle. When it leaves the glass or water the ray again moves in a straight line. However, it is traveling at a different angle than before it encountered the glass or the water.

Our chief source of light is from the sun, but we create light by artificial means, such as electricity, as well.

It is important to remember that light is related to heat. It is the sun's tremendous heat that causes it to give off light. A burning fire also creates light. And if you hold your hand near, but not touching, an electric light bulb you'll feel the heat it gives off.

Heat can also cause light. It is the heating of the filament inside an electric light that creates the artificial light we see in the bulb. When things are heated enough, they change. Vegetables, for example, become tender when they are cooked. A room gets warm when the furnace comes on. Ice melts and water boils if heated enough. Air and many other materials expand when heated. It is the expansion of air that makes some of the experiments in this chapter work.

Breaking Up Rays of Sunlight

It is possible to break up or separate the sun's rays. When this is done, a ray of light suddenly shows a rainbow of colors. And you can do it in about two minutes on a sunny day.

What to do: Pour about 1 inch (2.5 cm) of water into the baking pan. Now you need a small mirror.

Put the pan of water where the sunlight shines directly on it, either indoors or outside.

Lean the mirror against one edge of the pan, like this:

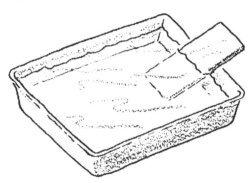

Direct the mirror's reflection onto a white ceiling or wall or the sheet of white paper. If you are outside, you'll probably have to use the paper as your viewing screen.

What happens: You'll see a rainbow of colors on the ceiling or wall or sheet of paper. These colors start with red and end with violet.

Why: Water causes the rays of sunlight that are reflected from the mirror to bend. When light rays bend, each color in the ray bends at a different angle. This causes the rainbow effect.

All the colors we normally see—red, orange, yellow, green, blue, and violet—are contained in sunlight. We see objects as having color depending upon which light rays they reflect.

Upside Down in a Spoon

YOU WILL NEED:
shiny soup spoon or serving spoon

150 How can a spoon turn you upside down? This experiment is great fun for younger children you have to entertain.

What to do: The scoop of a spoon makes an interesting mirror. Just be sure the spoon you use is shiny and the larger the better. Hold the spoon up so you see yourself in the scoop.

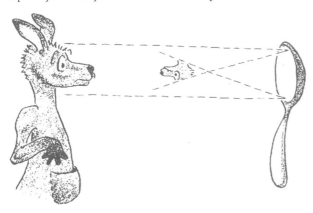

What happens: When you look at the spoon you'll see your reflection upside down. Tip the spoon so it reflects other things that also appear upside down.

Why: Light rays travel in straight lines. They are reflected in straight lines, too. But when light is reflected from a curved surface, the rays leave the surface at different angles. The illustration shows how this works with the spoon. The reflected image appears upside down because of the angle of the reflected rays of light.

151 The Case of the Vanishing Reflection

In this experiment you'll see your reflection one minute and have it vanish the next.

YOU WILL NEED:
10 inch (25 cm) length of kitchen foil
scissors

What to do: Use the scissors to cut a piece of kitchen foil off the roll. Don't tear it. Cut it to avoid wrinkles.

Look at your reflection on the shiny side of the foil. It won't be perfect, but you'll see yourself clearly.

Now crinkle the foil into a loose wad. Don't press it together tightly because you'll have to straighten it out again.

Flatten out the wadded foil, like this:

Now look for your reflection.

What happens: No matter how you turn the foil you won't see your reflection. It has vanished.

Why: Remember that light rays are reflected from a surface in straight lines. The once-smooth foil surface is now a mass of ridges and valleys. The reflected light bounces off it in all directions.

Because these reflected rays are going off at different angles, your image does not form in the way it did when its smooth surface reflected the rays right back to you.

A Water Droplet Magnifier

Yes, it's possible to make a tiny drop of water into a magnifier. You can't use it to read with, but it will magnify one letter at a time.

YOU WILL NEED:

paper clip
pliers
glass of water
newspaper page

What to do: Straighten the paper clip and make a small loop, as round as possible, at one end. You'll need a pair of pliers to form the loop. Paper clips are hard to bend when you work with just the end. The loop should be about 1/8 inch (3 mm) across or just a tiny bit larger.

Dip the loop into the glass of water. You'll see that a film of water fills the inside of the loop. Tap the wire against the side of the glass. This helps form the tiny lens of water.

Hold the loop above a letter on the newspaper page.

What happens: If all went well, the letter you're looking at will appear several times larger than it is.

If the letter seems smaller than usual , the water formed the wrong kind of lens. Tap it against the side of the glass and look again.

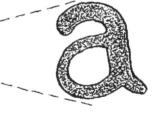

If you lose the water inside the loop, just dip the wire again and collect a new water lens.

Why: The drawing above shows how light enters and leaves the lens you just made. Always remember that light rays may be bent by a lens, but they always enter or leave the lens in a straight line.

The Hot Water Tap Always Leaks

153

YOU WILL NEED:
2 paper cups
straight pins
small drinking glass
water
ice cubes

It wastes water to have any tap leak. But it's even worse to realize that it is always the hot-water tap that seems to be leaking.

What to do: Right in the middle of the bottom of each paper cup make a tiny pin hole. Then set the paper cups on top of the glasses like this:

Fill one cup half full of cold water. Drop in a couple of ice cubes to make sure it is really cold.

Fill the other cup half full of hot water out of the hot-water tap.

Now sit back and observe the tiny drips from the pin holes in the bottoms of the cups.

What happens: If the holes are the same size, you'll see the hot water leaking faster than the cold water. In fact, if the cold water is cold enough it may not leak at all.

Why: The molecules in hot water move much faster than they do in cold water. The faster they move, the easier it is for them to slip past each other. That's why hot water is more likely to leak than cold.

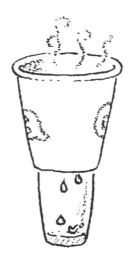

Undersea Water Fountain

YOU WILL NEED:

pot
cold water
small glass bottle
hot water
marbles or washers
ink, food color, or
watercolors

What happens when warm water suddenly appears beneath a mass of cold water?

What to do: Fill the pot nearly full of cold water, the colder the better. If you want, instead of using a pot, just put the stopper in the kitchen sink and run about 5 inches (12.5 cm) of cold water into it.

Next, fill the small bottle about three-quarters full of hot water. A glass bottle works best, but if you only have a plastic bottle it will do. Drop a couple of clean marbles or washers into the bottle. These will give it enough weight so it won't float when you put it into the cold water.

Add a few drops of ink or food color to the hot water. If you don't have any, then use a bit of paint from a set of watercolors.

Immediately put the bottle in the bottom of the pot or in the sink.

What happens: The colored water will rise upward from the bottle toward the surface of the cold water. It looks just like a little underwater volcano erupting. When the colored water begins to cool, it will thin out and settle toward the bottom of the pot.

Why: Hot water rises because the molecules in it are moving rapidly. As they bounce and dart about they expand the water. When water or air expands, it gets less dense, because the same amount of matter takes up a larger space.

This expansion causes warm water or air to rise above colder, denser water or air. This kind of movement is called convection.

What a Way to Cut an Ice Cube

If you ever need to cut an ice cube in half, here's a way of doing it that has a result so surprising it seems impossible.

YOU WILL NEED:

18 inches (45 m cm) of thin wire or thin nylon cord

2 round pieces of wood (dowel rods) or 2 bolts, 6 to 8 inches long (15 to 20 cm)

ice cube

pieces of wood or a tin can

What to do: Tie the ends of the wire or nylon cord to the round pieces of wood. Dowel rods are perfect but so are pieces of broomstick. Fairly long bolts will work well, also.

Make sure the wire or cord is tied tightly to the wood rods or bolts. You'll use them as hand-holds so you don't cut your fingers instead of the ice cube. The cutter looks like this:

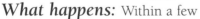

Put the cube of ice on something solid that is high enough so you can stand over the cube and push down on the cutting tool. Several short pieces of wood work well when stacked on top of each other or you can use a tin can as a cutting stand.

After placing the cube on the wood or can, position the cutting tool like this:

Take hold of the two handles and press down good and hard. Move the wire back and forth over the surface of the ice cube in a sawing motion while you keep pressing down.

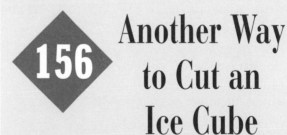

What happens: Within a few seconds the wire or cord will begin to work its way slowly into the ice cube. As you continue to push down and the wire cuts deeper, you may wish to stop the back and forth motion and just keep pressing down.

The wire sinks into the ice cube even if you don't keep up the sawing motion! And the amazing thing is that the ice cube seems to freeze over above the wire.

When the wire is nearly through the ice cube, let up just a bit on the downward pressure. This keeps the wire from coming through the bottom of the cube with a sudden jolt.

When the wire is finally all the way through the ice cube wouldn't you think you'd have two cubes? You don't. You still have only one because the two halves froze together.

Why: Pressure on the wire causes the ice under the wire to melt. This is because pressure creates heat. However, the ice cube is cold enough to refreeze when the water oozes its way to the top of the wire where there is no pressure.

156 Another Way to Cut an Ice Cube

Hang two heavy weights on either end of the wire. Then stand back and watch the wire work its way through the ice cube all by itself.

The Hot Air Twirler

Here's a twirling toy that uses the heat from your hands for power.

YOU WILL NEED:
sheet of thin paper
scissors
straight pin
pencil with an eraser

What to do: Begin with a sheet of the thinnest paper you can find. Cut a square that is exactly 3 inches by 3 inches (7.5 cm x 7.5 cm.)

Fold the square diagonally and then unfold it. The solid line in the illustration shows this fold. The dotted line shows the next fold to make.

When the two diagonal folds are in place, push in a little on opposite sides of the paper. This causes the center to rise about ½ inch (1.25 cm) higher than the sides. The arrows in the illustration below show where to push.

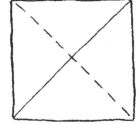

Next, push the straight pin into the eraser of the pencil. Leave 1 inch (2.5 cm) of the pin sticking straight up from the eraser. Sit down and hold the pencil between your knees as seen in the illustration.

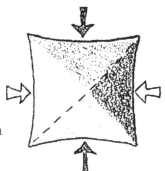

Set the square of paper on top of the pencil so the head of the pin is right at the center peak, where the two folds come together.

Place your cupped hands on either side of the paper so they are about an inch or so away from it.

Now just sit and think warm thoughts without moving your hands or knees.

What happens: Within just a minute the little paper twirler will begin to turn. If you see that the corner of the paper is going to hit your hands when it turns, move your hands back enough to give it room. But keep your hands as close to the paper as possible.

When it gets going, the twirler will spin slowly around and around. The lighter the paper and the warmer your hands, the faster it turns.

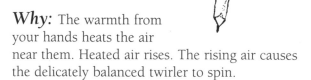

Why: The warmth from your hands heats the air near them. Heated air rises. The rising air causes the delicately balanced twirler to spin.

BLOWN AWAY

Air is all around us. We breathe it. We see such things in the air as dust, smoke, and other kinds of pollution we all dread.

Air is moving constantly. We are aware of it when the wind blows. We also see clouds moving rapidly across the sky or watch a plume of smoke or steam as the wind blows it one way or the other.

Automotive engineers design cars so their movement through the air will be smooth. Airplanes fly only because air provides the "lift" necessary for them to remain in flight. It is the shape of their wings that changes the wind speed and results in the lifting effect.

Air also exerts pressure. Anyone who has ever tried to carry a large sheet of cardboard when the wind is blowing knows

how great that pressure can be. And it is the force or pressure of moving air that drives a sailboat across the water.

Air doesn't have to move to exert pressure. Every minute it pushes down on us and from every side as well. We have about 14 pounds (6.3 kg) of air pressure pushing down on every square inch of our bodies at every moment.

What we call a vacuum is really just lower-than-normal air pressure. When you suck on a drinking straw, you are lowering the air pressure inside the straw. Then the normal pressure outside pushes the liquid up into the straw.

Air presses from all sides. So, when something like a kite or an airplane is up in the air, air pressure is pushing up and from all sides as well as pushing down from above.

The things that happen because of air speed and pressure are what make the following experiments work.

158

The Impossible Fluttering Paper

Do you have enough lung power to make a paper flutter that is hidden behind a bottle?

What to do: Fold the paper strip ½ inch (1.25 cm) from the end so it looks like this:

Place the strip of tape over the folded end and tape the paper onto a tabletop so it looks like the illustration below.

Put the large bottle on the table between you and the paper. Place the bottle about 3 inches (7.5 cm) in front of the paper strip. Blow directly at the bottle in front of you. Keep your eye on the paper strip as you blow hard, then soft, then fast, and then slow.

What happens: When you blow just hard enough, the paper will begin to bend and flutter although you are blowing on the bottle instead of the paper.

Why: Moving air will follow a curved surface. It does not always travel in a straight line the way light rays do. Although your breath of air is deflected when it strikes the bottle, some of the air continues around the bottle, striking the paper strip.

159

The Even More Impossible Fluttering Paper

See how far away from the bottle you can blow and still make the paper flutter. Move the paper closer to the bottle or farther away and check your results. Just remember to rest a minute between blowing efforts so you don't get dizzy.

The Stubborn Ping-Pong Ball

Anyone can blow a ping-pong ball a few inches. Or can they?

YOU WILL NEED:

large funnel
ping-pong ball
sheet of paper and
tape (if you don't have
a funnel)

What to do: Wash the funnel carefully to make certain it is absolutely clean. A funnel used around the kitchen is the only kind to use for this experiment. Don't use a funnel that has been used around oil and gasoline in the garage.

If you don't have a funnel, it takes about ten seconds to make a paper cone. Roll a sheet of paper into a cone that is large at one end and 1/4 inch (6 mm) across at the other. Tape the loose end so your cone looks like this:

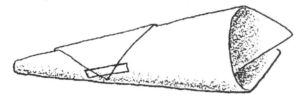

Drop the ping-pong ball into the paper cone or funnel. Hold the funnel directly over your head and blow into the small end. The drawing shows how.

The object is to blow the ball out of the funnel. Blow hard, but steady.

What happens: Unless you are using a very small funnel, you'll find it is impossible to blow the ball out of it.

Why: The passage of air around the ball makes it jump and bounce, but it will not fly out of the funnel. This is because the fast-moving air flows all around the ball instead of pushing it upward. The ball tends to jump up (even higher at times than the rim of the funnel) but it won't jump to one side.

Puzzling Paper Loop

Here's a paper loop that does just the opposite of what you'd expect it to do.

What to do: Cut a strip from paper about 8 inches (20 cm) long and 1½ inches (3.75 cm) wide. Glue or tape the loose ends together to form a circular loop like this:

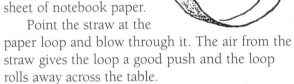

The next step requires a drinking straw. If you don't have one, just roll a hollow tube from half a sheet of notebook paper.

Point the straw at the paper loop and blow through it. The air from the straw gives the loop a good push and the loop rolls away across the table.

Now place the loop on the table in front of you. Aim the straw so it is above the loop, pointing to the side that's away from you at an angle, as shown in the illustration.

Now blow sharply through the straw.

What happens: The loop will either stay where it is or roll away from you. If it doesn't roll away from you, toward the burst of air coming out of the straw, then change the angle of the straw. Blow again.

When you have the correct angle for the straw and get the feel of exactly how hard you need to blow, you can astound friends by making the paper loop follow the air rather than run from it.

Why: Moving air creates a low pressure area as it flows along. The paper loop is moved into that low pressure area by the normal air pressure behind it and on its sides.

The fact that moving air—or something moving through the air—creates a low pressure area is one of the things that enables airplanes to fly. Air flowing past a curved surface tends to speed up.

The faster it flows the lower the pressure it creates. This tells you something about creating low pressure on top of a curved airplane to supply the "lift" the plane needs to fly.

The Great Coin and Paper Race

162

The outcome of this race between a coin and a piece of paper is amazing.

YOU WILL NEED:
fairly large coin
paper
scissors

What to do: Cut a round piece of paper that is a little smaller than the coin. It doesn't have to be perfectly round, but keep it as nearly round as possible. Just be sure the does-n't stick out at any point past the edge of the coin when you place the coin on top of it.

You're going to use the coin and the paper in a scientific race. Hold the coin in one hand and the paper in the other about 3 feet (90 cm) above the floor. Drop them both at the same instant.

What happens: The coin takes off for the floor in a straight line while the paper flutters this way and that and reaches the floor long afterward. Their paths look like this:

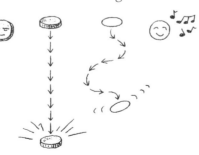

Why: The coin is heavy enough so its fall is not disturbed as gravity draws it down.

The paper is extremely light in weight, but it has about the same amount of surface as the coin. This combination of lots of surface plus light weight causes the paper to flutter because the air pushes at it as it falls.

The Great Coin and Paper Race— Second Stage

163

It's only fair to let the loser in any race have a second chance at winning.

YOU WILL NEED:
coin and paper from the previous experiment

What to do: Hold the paper and the coin in the same hand with the paper sitting on top of the coin. Hold them like this:

Paper

Coin

Hold the coin by its edges so you don't touch the paper at all. Drop them now.

What happens: The coin and the paper should travel together all the way to the floor. If any air gets between them they will separate and the paper will finish its journey fluttering instead of falling with the coin. If that happens, repeat the experiment.

Why: The paper and the coin travel together because of moving air. When something moves rapidly through the air (such as the falling coin), it pulls some air immediately behind it.

The paper "rides" the coin down because it is caught in the pocket of air traveling with the speeding coin.

164 The Great Coin Blowing Demonstration

YOU WILL NEED:
drinking glass
small coin

Do you know anyone who can blow hard enough to blow a small coin all the way across the mouth of a glass? Of course you do. You can!

What to do: Put the drinking glass on a table. Balance the coin on the rim of the glass like this:

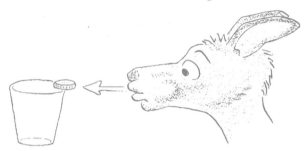

Blow sharply on the edge of the coin. The arrow in the drawing shows where to direct the stream of air.

Now, balance the coin on the rim of the glass again. This time you are going to blow the coin all the way across the open mouth of the glass so it lands on the table on the opposite side of the glass.

Impossible? No, You can do it!

Blow hard. The coin will probably fall into the glass the first few times you try.

You must blow right at the edge of the coin. Check the arrow in the illustration again. Don't blow over the coin and don't blow under it. Don't place your lips too close to the coin. Stay back several inches and blow straight at the coin's edge. Blow hard and fast.

What happens: The first time you tried it, the coin fell off the rim of the glass. It may have fallen into the glass or onto the table. But that's what you expected, wasn't it?

When you lined up everything correctly, the coin sailed across the glass and hit the opposite rim, but the force of the rapidly moving air kept it going.

Why: The coin is light enough for the moving air from your lungs to set it in motion. It had very little friction to overcome, because it was balanced delicately on the rim of the glass.

It's all a matter of directing the coin in the path it needs to take. Air speed does the rest.

What's the Matter With This Bottle?

165

YOU WILL NEED:

large, empty plastic
soft drink bottle
funnel
sticky cloth or plastic tape
large pitcher
water

Here's a bottle of water with an open top, but you can't empty it.

What to do: Place the funnel in the mouth of the bottle. Carefully and tightly seal the funnel onto the bottle as seen here:

Use very sticky black cloth or plastic tape or electrician's tape. Take your time and work with strips of tape 8 or 10 inches (10 or 12.5 cm) long. Make certain you tape the funnel onto the bottle so the seal is airtight. Pull the tape tight and press it down firmly.

Put the bottle and funnel in the kitchen sink. Fill the pitcher with water and start filling the bottle. Be sure you pour water into the funnel fast enough so the water level rises in the funnel. This is extremely important! Keep pouring so the water level is near the top of the funnel.

Now, place your hand tightly over the top of the funnel (which is full of water) and quickly turn the bottle over so it looks like this:

Keep your hand over the mouth of the funnel until the air inside the bottle rises to what is actually the bottom of the bottle. Don't let even a tiny bubble of air get past your hand into the mouth of the funnel.

What happens:
The water stays in the bottle.

Why: With the space between the funnel and bottle taped airtight and the funnel full of water, air is trapped inside the bottle with no way to escape. As water fills the bottle the air molecules are so compressed that the air pressure inside the bottle is equal to the pressure of the water pushing against it.

As long as not even a bubble of extra air works its way into the bottle, the air pressure on the outside will hold the water in the bottle.

A Person Could Die of Thirst

YOU WILL NEED:
soda bottle
water
drinking straw
sticky cloth or plastic tape

What could be more annoying than to stick a drinking straw into a bottle and then find it impossible to suck any of the liquid up into your mouth.

What to do: Fill the soda bottle nearly full of water. Place the drinking straw in the bottle.

Pull off a strip of sticky cloth or plastic tape about 8 inches (10 cm) long. Wrap it carefully and tightly around the mouth of the bottle so it forms an airtight seal around the straw. Use a second and maybe even a third strip of tape to make sure no air can get through the seal.

Place your mouth on the end of the straw and begin to suck on it as you normally would. Don't take your mouth away from the straw after you begin trying to drink through it.

What happens: You won't get more than just a tiny bit of water out of the straw, if you get anything at all.

Why: Early in this chapter we mentioned that it is the outside air pressure that enables us to drink through a straw. Unless air can push down on the liquid in a glass or bottle, it is impossible to drink through a straw.

As you suck on the straw you lower the air pressure inside the straw. Outside pressure normally pushes the liquid up into the straw. But, since you sealed the top of the bottle shut, the outside air can't push on the water in the bottle, and you're out of luck when it comes to drinking through that straw.

The Paper Wad That Won't Go Into the Bottle

167

small-mouthed bottle
piece of scrap paper

No great effort is required to put a small wad of paper into a bottle. So why won't this paper wad do what you ask it to do?

What to do: Place the bottle on its side on a table.

Wad a small piece of paper into a ball about the size of a green pea. Then place the paper wad in the bottle's mouth as seen here.

Blow hard and fast as shown by the arrow in the drawing.

What happens: Instead of flying into the bottle the paper wad is more likely to fly out of the bottle's mouth and come back toward you.

Why: The fast-moving air goes past the paper wad and strikes the bottom of the bottle. This increases the air pressure inside the bottle. As that compressed air rushes out, it carries the paper wad out with it.

How to Empty a Glass by Blowing on It

YOU WILL NEED:

water
2 drinking glasses the
same size
pan
drinking straw

It's easy to empty a glass by pouring the water from it. But it's more fun to blow on it to accomplish the same thing.

What to do: Run enough water into the kitchen sink so the water level is a little higher than the width of the glasses when they are turned on their sides. Here's how:

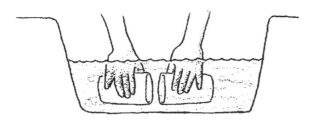

Be sure the glasses are full of water. Press the two rims together. Get a firm hold on both glasses and lift them out of the sink with their rims still pressed together.

Now turn them a quarter turn so that one glass is on top of the other. Set the two glasses in the empty pan.

Very carefully slide the top glass a bit to one side so the rims of the glass no longer meet exactly. Do this slowly and no water will run out of the top glass. Here's how the glasses look in relation to each other:

Aim the drinking straw right at the point shown by the arrow where there is a tiny space between the rims of the glasses. Now blow gently through the straw. Then blow a bit harder.

What happens: Air bubbles will rise inside the top glass and a stream of water will flow down the side of the bottom glass into the container. Within a short time the top glass will be totally empty.

Why: Air pressure outside the glasses combines with surface tension to keep the water on the top glass from running out and into the container when you move their rims apart slightly.

When you blow, the air pressure from the end of the straw overcomes the water's surface tension and forces air between the two glasses. Once inside the glasses, the air rises since it is lighter than water.

169 A Great Experiment or a Wet Trick?

Try this as a great science experiment. Then decide whether to use it as a wet trick.

What to do: Begin by making twelve very small holes in the bottom of the bottle. A small nail is all you need for this. Hold the nail in the pliers and use the pliers to push the nail's point into the bottle's bottom.

After you've made the little holes, set the bottle in the kitchen sink. Run about 2 inches (5 cm) of water into the sink so the water rises well above the holes you just made. Hold onto the bottle to keep it from floating and tipping onto its side.

Now fill the bottle to the top with water. The water in the sink keeps the water you pour in from coming out the holes in the bottom. Lift the bottle above the water in the sink for a second to make sure water comes out the holes.

When the bottle is completely full, screw on the cap and slowly lift the bottle up above the water in the sink.

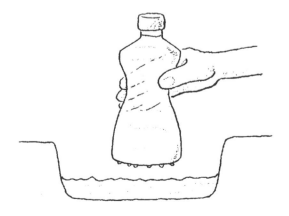

What happens: A few droplets may form around the holes, but the bottle will not leak. While you're still holding the bottle over the sink, remove the cap and the water will flow out through the holes you punched. Your experiment looks like this:

Why: As long as no water can push down through the open mouth of the bottle, the outside air pressure holds the water inside the tiny holes. When you open the cap, air pressure pushes down through the bottle's mouth and out the water comes.

You can use this as a practical joke, but you must do it outdoors. Pretend you can't open the cap, which you have screwed on fairly tight. Ask someone to help. Of course, that person will be able to open the lid and may even laugh at you for being so weak. But when the lid loosens, whoever is holding the bottle is going to get wet.

BEING EARTH CONSCIOUS

The chapters that follow give you a world of information, dozens of earthly exciting activities and experiments, and teach you the hows and whys of becoming a real conservationist—a person who is "earth conscious" and does everything possible to save and protect our lands, forests, and waters.

You'll learn through experimentation how plants give off oxygen and moisture and how, without them, life could not exist. You'll learn how magnetism and electricity are related earth forces. You'll see how earthquakes are produced and even make your own seismograph, the instrument for measuring them, and you'll build a glacier model that melts, moves, and leaves behind the sand and rock it carries.

Learn about soil, sand, the sun, and fossils, and then make a down-to-earth water filter, solar water heater, and a different type of "chemistry volcano" that foams, steams, and hisses.

In addition, you'll learn through facts and experimentation about ozone, fossil fuels, acid rains, rain forests, and global warming. You can even recycle old newspapers to make your own paper and notecards.

Worldly Matters

The planet Earth—a huge ball with an outer crust, inner mantle, and core—travels through space, as do the sun, stars, and other planets. Beside this movement through space, the surfaces of the earth are also changing constantly. High mountains and deep valleys, both on land and under the oceans, are all part of the earth's movement. Nothing stays the same. Think of the earth as an apple sitting in the sun. As the sun warms and dries the apple, its water is lost and the apple shrinks and wrinkles.

The earth, like the inside of the apple, shrinks or contracts. As the hot interior parts of the earth cool and shrink, the outside covering is forced to move. The apple's surface makes wrinkly peaks and valleys and, similarly, the earth's crust forms mountains, valleys, and breaks or cracks called faults.

In this chapter we'll take a look at some of the forces that affect our earth, as well as other worldly matters.

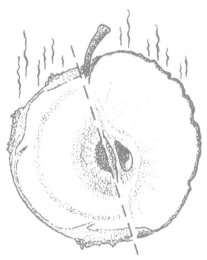

Earthquakes: They're Definitely Not Your Fault!

YOU WILL NEED:
3 similar-size hardcover books

The pressures within the earth cause great forces, which, in turn, break and crack the earth's crust. These cracks are called faults, and movement along a fault produces earthquakes. How does this happen?

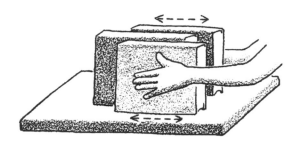

What to do: With the three books held firmly together, bring them close to your chest, book spines (with titles) upward. Reaching under, push upward on the middle book so that it slides upward between the two outer books. Do this several times to make a smooth, straight lift.

Next, firmly hold the books out away from your body, keeping them tightly and evenly together. Hold them sideways again, with the titles up and the pages going down. You'll have to apply a lot of force to keep them from slipping. Now, release some of the pressure so the middle book slips.

Finally, hold the books evenly together, spines upward, and rest them on a table. With your hands holding only the two outer books, slide them back and forth.

What happens: The different movements of the books resemble earthquake faults, with much uplifting and slipping.

Why: In the first two experiments, in which you held the books first close to your chest, and then away from your body, you demonstrated dip slip fault movement, a repositioning up and down. The middle book that was forced up (thrust fault) and the one that slipped down (normal fault) are good examples of this type of fault. The books that rested on the table and were moved to slide past one another show the action of a strike slip fault. In this type of fault, movement is sideways (side by side) or parallel.

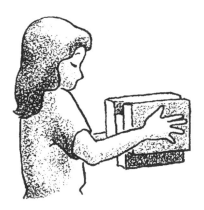

Get the Lead Out!—Build a Seismograph Shaker-Maker

That's right! With a sharp lead pencil with an eraser, you can build a simple seismograph, an instrument used by seismologists (earthquake scientists) to record the strength or intensity of earthquakes. (Adult help may be needed.)

What to do: Carefully cut a tiny slit in the middle near one end of the shoebox lid. Place the open box upright, on one end, and put something small and heavy inside to keep it in position. Tape the lid onto the top of the box forming an upside-down L. (It doesn't matter if the open part of the box or the bottom of it is toward the slit in the lid.)

Now, place the weights near the tip of the pencil point, but do not cover it, and tape them on securely. A small piece of clay around the pencil near the taped weights will keep weights from slipping off. The weights must be fairly heavy so the seismograph recorder pencil will make good contact with the paper and draw fairly dark drag lines on it.

Next, open one end of a paper clip and push it securely into the eraser. Tie the string to the unopened end of the clip. Attach the second paper clip to the other end of the string. Wind the string around the paper clip, as you would wrap a kite string around a stick.

Slip the top clip through the slit and adjust the pencil marker so the tip rests on the table, not perfectly straight but dragging as it moves. Slip the remaining string under one side of the clasp to fasten the upright pencil in place.

Now, cut each paper sheet lengthwise into three strips. These strips will act as roll paper and will record your "earthquake movements."

Place a paper strip against the box (below the slit you made in the lid) and slowly pull the strip forward. Notice how straight the drawn line is as you move the strip of paper.

Have someone bump and shake the table as you pull the paper strips under the dragging pencil marker. Your seismograph makes sideways and up and down movements. Compare the separate strips of paper, how do the lines differ? How do they show the effects of a dip slip fault versus a strike slip fault? (See the experiment opposite.)

You Can Move Mountains

Have you ever wondered how mountains are formed? One way is the great pressures from deep within the earth that cause folds or waves to appear on its surface. These forces cause fold mountains. You can reproduce a version of this force and effect in a simple and easy way. All you'll need is a lump of clay—and a lot of imagination.

What to do: Lay some newspaper on a work table. Place a lump of clay on it and make a clay rope by rolling the lump back and forth over the table with your fingers. When the rope is about 8 inches (20 cm) long, lay it out flat on the newspaper and push inward on the ends, trying to make hills and valleys. After you've done that, roll and smooth out the rope again and place

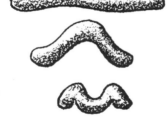

different forces on it. Try to make it bend in new and different ways.

What happens: The clay rope, with its outside forces, demonstrates the hills and valleys of mountain making.

Why: Great broken pieces of the earth's crust, called plates, float on the layer beneath the surface called the mantle. This is similar to cracked sheets of ice floating on water.

When these plates meet, pass, or bump into each other (the science of plate tectonics), great and forceful pressures are created. These tremendously strong forces can fold, bend, uplift, and break the earth's surfaces to form whole mountain ranges.

When the clay rope was pushed and forced inward from the ends, it made hills and valleys similar to mountain building. The hill shape, higher in the middle, is called an anticline formation. If the clay makes a wavy S-like pattern that dips in the center, it is a syncline formation. The North American Appalachian mountain chain is an example of mountains formed by folding.

Tsunami: It'll Tide You Over

YOU WILL NEED:
deep baking pan
water
2 blocks of wood

If you receive some money when you're very broke, we say it will "tide you over" or help you out until you get paid. But tsunami, a Japanese term for great ocean waves, will really tide you over . . . tidal wave, that is!

In this activity, you can create conditions that will produce your own tsunami wave, then you'll understand much better how they are formed and the changes these giant tidal waves produce. This is a great experiment for a hot summer day because it's likely you will get very wet! So either wear your old clothes, or be very careful.

What to do: Fill the pan with water, then place the blocks of wood in the bottom of the pan so they are completely below the surface of the water. The object of this experiment is to rapidly compress, or squeeze, the water between the blocks.

So, take hold of the blocks and quickly bring them together. Do it again, and again. Continue the squeezing action until the blocks can no longer compress the water.

What happens: The movement of the two blocks coming together rapidly under the water forces swells of water to the surface, where they form waves that splash over the sides of the pan.

Why: The action of the blocks and the water in this experiment is similar to the conditions in the ocean depths that produce tsunami tidal waves. Great earthquakes and volcanic forces on the ocean floor cause large amounts of ocean water to be compressed, or squeezed together, and pushed to the surface. There, great walls of water are formed and threaten nearby coastal cities. These great waves sometimes reach heights of 50 to100 feet (15 to 30 m). Because they form so suddenly and without warning they are extremely dangerous and often kill many people.

Photoplay: Say Cheese!

174

YOU WILL NEED:

shoebox with lid

black tempera paint (available from a craft, hobby, or variety store)

paintbrush

scissors

piece of tracing paper or wax paper, cut into a 3 inch x 5 inch (7 cm x 12 cm) rectangle

tape

Light energy from the sun is so important that without it there would be no life on earth! Still, we can put this great energy to use right now by making a simple but exciting pinhole camera. It uses light rays from the nearest star—our own sun.

What to do: Prepare your camera by painting the insides and the lid of the shoebox with the black paint.

Cut a 2 inch x 4 inch (5 cm x 10 cm) opening in the middle of one end of the shoebox and tape the larger piece of tracing paper or wax paper over it. You should now have a screen on one side of your pinhole camera.

At the other end of the box, again in the middle of the panel, carefully punch a small ⅜ inch (½ cm) hole in the side with the scissors.

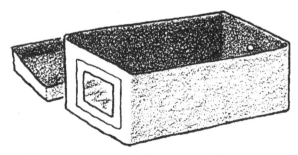

Now you are ready for action. Take your camera outside, find a sunny location, and place something—a friend, a toy, or another object—in front of it. Point the pinhole side of the camera toward the object, and keep the screen in position in front of you for viewing.

The next experiment will tell you about getting picture-perfect images.

What happens: When you aim the small opening of the pinhole camera at something, a fuzzy but noticeable, upside-down image of that object appears on the screen.

Why: The image or picture on the pinhole camera is reversed because light normally travels only in straight lines. Light rays from the top part of the image are reflected to the bottom part of the screen while rays from the bottom part of the image fall on the top.

◆ 175 Picture Perfect: Watch the Birdie!

To view a perfect picture, or image, through your pinhole camera, place a covering over your head. Wrap it around your head and the screen so that it is completely dark. No light is able to get in. (This may remind you of photographers long ago, with their big cameras on tripods, who had to cover their heads with large dark cloths attached to the cameras to take pictures.)

Find something or someone (your subject) in the light through the screen held before your face. A part of a house or a person at sunset is a perfect image. Move the camera away from your face, up or down, closer or farther until the object is in view. Take your time—it may take several trials to adjust your eyes to the dark, get enough light into the box, and find the object, but you will eventually succeed.

176

I Steam Cone

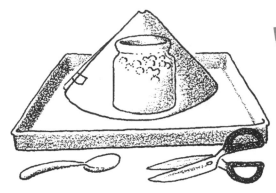

In this great party-trick experiment, you'll build a different type of volcano based on earth science and chemistry. It's definitely something to get all steamed up about! It's simple, easy, and you won't need a lot of materials. So, what are you waiting for? Get going and dig in! (Caution! Throw away all chemical solutions and thoroughly wash out all containers when you're finished.)

What to do: With the cardboard strip, form a cone shape that will fit over the small container and fasten it with the paper clip or tape. Cut the end corners off so the cone will stand upright in the tray or pan. Place the small bottle or jar in the tray and get ready for action.

The jar should be large enough to contain the hydrogen peroxide but fit under the cardboard cone or extend slightly above the cone's mouth. With the cone over the small container, pour in the hydrogen peroxide followed by the quick-rising yeast. Stir the mixture thoroughly. (If it is easier, you may place the cone over the bottle after stirring, but you must be quick!) Continue to stir the mixture, for best results, until the experiment is finished.

What happens: The mixture of hydrogen peroxide and yeast causes foam, steam, and a hissing noise to come from the cardboard "volcano."

Why: The ingredients placed in the container under the cone produced a chemical reaction, or change. It is called exothermic because, in addition to foaming, steaming, and hissing, heat is given off. If you touch the rim and sides of the container or the stirring spoon you can feel this warmth.

In a real volcano, hot melted rock called magma, deep within the earth, erupts or shoots through fissures or cracks. This moving rock, known as lava, sometimes flows from openings in the volcano's sides, or explosively shoots or blows out steam, smoke, ash, and rocks. Although your model volcano is small and simple, it does give you a good idea how a real volcano erupts.

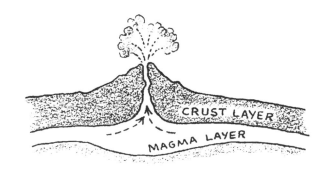

Hotwire High Jinks

Rocks inside the earth can be changed due to the pressure and folding within the earth.

YOU WILL NEED:
wire coat hanger
candle

The pressure causes heat. Do this experiment and see what we mean.

You will need the help of an adult.

What to do: To prepare for this experiment, ask an adult to unhook the wire hanger or cut it apart. Take the hanger and bend one section rapidly back and forth, in the same place, 30 to 50 times.
Quickly, place the bent section against the candle. Don't touch the wire.

What happens: The wire has heated up. This warmth placed against the candle causes some melted grooves or ridges to appear in the wax.

Why: Deep within the earth, certain rocks, called metamorphic rocks, are caused by the constant folding of the earth. This causes heat and changes the composition, or make–up, of the rocks. Marble and quartz are examples of metamorphic rock.

In this experiment, the rapid and constant bending of the wire caused heat that changed or partly melted the wax, the same way that pressure and heat within the earth melts and changes rocks.

An Earth-Shattering Experience

YOU WILL NEED:
piece of chalk
½ cup of white vinegar
small jar

Limestone caves are hollowed out by slightly acid rainwater that, over thousands of years, has gradually dissolved the soft rock.

What to do: Place the piece of chalk in the jar with the vinegar for 5 minutes.

What happens: The chalk dissolves in the vinegar.

Why: School chalk is a form of limestone, or calcium carbonate. It is made up of small bits of sea shells and the mineral calcite and is similar to the soft rock caves of limestone. These caves have been formed when the rock has been dissolved by the acids in rainwater, similar to the chalk that is dissolved by the vinegar, which is acetic acid. England's famed White Cliffs of Dover are made of great sheets of chalk, a form of calcium carbonate.

Shell Shock

179

YOU WILL NEED:

small sea shells
2 small jars
½ cup of white vinegar
½ cup of water
newspaper
metal spoon

Replace the chalk with a few sea shells, another form of calcium carbonate and limestone, and see how fast or completely they dissolve.

What to do: Place some sea shells in one jar with the vinegar, and a few in the other jar with the water (as the control, for comparison). Leave the shells sit in the jars for 4 days.

Remove the shells from the jars, place them on newspaper on a counter or worktable, and carefully try to break them with the spoon.

What happens: The shells from the jar of water remain as hard as ever, while the shells placed in the vinegar should break and crumble quite easily. They will also be covered with a white chalky substance (calcium carbonate).

Why: The shells in the water are the experiment's control, to be compared with those in the other jar that were affected by the vinegar. Again, there is acid in rainwater as there is acid in vinegar. Acid will dissolve calcium carbonate whether it is in the form of cave rock, chalk, or shells. In some areas of the world, the rain is as acid as vinegar.

Snow . . . Er! Iceballs!

180

This simple activity can help you to understand how huge glaciers are formed.

Glaciers are created when snow becomes compacted, or packed tightly. During the winter, when snow is on the ground, go outside and get some. At other times, ask an adult to make you some shaved ice in a blender or food processor, so you can learn about glaciers.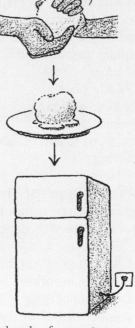

Compact or squeeze the snow or shaved ice into a tight ball (notice how solid it becomes). Let it melt a little and then put it into the freezer for about 30 minutes. When you remove the chunk of snow it will be changed into a solid ball of ice.

Think of all the snow that falls in the mountains, day after day, compressing the snow underneath, and what happens to that snow, and you can imagine how the great glaciers are formed.

Glacier Melt

You can learn a lot about glaciers by making a model of one. It's best to do this outside. Adult help may be needed.

What to do: Place a 1 inch (2.5 cm) layer of sand and pebbles in the cup. Add 2 inches (5 cm) of water. Place the cup in the freezer. When the water has frozen solid, repeat the process, adding sand, pebbles, and water, then freezing. The cup should be filled to the top.

Next, carefully hammer a nail partway into the middle of one end of the board. Place that end against something immovable to create an incline or slant. Now you are ready.

Remove your model glacier from the freezer. Warm the sides of the container under warm tap water, only just enough to get the model glacier to slide out of the cup when tapped. With the sand-side down, place the glacier at the top of the incline and fasten the rubber band around its middle and around the nail. How long will it take your glacier to melt, move, and leave rock and sand deposits? Time it.

What happens: Depending on the weather, melting should begin immediately, even on cooler days. Pebble and sand deposits will fall off in clumps, some will slide down the board, while other separate bits and pieces will form along the

board surface in strange patterns, much like moraine, or glacial matter.

Why: Glaciers are large masses of ice that move down mountainsides and valleys cutting gouges out of the rock and soil. Deposits from glacier movements can be found in such places as the Arctic, Antarctica, Finland, and Greenland.

These giant masses of ice would not move at all if it weren't for the great pressures they also exert. The force of these pressures causes periods of heating and melting. The ice refreezes, but just enough thawing occurs to cause the slipping movement.

As glaciers move, they break off and pick up tons of rock and soil and deposit it someplace else. The unusual rock formations or deposits left behind are called moraine. Like the real thing, our miniature-glacier experiment shows how and why those rock and sand deposits are so unusual and often unevenly placed.

WORLD TRAVELLERS

While the earth's surface, or crust, is always changing, and our planet continues to move through space, time and the seasons go through constant cycles—day after day, year after year.

While reading about the earth and its place in the solar system of planets is good, it is even better to do simple experiments that help you to understand time and space and why things happen as they do.

So, gather up your materials and get ready to do some simple, interesting, and timely experiments. Definitely, a fun time will be had by all!

Stick Around

YOU WILL NEED:

stick
pencil
paper
stones or other markers

Make a simple sundial or sun clock and watch the shadow from its stick or rod, called a gnomon, move around on the ground to tell time. The angle of the shadow produced by the sun will change as the earth rotates, or spins, and changes from day to night. So stick around to watch the shadows, and the time, change—it's time well spent!

This experiment can only be done on a sunny day.

What to Do: Find a sunny location in your yard and push the stick into the ground. On the hour, mark the time of day on the piece of paper and place a stone or marker on the spot where the shadow strikes the ground. Again, one hour later, record the time and mark the shadow with a stone or marker. Continue these steps until you have a completed and marked (calibrated) sun clock.

What happens: The shadow cast by the sun on the gnomon, or stick, will change angle and length as the sun moves from east to west in the sky.

Why: Although the sun appears to be moving from east to west, it is really the Earth that is moving, or revolving, around the sun. Besides orbiting, or circling, the sun, the earth also spins on its axis, or turns like a top. It is this spinning, or rotating, in relation to the sun that makes it possible to record the time, and night and day. Where the sun casts the gnomon's shadow at a certain time of the day, it casts the same shadow the next day, and the day after that.

In the morning, the shadow will be long and narrow and will point to the west. At noon, when the sun appears at its highest point, the shadow will be short and will point north in the northern hemisphere (but south in the southern hemisphere). In the afternoon, the shadow will be directed toward the east.

Time on My Hands

YOU WILL NEED:

piece of clay
2 pencils
pencil
paper

It is important to check and double-check all experiments to make certain that the results come from your hypothesis, or scientific guess, as to what will happen. If you are not careful, other causes or variables could affect the results you get.

To be certain that shadows always perform the same, do the previous experiment again, but this time use the shadow of a hand-held pencil gnomon to compare with your shadow stick. This is a "controlled" experiment, comparing the shadow of the short pencil rod to the longer stick rod.

adjust the shadows of the two gnomon rods so that they are parallel, or next to, one another.)

Is one shadow in alignment or in the same position as the other? Mark the base of your hand gnomon with the side of the other pencil. Put pressure on the clay, marking where the shadow strikes it. Continue to compare the shadow of the pencil gnomon with the rod in the ground. Mark each, with stones and markings, every hour. What are the similarities or differences? Do the shadows change position equally? Do the shadows of the rods grow longer or shorter? If so, when?

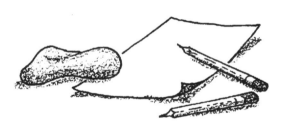

What to do: To make a base, flatten the piece of clay into a disk about 2 inches (5 cm) across. Push the pointed end of the pencil into the clay. You now have a simple hand gnomon. Position the gnomon, aligning and adjusting it according to the shadow cast by the stick version. Write down the exact position in which you place the hand rod next to the shadow stick and keep it in that position every time you do a reading or test the experiment. (Example: Place the clay base of the hand rod next to the ground stick and align or

Spotlight Time Machine

184

YOU WILL NEED:

cardboard square,
about 4 inches x 4 inches
(10 cm x 10 cm)

watch or clock

scissors

tape

2 pieces of paper

pencil

The sun is a kind of time machine, as this simple experiment will show. It will only work, however, on a sunny day.

What to do: Cut a 1 inch (2 cm) hole in the center of the cardboard square. Tape the square on a south-facing window in a position so the spot of sunlight will shine on a clear area of floor. Place the paper where the spot of sunlight hits the floor so that it lands on the paper.

Draw a circle around the spot of light and write the time next to it. Continue to watch the sunlight spots every 30 minutes. Use more paper and record the times and movement as you watch.

What happens: The spots of light move from left to right and change their positions as the time changes.

Why: The earth rotates, or turns, from west to east every 24 hours while it travels around the sun. This movement of the earth causes the spot of sunlight to move across one paper and to the next as your part of the earth moves from sunrise to sunset.

Season Tickets

185

Would the spots of sun fall in the same location at 8:00 A.M. in the summer as they would at 8:00 A.M. in the winter?

If you enjoy long-term experiments, those that take a while, and you can find an unbusy room with a south-facing window, try it! An undisturbed bedroom with plenty of floor space would be an excellent place to do this experiment.

Repeat the last experiment, but this time use pieces of paper about 4 inches (10 cm) square.

Tape them to the floor, over the spots, at the same time at different times of the year. Example: 8:00 A.M., October 1st, and 8:00 A.M., December 22nd.

Is there a difference in the positions of the spots from one season to the next? Record your results.

Skylight Direction-Finder

Early explorers and sailors used a simple direction-finder called an astrolabe to find their location on the open sea. You can make your own astrolabe and find your location on the earth with a few easy-to-find and inexpensive materials.

What to do: Tie a piece of string from the middle of the flat side of the protractor. The string should extend a little beyond it. Now tie the weight to the end of the string and place the flat side of the protractor next to the pencil and tie it to it with two additional short pieces of string.

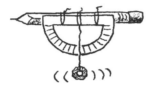

You are now ready to use your astrolabe. On a clear, starry night, point your instrument and center it on the North Star, sometimes called the Pole Star. The weighted string will drop next to the side of the protractor and will show the degree or the number of your latitude. Be patient and do this several times to get an accurate reading.

What happens: Your instrument, when pointed to the North Star, will help you find your latitude on earth. Latitude is a series of imaginary side-to-side earth lines that tell you in numbers where a certain place on earth is located.

Why: The protractor in your astrolabe is a half-circled instrument used to measure angles. It is marked in units of ten called degrees. When you pointed your instrument to the North Star, the weighted string aligned itself to the unit angle on the protractor. This, in turn, gave you your exact location on earth or your latitude.

How to Find the North Star

The North Star, also called the Pole Star, is seen only in the northern part of the sky. This star seems almost fixed in place because of its position above the North Pole. Like a clock, it also appears to change position from hour to hour and season to season. It appears very faint because it is more than four hundred light years away.

The North Star can be found opposite the constellation Ursa Major, commonly known as the Big Dipper. It is seen as a cup with a long handle on it, if you were to draw imaginary lines from each of the seven stars that make up the pattern (as you would in a dot-to-dot puzzle). The stars furthest from the handle, which make up the cup, point directly to the North Star.

188 Can You Find the Southern Cross?

Do people in the southern hemisphere, or the southern half of the world, also see the stars visible from the northern half of the earth?

If you live in the northern hemisphere, you cannot see all the stars in the sky over the southern half of the world. If you live in the southern hemisphere you cannot see all the stars over the northern half of the world.

If you live on or near the imaginary line that circles the middle of the earth, known as the equator, however, you can see all the stars of both halves of the earth.

While people in the northern hemisphere can find Polaris, the Pole or North Star, which appears to be fixed directly above the North Pole, star gazers in the southern hemisphere have no such marker.

The Southern Cross, in the southern hemisphere, is a constellation, or group of stars, made up of four crossed stars and other stars, two of which, like the north's Big Dipper, point to the South Pole. The Southern Cross, however, is not a good locator of its pole. It does not always appear as a cross and it is often hard to find and to see. In addition, the southern hemisphere has no visible "pole" star to mark it in the sky.

189 Meteor Burnout: Truth or Friction?

Meteors are small rocklike chunks, most probably broken fragments of comets or asteroids, tumbling rapidly around the sun in outer space. As they enter and pass through the earth's atmosphere, they burn up. Now you can try this simple experiment and discover how this happens.

What to do: Drop the tablet into the bottle of water and watch what happens as it falls or floats down to the bottom.

What happens: The tablet dissolves or breaks up into many small pieces, or fragments, that disappear as it journeys to the bottom of the bottle.

Why: The water represents the earth's atmosphere and the seltzer tablet, the meteor.

Like a meteor, the tablet breaks up into many small fragments as it drops to the bottom of the bottle (the earth's surface). Unlike the tablet, the meteor rushes through outer space at such great speeds that friction, or the rubbing force of its surface against the earth's atmosphere, causes the space rock to heat up and the white-hot fragment to break up and explode into cosmic space dust.

Most meteors are no bigger than small stones, but every so often a few larger chunks make their way to the surface of the earth as meteorites.

YOU WILL NEED:

large soda bottle filled with water
½ seltzer tablet

157

Starry-Eyed

Make a star-lit light box and learn about the constellations, groups of fixed clusters of stars. It's fun and it's easy, and you and your friends will be headed for stardom.

YOU WILL NEED:
oatmeal box with lid (several lids are best)
nail
flashlight
pencil

What to do: Using the nail, punch "star" holes in the box lid. Follow your favorite star–chart patterns from astronomy books, or from looking overhead at the night sky where you live.

Depending on the size of the box and the lid, you should be able to punch in a large pattern or two or more smaller constellations on one lid.

Now, press the narrow end or handle of the flashlight against the center of the other end of the box and draw a circle around it. Then cut a hole in it and fit the flashlight into the box. (This can be done by removing the lid and pushing the handle through the hole.)

What happens: Your light box projects groups of small, starlike, light spots on the ceiling or wall.

Why: Different constellations seem to sweep across the sky, and are seen only at certain times of the year. From week to week, and at the same time every night, their positions change, as they move a little farther to the west.

The orbit or path the earth takes around the sun, and its position at certain times of the year, determines whether you can see certain constellations or not. In winter, the summer constellations are blocked out by the sun's light while the winter constellations are blocked out in the summer.

You are now ready to dazzle your friends with your new star-lit light box. By rotating a lid or turning the box, you can even make the constellations move. Take it into a dark room and point it, with the flashlight on, at the ceiling or wall and enjoy the starry-eyed show.

191 Parallax Puzzle

YOU WILL NEED:
pencil

Scientists can calculate, or figure out mathematically, the distances of different stars from the earth.

As we look at the stars, we understand from what we have learned that the stars stay in an exact position and are very far away. But what our eyes and our brains tell us may not be totally correct.

If we walk past a house, the house does not move but the position of it does because the angle we view it from after passing it is different. This is parallax, and this simple experiment will show you how parallax works.

What to do: Hold the pencil out vertically, or straight up and down, right before your eyes. Now, close your left eye, then quickly open it and close your right eye. Do it again. Continue to rapidly close first one eye and then the other and observe what happens to the pencil before you.

What happens: The pencil jumps, moving from side to side! Where is it really? How can you know?

192 Moving Picture

Do the parallax experiment again the same way, but this time, as you view the close–up pencil, also look at a distant object, like a lamp or a table, in the background. What do you see? Does the position of one object change more than the other?

What happens: Although the pencil appears to shift position, or move, from one side to the other as it did before, the distant object did not.

Why: The pencil did not really move, but the angle of viewing did. The angle between the pencil and your eye changed and so the pencil's position did, but only according to your eyes and your brain. This shift difference is called parallax, and it is the key to finding distance. The closer an object is, the more it will seem to shift, while objects that are farther away do not. In the same way, parallax makes closer stars seem to move and those very far away seem fixed.

To see the shifting of stars, astronomers (scientists who study and observe the universe from our solar system to the farthest galaxies) measure the different positions of stars at two different times of the year as the earth moves in orbit around the sun. In that way they can calculate the stars' exact distances from the earth.

Track Star

193

YOU WILL NEED:

sheet of paper
drinking glass
half-filled with water

Our sun, a star, is a giant ball of hydrogen gas many million of miles away. Yet it is possible to learn something about the sun from tracking, or following, the wavelengths of light coming from it. This can be done in a simple way in a sunny outdoor location.

What to do: Find a place outside in full sunlight for your experiment. Place the sheet of paper on a table or lay it on the ground where the experiment is to be done.

Now, hold the glass with the water firmly and carefully between your thumb and a finger over the sheet of paper. The glass should be held about 3 to 4 inches (7 to10 cm) above the paper. Do not hold the glass in the usual way, around the glass. It's important that you hold the glass so that your hand does not block the sides.

Move the glass up and down and slant it slightly, focusing the light on the paper until a clear colorful pattern appears.

What happens: The glass of water acts as a prism and casts a rainbow on the paper.

Why: A glass of water is able to act as a prism, or something that can change the direction of light so the bands of color in it can be seen and studied. White light is really a combination of many colors.

When a wavelength of light is split and changed by the glass of water, color occurs. Light from the sun shows many colors. Astronomers can tell what elements or gases make up a star by studying the bands, or spectrums, of the light it gives off.

194

Glassify

Do different types of glass make better prisms for casting rainbow patterns on paper?

Do the same experiment again, but instead, use a different size glass, then use a glass with a different shape. What about colored glass? Will glasses made of colored glass refract, or split, light into colors, too? Will a full glass of water work better than a glass half full of water?

Do a variety of experiments and write down your observations and results. When you're finished, you'll know what glass works best.

195 ◆ Highly Focused

YOU WILL NEED:
thermometer
paper
pencil
flashlight
watch or clock
can or other support
for thermometer

The seasons of the year depend on the tilt of the earth and the concentration of sunlight at different times of the year in the northern and southern hemispheres. This simple experiment explains it all.

What to do: Record the temperature on the thermometer. Run the thermometer under warm or cool water to get the temperature where you want it, so that it is easy for you to record and calculate.

Prop the thermometer, glass side outward, against the lighted end of the flashlight. Leave it in that position, timing it with a clock or watch, for 3 minutes. Record the final temperature.

After the first reading against the flashlight, hold the thermometer under cool water until the temperature returns to what it was at the beginning of the first trial.

Now, lean the thermometer against a support to hold it upright and shine the flashlight on it from a set distance away, about 1 foot (30 cm). Again, record the reading after 3 minutes.

What happens: The thermometer leaning against the flashlight and in direct contact with the light, so it was more concentrated or had greater strength, registered a few degrees warmer. No noticeable change was seen when the light was shined on the thermometer from a short distance away.

Why: The concentration of light on various parts of the earth, at any one time of year, is similar to the concentration of light in our experiment.

The greater an area covered by light, the lower the temperature. In our experiment, the thermometer that was farther away from the light was not affected by it as much, if at all.

The northern hemisphere, or upper half of the earth, which is tilted away from the sun in December, receives a greater spread of light, while the southern hemisphere, or lower half of the earth, is tilted toward the sun at that time and receives stronger, more concentrated light. This explains why, in December, it is winter in New York City and summer in Sydney, Australia.

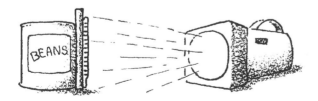

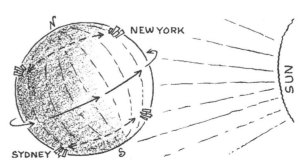

LEAFY LESSONS

We could not live without plants. Consider these facts:

Plants, humans, and animals keep the Earth's atmosphere balanced.

Plants, through photosynthesis, make their own food, while taking in carbon dioxide and giving off oxygen.

Animals and humans need oxygen and breathe out carbon dioxide.

Animals and humans get much-needed sugars and starches from eating plants.

Millions of tons of water are released into the air every day by plants in a process called transpiration.

Some scientists believe that the loss of trees and an increase in human and animal breathing, or respiration, can increase the amount of carbon dioxide in the atmosphere and cause the earth to warm up.

The experiments in this chapter will answer your questions about plant growth, but more important, they'll show you why these living things are so very important to our lives.

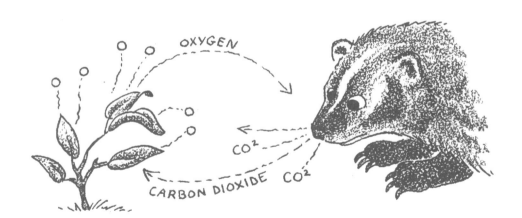

 196   Oxygen Leaves

YOU WILL NEED:
1 clear, wide-mouth jar
water
1 leaf
magnifying glass

Oxygen leaves? That's right, oxygen leaves! Leaves what? Confused? Try this experiment and you won't be. You'll also learn about two important plant words—stomata and photosynthesis.

What to do: Fill the jar with water and drop the leaf into it. Place the jar in a sunny location outdoors or on a windowsill. Leave it there in the sun for at least one hour, or until the outside of the jar feels warm. With the magnifying glass look at what happens in the jar.

What happens: Thousands of tiny bubbles appear on the surface of the leaf and inside the jar.

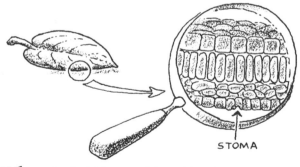

STOMA

Why: The bubbles are formed by the oxygen gas given off by the leaf.

A plant needs certain elements and sunlight to make its food. This process is called photosynthesis. "Photo" and "synthesis" mean "light" and "putting together." When water, air, chlorophyll (which causes the leaf's green coloring), and sunlight are put together in a certain way by the plant, it makes its own food. If any one of these elements is missing, a plant cannot live.

Carbon dioxide, a gas, enters the tiny, pinlike holes, called stomata, in the underside of the leaf. The plant uses sunlight and chlorophyll and, combined with water and carbon dioxide, turns these elements into the food it needs. The food is actually a form of sugar that is eventually turned into starch. Oxygen is given off as a waste product. Now you know why you saw the bubbles in the container and on the leaf.

197   Don't Leaf Me Alone

Now see what happens when you do the same experiment again, but place the jar in the shade.

Does it matter if a leaf is in the sunlight before you test it? Try placing a leaf from outdoors in the sunlight into one container of water. Into a second container of water put a leaf from an indoor plant that is kept in the shade. Put both containers outdoors in the sunlight. Is there any difference?

Try this experiment indoors now. Do bubbles appear on the leaf or container?

Remember always to keep good notes and records and to log, or write down, all your observations and the results of your experiments.

Phototropism: Waiting for the Weekends

198

Plants will always grow toward the sun. They will turn upward, even if they are turned on their sides.

What to do: Take the two flat squares of plastic. Fold the napkin to fit onto one of the plastic squares and arrange the roots of the weed on top of it.

Place the second square of plastic on top, like a sandwich, making sure that the stems and leaves of the plant are outside the plastic sandwich. Wrap the rubber bands tightly around the squares to keep everything in place.

Fill the shallow container with water. Place the "weed sandwich," propped on its side in the container, near a sunny south-facing window. You will have to wait at least four days for results. Make sure there is always ½ inch to 1 inch (1 to 2.5 cm) of water in the bottom of the container. Make drawings showing the position of your plant each day. Be patient.

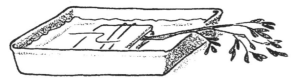

What happens: The leaves and stems of the weed grow upward, toward the sun, even though the weed was placed on its side.

Why: A plant's leaves and stems always grow toward the sun, no matter if they are placed sideways, or even upside down. This could involve moving, bending, and turning to go toward the light. This process is known as phototropism.

YOU WILL NEED:

2 small pieces of plastic, about 3 inches (8 cm) square, cut from a plastic container

paper napkin

medium-size weed with well-developed leaves and stems and a good root system

2 rubber bands

small shallow container or a meat tray from a frozen food package

water
pencil
paper
scissors

Drying the Insides of Bottles

199

Some experiments call for completely dry soda bottles. But how do you get the inside of a wet soda bottle dry? Just stuff a sheet or two of paper toweling inside the bottle and use a long-handled screwdriver, stick, or something else that is long and thin to press and stir the absorbent paper against the sides and bottom—and slide it up and out of the bottle when you are finished.

200 Perspiration or Transpiration: Don't Sweat It!

People sweat, or perspire, while plants transpire. A plant gives off water through its stomata, the tiny holes located under the surface of each leaf. Now see what it's all about.

What to do: Roll the clay between your hands to form a 2 inch (4 cm) plug. The plug will have to reach about 1 inch (2 cm) into each bottle neck to hold one bottle vertically, upside down, above the other.

Using the nail or pencil, poke a hole in the plug and insert the stem of the leaf through it, being careful not to break the stem or crush the leaf. Now, gently, press the clay plug inward around the stem to seal it in. Fill one bottle with water and push the plug with the leaf in it into the top of the bottle. (The plug should rise above the bottle neck and the stem of the leaf must touch the water.)

Wipe any moisture from the plug and leaf and make certain that the plug itself is not touching the water—this could cause moisture to get into the bottle above and negate the experiment.

Carefully, turn the other bottle upside down on top, working the leaf into it, and the plug into place. Press the clay gently around any opening to seal it. After one hour, take the magnifying glass and observe your experiment closely.

What happens: A small, but noticeable amount of moisture (areas with small water droplets and steamy haze) appears on the glass inside the "dry" upside-down bottle.

Why: Transpiration in plants is much like a person sweating. A plant loses water vapor through holes or pores called stomata. Plants often obtain too much ground water through their roots and get rid of what is not needed through these holes.

All the world's water is always the same—none is ever lost. The earth's waters are naturally recycled through rain, clouds, lakes, rivers, oceans, and especially by plant transpiration.

Although you may not see it, plants give off gallons of water each day. Leaves release millions of tons of water vapor into the air every day. This is an earth process we never consider, but without it we could never live on this planet.

201 Three Leaves and a Maybe

In the last experiment, you used a broad leaf in a bottle and saw water droplets and steam form. But would the rate of transpiration be the same if different types of leaves were used?

Find more bottles and try the experiment using different leaves—broad leaves, narrow leaves, leaflets, and fern-like leaves. Place one set in the sun, another in the house. Is the amount of water seen in the "dry" bottle more, less, the same? What's your hypothesis?

Doing the same experiment without the leaf can serve as a control, to show that other things are not producing the water droplets.

For the Birds

Birdseed, radish seeds, onion seeds, or any other kind of seed will grow if placed on a water-soaked sponge.

YOU WILL NEED:
sponge
shallow container or dish
water
seeds
magnifying glass

What to do: Place the sponge in the container with enough water to soak it. The sponge should rise above the water level. Water should be added to the container from time to time as the water evaporates, to keep the sponge moist.

Sprinkle a small amount of seeds on the surface of the sponge and lightly pat them into it. Place the container of sponge-soaked seeds in a sunny location, perhaps on a windowsill. Check them in two or three days for some cracking and sprouting. You'll need your magnifying glass to see them. The seedlings should be fully developed in five to seven days.

Why: When the dry seeds are placed on the water-soaked sponge, they swell until they break

open. The seeds germinate, or start to develop, on the sponge. The water softens the outer part of the seed called the seed coat. At this point, seeds need only food, water, and air to grow. The new plants use the seeds for food, but eventually they need soil and sun to make their own food.

What Now?

Now you have a quick and easy and fun way to sprout seeds, because you can actually see them. After the seeds have sprouted, gently scrape them off the sponge and let them fall into a container of potting soil or another gardening material like vermiculite. (See the next experiment for instructions.)

Waterbed

204

Can plants be grown if you don't have any soil? Hydroponics is the science of growing plants without this needed element! How is it done? Does it really work? You'll find out, dirt free, in this important scientific investigation.

YOU WILL NEED:

flower pots (with holes in the bottoms)
stones or broken pottery, for pot drainage
tray or shallow dishes
spray bottle
flower or vegetable seeds
water-absorbent plant material, like vermiculite, perlite, or peat moss
liquid or granular plant food

What to do: Place the stones or broken pottery in the bottoms of the flower pots, to cover the holes and provide drainage. Fill the remaining areas with the planting material. Put the pots on the tray or on shallow dishes.

With the spray bottle, water the material well—it should be moist but not soaking wet. Now, lightly and evenly scatter the seed over the planting material and press it down. If you have a lot of several kinds of seeds, it is best to use several pots for good spacing and better growth. Place the pots in sunny, south-facing windows and continue to keep the planting materials moist.

What happens: The seeds grow into healthy seedlings or young plants without using any type of soil.

Why: Plants need air, water, and light to grow, but they don't necessarily need soil. Plants can be grown without soil by replacing the minerals they would normally get from the soil with liquid or dry plant food. Hydroponics, or growing plants without soil, may be the new way of growing plants for the future.

After the plants germinate, or sprout, water them with a combination of water and plant food. (See package directions on how to dilute the food with water.) Continue to water the plants whenever more moisture is needed, but be careful not to water them too much.

Phil O. Dandrun's Root Bare

A new brand of soda? No. Phil O. Dandrun is our nickname (an alias) for the philodendron. If you have this common house plant at home, try this experiment—if you don't, use a different plant. One way or another, leave it to us and you'll be raising a plant from a stem in no time.

What to do: Cut the stem off the plant below the leaf scar or the bulge, which is called the node, as in the illustration. Remove the side leaves.

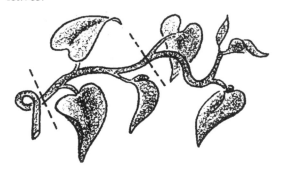

Place the piece of philodendron in the jar of water. Make sure the water covers the spot where the leaves were pulled off. Now you must wait patiently for roots to develop. It may take several weeks for good root growth.

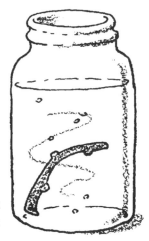

What happens: Long brown, threadlike roots form from the scarred areas where the leaves were removed.

Why: Some plants can grow from roots, leaves, and stems. Philodendron sections or stems, called cuttings, that are placed in water will grow roots from the leaf areas around the bulge or node. Geraniums and other plants also do this, so if yours didn't work, don't give up. Try again.

206 Little Sprouts or Hothouse Tomatoes

A greenhouse is a hot, closed space for growing plants. The earth can have a kind of greenhouse effect, too, when gases from burning fossil fuels act as a lid and prevent heat from escaping into space.

Now let's put this greenhouse idea to work for the fun of raising some sweet little sprouts that may even turn into tomatoes. There's nothing like tasting the juicy, sweet, delicious results of this successful experiment.

What to do: Prepare the pots with packed-down potting soil. Scoop the seeds from fresh tomatoes, or use packaged tomato seeds, and scatter them evenly over the soil, avoiding clumps of seeds. Then cover them with a light and thin layer of soil.

Water well, then cover each pot with a piece of clear plastic wrap and fasten it with a rubber band. Place the pots on a sunny windowsill and watch for little sprouts.

207 Planting Seeds and Seedlings

Plant cuttings that have rooted, seeds, and seedlings, can be planted or moved into soil. Easy enough, but some rules must be followed.

For seeds to start growing and plants to grow well they need water—but not too much (they'll "drown" from lack of air) or too little (they'll dry out and die). Good light and soil with the proper minerals are also needed to boost growth.

First, plant seeds, seedlings, and new plants in clay or plastic pots with drainage holes in the bottom. (Egg and milk cartons with holes punched in them also make great planters.) Adding bits of broken clay pots, gravel, or stones also helps the water drain. Use a good potting soil with equal parts of peat moss, sand, bark, wood, and a good nitrogen and iron content.

Containers should be nearly filled and plantings should be given "elbow room" away from other seeds, seedlings, or plants. In other words, don't crowd! A light covering of soil, about ¼ inch (1 cm), should cover seeds or seedling roots and be lightly compressed, or pressed down. New plantings should be placed in a sunny, south-facing window, and the soil should be kept moist. A small sprayer or medicine dropper might deliver just the right amount of water and help prevent over-watering.

If necessary, get an adult to help with your new plantings until you know what to do and how to get the results you expect. Good luck and happy planting!

DIRTY WORDS: SOIL, SAND, HUMUS, AND MUD

The next time you fill a pot or planter with soil, think about its properties—how it looks, feels, and smells, what it's made of, and what lives in it. As you investigate, you'll discover bugs, leaves, pebbles, and small rocks, but that is just scratching the surface. You won't see the billions of microscopic plants and tiny animals that live there in the soil, too, but they are responsible for making up good, rich soils.

In this chapter you'll learn about soil, sand, humus, and mud, and how dirt acts under certain conditions. And asking questions about these dirty words won't get you grounded!

Dirty Questions
Call For Dirty Answers

What is soil made of? Is all soil the same? What's the difference? What kind of soil is best for plants ? How can I find out about it?

Read this whole introduction, and then do the "Earthshaking" experiment and you'll definitely dig up more dirt on the subject than you ever imagined was there.

What is known as soil or dirt is made up of broken rocks, minerals, the remains of dead plant and animal life, and germlike plants called bacteria. These tiny, one-celled plants are too small to be seen, unless you look through a good micro-

scope, but they are everywhere in the soil and they do a big job.

Small animals, worms, oxygen, and water are also needed in the soil. With the help of the larger animal life, the bacteria use the air and water to break down and chemically change the soil. When their job is done, poor soil that was not good enough to grow anything becomes a nitrogen-rich fertile soil that can grow just about anything.

Soil by Any Other Name is Still Dirt

Scientists have identified four different kinds of soil according to the way it feels (texture) and what it contains. The types of soil are sand, silt, loam, and clay.

Sand is made up of broken shells and worn-down bits of rock and minerals like quartz and basalt, a volcanic-like rock.

Although all good soils need sand, too much of it can cause too much water to drain away from plant roots, leaving them to dry and shrivel up. Sand is found in deserts, on beaches, and along river bottoms. Larger grains of sand are called gravel.

Silt, on the other hand, is a very fine-grained, sandy soil. Its parts are smaller than sand but larger than particles of clay.

Clay is a fine soil and it is much needed in all soils. Without clay, soils fall apart and fertilizers are washed away. Too much clay in any soil, however, will cause problems with water drainage and eventually produce rotted roots in plants.

The best type of soil for most plants is loam. Loam is a mixture of clay, sand, and silt with enough humus (broken-down plant life and animal matter) to make it rich and fertile.

Sand
Silt
Clay
Loam

208 Earthshaking Discovery: It's Sedimentary

The sediment, or different types of soil particles, and how they float and settle, are unusual and interesting. Just shake up these soil-shakers and watch out.

What to do: Fill each jar with ½ cup of soil. Add water. The jar should be about three-quarters filled. Screw the lid on the jar tightly and shake well. Repeat the procedure with other soil samples to be tested.

Be patient and wait about 2 hours for the soil to settle. (You could sit and watch, but you don't have to.) Then, with the magnifying glass, observe what happened to the soil samples. Draw a picture of the settled sediment in each jar.

What happens: The soil settles into bands, or layers, depending on the content of the soil.

Why: In sandy mixtures, heavier, rocklike particles settle first, followed by light-colored silty, sand-like grains.

In most loamy, gardening top soils, the heavier gravel mix settles to the bottom, while the dark-colored, lighter-in-weight humus floats to the top of the jar. As you see, this is a good test for determining good, loamy, rich soils.

209

More Dirt

Collect soil samples in different areas when you go on long car trips and vacations. When you come home test the soil you have collected and discover how much humus and different kinds of soil are in each sample.

210 Air Condition

What if you can't see
what condition the soil
is in?

YOU WILL NEED:
small jar
½ cup of dirt
1 cup of boiled and
cooled water
magnifying glass

What to do: Place the soil sample in the jar.
Pour the cooled, boiled water slowly onto the soil
and watch closely.

What happens: Air bubbles appear and circle
the top surface of the soil.

Why: All dry soil has air trapped in and around
the particles. The bubbles that rise from the soil's
surface are formed by air forced from the soil by
the water.

    Water also normally contains its own air,
which is why, for this experiment, it is necessary
to use boiled and cooled water. During the boiling, the heated air in the water is boiled away.
This experiment, then, reveals that it is the air
from the soil that causes the bubbles and not the
water.

211 Bubble Blowers

Find some porous
rock (rocks that are
lightweight, with
some holes or spaces
in them) and place
them in a pan filled
with water for a rocky bubble-blower show.

YOU WILL NEED:
porous rock or broken
pieces of brick or
pottery
shallow baking pan
water
magnifying glass

What to do: Place the rocks in the baking pan
and pour in enough water to cover them. Using
the magnifying glass, observe what happens.

What happens:
Streams of bubbles
flow from the rocks.
The more porous the
rocks, the more bub-
bles you will see.
Depending on the

weight of the rocks and the force of the air escaping from them, the rocks might move slightly, rock
back and forth, or bounce and rattle against the
pan.

Why: Oxygen is present, even in the rocks. Air
bubbles flow from the spaces in the minerals that
make up the rocks and rise to the water's surface.

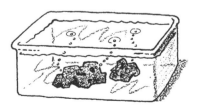

212 Sand Trap

YOU WILL NEED:

sheet of newspaper
large bowl
measuring cup
1¼ cup of cornstarch
1 cup of water
mixing spoon
2 tablespoons of
ground coffee

Quicksand is a thick body of sand grains mixed with water that appears to be a dry hard surface. It may look solid, as if it can be walked on, so it can be unexpectedly dangerous because it really cannot support much weight. People have been known to be swallowed up in quicksand.

In this experiment, you'll make a type of quicksand goop that will magically and surprisingly support your hand one minute but not the next.

What to do: On the newspaper, because this experiment can be messy, combine the cornstarch and water in the bowl and stir with the spoon until the mixture looks like paste. The cornstarch mixture will be hard to stir and will stick to the bottom of the bowl. This is to be expected. Next, lightly and evenly sprinkle the ground coffee on top of the mixture to give it a dry and even look.

Now the fun begins. Make a fist and lightly pound on the surface. Notice what happens and how it feels. Next, lightly push your fingers down into the mixture.

What happens: When you used your fist to hit the surface of the mixture, it appeared to hit the surface only and seemed to be mysteriously and magically stopped from going any further. But when you placed your fingers or hand in the mixture, they easily and readily slid into the bottom of the bowl.

Why: The molecules of quicksand goop behave much like real quicksand. Unlike water molecules, the goop's molecules are larger. They swell and hook together, and seem to act more like a solid than a liquid. In addition, the coffee grains give the mixture a deceptively smooth and dry look, much like real quicksand.

Holding Pattern

213

YOU WILL NEED:

nail

equal amounts of four different soil samples, like clay, sand, potting soil, and rich loam gardening soil

4 paper cups or the bottoms of waxed cartons

small containers

water

paper

pencil

measuring cup

A soil is called "permeable" when it allows water to pass through it. Which soils are the most permeable? Which soils hold the most water, the least, or just the right amount? For this dirty experiment, it will be best to set up work space outside where you can just dig in!

What to do: With the nail, punch about six holes in the bottoms of the paper cups or the carton bottoms. Fill each container about half-full with a soil sample to be tested. Pour ½ cup of water into sample of soil to be tested. Place a small container under each to catch the water. Pour the water that drains into each container into the measuring cup. Record the type of soil tested and how much water the soil held. Repeat this step with other soils and again measure the amount of water.

What happens: There will be noticeably more soil and water in the bottom of some containers than in other. Water will drain faster from some soil samples than from others.

Why: Clay soils retain, or keep, too much water, while sandy soils drain too quickly. Too much water around the tender roots of plants can cause rotting, while with too little water the roots will dry out and shrivel up. Soils with a lot of humus, or decomposed, broken-down plant and animal matter, are best for most plants. It retains just enough water for healthy plant growth while stimulating the roots. Some plants, however, still do well or better in other kinds of soil.

214 ◆ A Down-to-Earth Water Filter

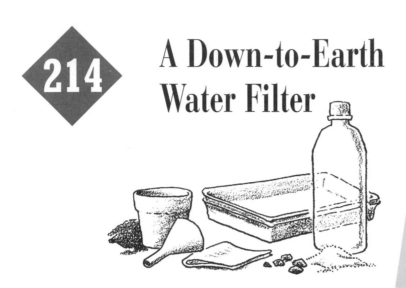

Have you ever wondered how water is cleaned before it reaches your home? How about making a simple water filtration system that will answer many questions? You can get lots of down-to-earth information as you test it.

Remember, though, that however good a job you think you have done, the water from this experiment should never be drunk. The experiment will give you a good idea how water filters work, but it is still not a real water treatment plant, and just a few drops of "bad" water can make you sick.

It will be best to do this experiment outside since it can be messy and the dirt you need to use should be easy to find nearby. Clean sand and gravel are available in small bags in garden or variety store.

What to do: Place the filter or a piece of paper towel in the bottom of the pot or carton. Fill the bottom of the pot with gravel or small stones, to a depth of about 2 inches (5 cm). Pour sand into the container until it is about three-quarters full. This is your filter system.

Using the funnel, pour about 1 cup of dirt into the soda bottle and fill it with water. Screw the cap on and shake it thoroughly.

Pour some of the muddy water from the bottle into one of the shallow containers. This will be the control or test container, to compare the filtered water against the original sample. Place your filter system in the other container and pour some muddy water into the top of it. Watch the water as it filters through and compare it to the control sample. Be patient, the first samples will not be as clear as later ones. Repeat this procedure several times until the water comes through fairly clear. Continue to compare these samples with the water in the control pan.

What happens: The first water the trickles out of your filter system will still be fairly dirty. However, as you continue to pour the water back into and through your system, it begins to get clearer. Although the water gets cleaner, there will likely still be a certain amount of sediment that remains.

Why: Although there are similarities, your simple water filter system is not like a city's large water treatment plant. In the city system, water is sprayed into the air to release unwanted gases, and substances are added to clump together dirt particles suspended in the water so that they can be filtered out.

As with your system, the water is also passed through layers of sand and gravel, but also through a layer of charcoal. The water is then chlorinated. The chlorine gas kills bacteria that may be present in the water. Cleaning water is a big job.

Now you know something of how water filter systems work, and why you wouldn't want to drink any water you "clean" yourself.

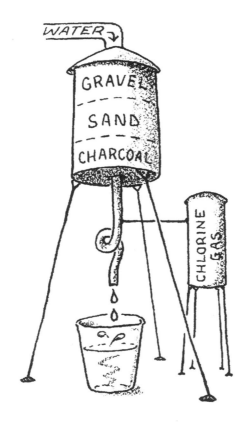

215 ◆ Sand-Casting

YOU WILL NEED:
sand or very fine soil
metal baking pan
water

The sea wears away coastal shorelines and rebuilds new sand formations. In this simple experiment, you will see how the earth is constantly being worn away, eroded, and how the process of erosion steadily changes the different shapes and formations on the earth's surface.

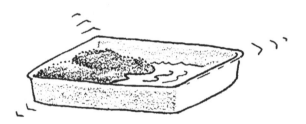

What to do: Pile the sand at one end of the baking pan and firmly pat it down. For the purposes of the experiment, this will represent the sandy beach or shore. Pour some water into the middle of the pan until part of the shore is slightly covered. At first gently, then increasingly faster, slide the pan back and forth until small waves are formed that roll up and onto the shore so the sand shifts, or moves.

What happens: The action of the waves in the container gradually changes the shape of the shore, moving the sand down the beach and into the water.

Why: All the seas and oceans of the earth are constantly changing the land they meet. Some wear away or carve out great rocky areas of land while others take away great sections of sand, depositing it elsewhere. This gradual but persistent action of water against land is called erosion.

Playing Dirty, or Groovy Soil Boxes

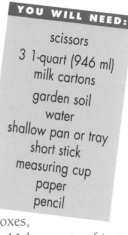

YOU WILL NEED:

scissors

3 1-quart (946 ml) milk cartons

garden soil

water

shallow pan or tray

short stick

measuring cup

paper

pencil

If you liked playing in mud when you were small, you're going to love this experiment. Do it outside wearing old clothes because you can get pretty dirty if you're not careful.

What to do: Cut away one side of each carton, the side away from the opening or spout. (The spout should rest on the ground as in the illustration.) Pack each opened carton with the same amount of soil.

Wet the soil in each carton thoroughly and mix it up. If the soil is too wet, put in some dry soil and mix it thoroughly by hand.

Next, pack down the muddy soil in each container to form a hill, or a slant with the high side toward the unopened end of the container. With your hand or the stick, form sideways, or horizontal, gullies or ridges in one carton, steps in the second carton, and leave the third "hill" alone.

Let the soil containers dry out for about 30 minutes. After they have dried, prop the first carton against something immovable so that it is at a slight slant. Place the shallow container under the spout opening so the opening rests on the bottom of the container.

Measure 1 cup of water and pour it steadily but gently on the top of the soil hill. Wait a few minutes for the water to settle and drain into the pan.

Pour the water from the container back into the measuring cup and see how much you have gotten back, or recovered. Write this down. Repeat this with the other two soil boxes, and again record your results. Make a note of just how clear or muddy the water is, or how much sediment or soil particles are present, as well as how long it took for the water you recovered to flow from each soil box into the drainage container.

What happens: In our experiment, we recovered 1 cup of water from the step and plain boxes but only ½ cup from the box with gullies. Is that what you found?

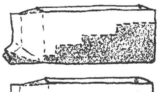

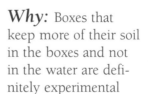

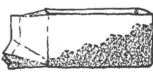

Why: Boxes that keep more of their soil in the boxes and not in the water are definitely experimental winners. Soil erosion, or the wearing away of topsoil, can be lessened by good farming or conservation techniques designed to protect and save the soil. The two such methods used in your experiment were contour farming, in which gullies or horizontal ridges are dug, and terracing, in which steps or elevated planes or levels are formed.

GRAVITY AND MAGNETISM: ATTRACTIVE FORCES

Although gravity and magnetism are different earth forces, they both exert a lot of pull.

Gravity is the force that pulls everything downward, toward the middle of our planet—you, your house, a ball, your bed, your car—everything! Your weight on earth is simply the amount of pull this force has on you.

The planets, the sun, and the moon also have gravities, but with a force lesser or greater than the earth's. The sun's gravity holds the earth and other planets in orbit around it, while the moon's gravity pull lowers and raises the tides of the oceans. Sir Isaac Newton, an English scientist, discovered these and other laws of gravity.

On the other hand, magnets have polar or field forces where an attraction, or pull is stronger. The earth itself, due to its iron center, or core, is also a giant magnet.

The wonderful gravity and magnetic experiments in this chapter will certainly attract your attention and pull you away from anything else you're doing.

Weight Lifter

217

YOU WILL NEED:
nail
bottom of a waxed carton
heavy string
paper clip
thick rubber band
ruler
substances to weigh, like stones, gravel, beans, rice, dirt, sand, and marshmallows

Weight is simply the pull of the force of gravity on you and on other objects. This experiment will demonstrate how this works. To avoid the mess of spills (gravity again), it's a good idea to do this experiment outdoors. You will need a friend's help, too.

What to do: With the nail, poke a hole through one side of the carton about 1 inch (2.5 cm) down from the top and another hole directly across from the first, on the other side of the carton. Thread the ends of the string through the holes and tie them securely to form a handle. Attach the paper clip to the top of the string handle and the rubber band to the other end of the paper clip.

Have your helper hold your homemade spring scale so the top of the carton basket is even with the top of the ruler. From the substances available, select one and pour some of the gravel, stones, rice, dried beans, or whatever you wish to weigh into the carton. Do this gradually as you fill the carton.

Hold the top of the ruler to the top of the cup and calibrate, or measure, how many inches, or centimeters, the gradually filled cup passes as it drops past the ruler.

What happens: Your homemade spring scale, filled with different amounts of weight, measures the force of gravitational pull on the material in the basket. The carton basket is pulled down past the ruler's measurements according to the amount of force gravity exerts on it.

Why: The earth pulls everything toward its center. The more pull gravity is able to exert on an object, based on its denseness or mass, the heavier the object is. As the basket is filled, and the rubber band stretches, the amount of force measured by the spring scale grows.

Canned Laughter

218

THE FORCE

2 large, hardcovered, thick books
empty coffee can with lid
clay ball (golf ball size)
pencil

Roll a can uphill and play a trick on a friend while learning about an important force that affects everybody and everything on earth.

What to do: Place one end of a book on top of the other end of the other book to form a ramp. Place the clay ball inside the coffee can and press it firmly against the side so it sticks to the can's surface. The ball should be centered on the can's wall somewhere between the two ends.

On the outside of the can, mark the spot with a pencil so you'll know where the weight of the clay is concentrated.

Now, put the plastic lid back on the can and get ready to amaze yourself with an uphill roll.

Position the can on the lower end of the book ramp and experiment with it until you get it to roll up the book ramp. Now find some friends who are interested in seeing your amazing "scientific magic."

What happens: The can, surprisingly, rolls up the slightly uphill book ramp.

Why: All objects are pulled toward the earth's center by a constant strong force called gravity. The "center of gravity" of any object seems to be the particular place on it where all the weight of the object is "centered." At this one point, the object will balance rather than fall.

The clay ball place inside the coffee can was enough to reposition the can's natural center of gravity. The added off-center weight allowed gravity to pull the can forward and up the ramp.

219 Roll Playing

Test the last experiment using different surfaces. What happens if you place the can in the same "weighted position" but on the "downhill" side of the ramp? What happens if you place it on a flat surface?

Take the lid off the can and watch what happens to the clay weight inside it as you try different things. When the can does not roll, the weight in the can is concentrated in one place. When the center of gravity is shifted, the can is forced by the weight to move.

Where is the center of gravity? Press one end of a short string or piece into the clay ball and watch.

Rapid Transit

The Dancing Cobra

YOU WILL NEED:

plastic drinking glass
small sphere, like a
ball of clay, a small
toy ball, or a marble

City subways or monorail
trains are often called
rapid transit. Now watch
how rapidly a ball will transit, or
move out of, a drinking glass, and learn about
an important earth force.

What to do: Place the sphere in the drinking
glass and rapidly slide it, open end forward, across
a tabletop or a hard-surfaced floor. Stop the
movement suddenly and observe what happens to
the ball inside.

What happens: The ball
shoots out of the end of the
stopped glass and keeps on rolling
straight until something in its way
stops it or changes its
direction.

Why: Sir Isaac Newton, an English physicist,
discovered several natural laws of gravity and
motion. One of these laws is called inertia. This
means that something that is at rest will stay at
rest, not moving, until another force works on it
or moves it—and it will continue to stay in
motion until, again, something works on it to
stop it!

The ball in the moving drinking glass stayed
in it as long as it was moving. The inertia of this
force was not overcome until the movement was
suddenly stopped. The sudden stop was the force
that overcame the inertia of the ball in the moving
container and sent the ball rolling—until a
counter-force stopped it.

YOU WILL NEED:

cotton thread, about
8 inches (20 cm) long
straight pin
horseshoe magnet

This experimental trick
done with a pin and a
magnet will remind you of
an Indian snake charmer
and his swaying cobra.

What to do: Make a loop in the thread and tie
it around the head of the pin.

Hold the end of the thread with the pin
attached and, with the other hand, lift it with the
magnet. When you get the pin to an upright position, carefully lift the magnet from the pin so it is
slightly suspended in midair. Move the magnet
slowly in circles and watch the pin and thread, or
cobra, follow the movements. Unless you have a
very strong magnet, there may be only a very
small distance, or break, between the pin and the
magnet or the pin and thread will fall.

What happens:
The pin and thread
floats suspended in the
air slightly below the
magnet and follows its
path as you move it
around.

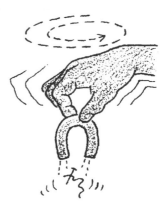

Why: The pin seems
to be slightly overcom-
ing gravity, floating
below the magnet while
not touching it. This is proof that the magnet's
attraction can pass through air and, at the right
distance, can "balance" the force of gravity.

222 Needlework on the Santa Maria

Christopher Columbus and other early mariners, or sailors, probably used a wondrous device to help them travel the seas out of sight of land—a magnetized needle floating in a bowl of water.

Modern seafarers now have access to several devices to help them navigate the oceans, even a system of space satellites surrounding the earth. But let's take a close look at that earlier version of the modern compass and see what a simple sewing needle can do.

What to do: Magnetize the needle by rubbing one end of it fifty times with the north end of the magnet. Do the same thing to the other end by rubbing it with the south side of the magnet. Be certain to stroke the needle with the magnet in only one direction, from the center to the end, and lift the magnet away from the needle each time you go to repeat the stroke.

Cut a small circle about 1 inch (2.5 cm) in diameter out of the wax paper. Place the bowl of water on a table or kitchen counter. Carefully stick the needle into the wax-paper circle, as you would a needle into cloth. Float the wax paper with the needle on top of the surface in the middle of the water. Try to move it around on the surface. Observe what happens.

What happens: The needle, when the movement stops, points north and south, no matter how many times you move it around.

Why: Your floating needle is reacting to the earth's invisible magnetic pull, caused by its giant bar-magnet core.

Don't Get Stuck: Control Your Needle!

How do you know if all needles, when movement stops, position themselves in a north-south position? To find out, set up a control compass or one that lets you know if other things are causing results.

Do the same experiment in the same way as in the previous experiment, but now substitute a non-magnetized needle for the magnetized one.

Move the compass to the middle of the water and again move the needle around. Wait patiently for the needle to stop moving. Do several trials or experiments and compare the control compass with the magnetized needle.

Don't Needle Me!

Make a magnetic compass that doesn't look like the usual one. It has no case and you won't have to needle it

YOU WILL NEED:
large piece of modeling clay (to make a stand)
very sharp pencil with an eraser
horseshoe magnet

What to do: Roll the piece of clay into a ball and flatten it to make a sturdy stand; then push the eraser end of the pencil into the clay stand. Carefully balance the magnet on the pencil lead.

What happens: The magnet gradually positions itself into a north-south direction.

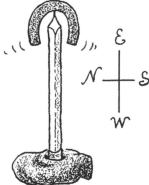

Why: The earth is a magnetic ball with north and south magnetic poles. The magnet positioned itself in a north-south direction because magnetic metals and liquids buried within the earth's core have turned it into a giant magnet that naturally attracts all compasses and magnets. These great magnetic forces are concentrated at its north and south magnetic poles, which, incidentally, are not exactly the same as the North and South Poles we usually speak of, although they are in the same area.

225 What's Your Point?

Magnetized straight pins with like poles repel each other, while unlike poles attract. True?

What to do: Magnetize one straight pin by laying it on a hard surface and rubbing one end of it with the north side of the magnet. Rub from the center to the end, one way only, and lift the magnet between the rubs. Do this about fifty times. Repeat the rubbing action on the other end of the pin using the south end of the magnet. Magnetize the second pin the same way.

Write down which end (point or head) is north or south. Tie 10 inch (25 cm) lengths of thread to the center of each pin and attach paper clips to the other ends. Dangle the two balancing pins about 2 inches (5 cm) apart, one on each thread, from the end of the table. Place the paper-clipped ends of the threads on the table and weight them down with the book. Now, try pushing the pins together.

What happens: Some ends move away from each other, while the other ends jump up at each other and bump.

Why: Like magnetic poles repel away from each other while unlike poles attract or pull together.

226 Bartender

If you tend, or pay attention, to this spinning bar magnet, you will notice some surprising things.

What to do: Tie one end of the long piece of string around the center of the bar magnet. Tie, or tape, the other end up to a light fixture, closet pole, or a rod between chair backs, where it can swing freely. Adjust the magnet so it is properly balanced and does not hang down on one side.

Now spin the magnet and wait about 3 minutes until it has stopped moving. Draw a picture showing its north and south poles as they look to you. Do this five or six times. Does the magnet come to rest, or stop moving, in the exact same position each time, with the poles aligned or the same?

What happens: The bar magnet should continue to align itself up similarly, with the same poles showing, no matter how many times you spin it.

Why: Hanging freely from a string, your bar magnet becomes a compass that aligns itself according to the earth's magnetic pull.

Coin Artist

Many coin-operated food and soda machines, called vending machines, catch fake coins, like slugs or washers, by using a magnetic part. How does this theft preventer work?

YOU WILL NEED:

3 large hardcover books
bar magnet
4 coins, like a dime, penny, quarter, and nickel
3 metal washers

What to do: Stack two books on top of one another and lean the third against the stacked books to form a slide. Hold the bar magnet in the middle of the book forming the slide, while you drop each coin and washer down the side of the book, past the magnets.

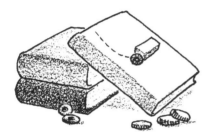

What happens: The coins slide past the magnet, but the washers are caught and held by it.

Why: The bar magnet "picked up" the washers because they are made of steel or iron, but did not pick up the official, government-minted coins because they are minted, or made into coins, from alloys or mixed metals that are non-magnetic.

United States coinage is a combination of copper and other metals. Since magnets will not pick up copper, they are useful in catching all the slugs, or fake coins, made of steel or iron that thieves may drop into vending machines.

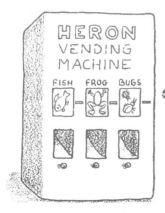

HERON VENDING MACHINE

FISH FROG BUGS

Drawing Paper

Riddle: What kind of paper can you draw on, but yet never use a pencil nor be an artist? Do this experiment and find out.

What to do: Over one sheet of paper, using an old scissors, cut the steel wool pad into fine small threads. (Be careful of splinters.) Lay the magnet down and place the second sheet of paper over it so that the magnet is underneath in the middle. Now, carefully and evenly, pour the threads onto the sheet over the magnet. Lightly pound the table near the thread-covered sheet with your fist and watch the movement of the threads. Examine the thread patterns through the magnifying glass.

What happens: The fine steel wool threads are drawn to and align themselves around the magnet in a circular pattern.

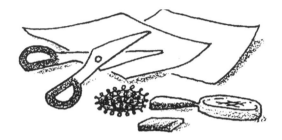

Why: Definite circular lines of steel threads form around the magnet. This pattern is called the magnetic field of force. The steel threads gather more at the magnet's poles, where the force is greater, and thin out in the middle, where the force is less. This is the same magnetic force that encircles the earth. Since the earth is a giant magnet, all steel and iron objects on its surface will behave this way.

DON'T FIDDLE WITH OLD FOSSILS

At one time or another we have all left the lights on when leaving a room or turned on the air conditioner when it wasn't that hot or the heater when it wasn't that cold. It's also very easy to forget to turn off the water promptly when finished, and even easier to just toss away aluminum cans, paper, and glass and plastic bottles when they are empty—without thinking about it. But the earth's resources, the natural substances we use to make energy and put it to work to make life better, are fast being used up. Some scientists predict that the earth's resources will be gone within fifty years—within your lifetime!

The earth resources of coal, oil, and petroleum are used to heat and cool our homes, make electricity, and fuel our cars. They are known as fossil fuels because they are made from the remains of ancient dead plants and animals. When these fuels are gone, they cannot be replaced.

There are other natural ways to create power. These include tapping into the heated water within the earth (geothermal), nuclear energy, solar panels, windmills, or water-driven devices that move turbines (hydro-electricity) or geared machines that circle back to again produce more energy. Until energy can be fully and inexpensively produced from such sources, however, fossil fuels will not be replaced.

So what can you do to help the earth? You can turn off lights when leaving a room, keep the thermostat or heater controls low so heat energy won't be wasted, dress warmly or use a blanket when it is cold, and drink cool water and wear light clothing when hot. Also, recycle paper, glass, aluminum, plastics, and metals (whatever is being collected where you live). Don't waste water. Use less when washing, take shorter showers, don't flush the toilet unnecessarily, turn water off while you brush your teeth. Just for the

record, one leaky faucet can waste thousands of gallons of water each year!

In this chapter you'll learn about conservation, fossil fuels, and recycling. You will even learn to make your own recycled-paper note cards. But remember, it is your efforts to be a conservationist, an earth-conscious, responsible person, that will help to save our planet, so don't fiddle with old fossils—save them!

Housewarming

A greenhouse is a closed glass house used to grow plants, where heat from the sun is trapped inside and moisture cannot escape.

Scientists see the earth today as becoming a type of greenhouse. By burning coal, oil, and other such products known as fossil fuels, by over-using and abusing the use of our cars, and by heating and cooling our homes with electricity or gas, carbon dioxide and other harmful gases are being pushed into the atmosphere. These gases act as a dome, or lid, over the earth's atmosphere, trapping the solar heat and preventing it from escaping into outer space.

When trees are cleared from large land areas, like the tropical rain forests, tons more carbon dioxide gas remains in the atmosphere, instead of being converted into breathable oxygen. It's like putting the earth into a big glass cooker, where heat from the sun is trapped and the air inside gets hotter and stuffier.

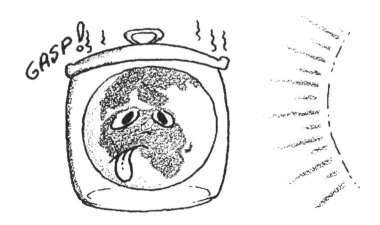

229 What Green House?

You may or may not find a greenhouse, or even a green house, on your block, but learning about the greenhouse effect and what it means to you and everything on earth is very important today.

What to do: Pour the teaspoon of water into the glass jar. Replace the lid and tighten it well so that no air can escape. Leave the container outside in a sunny location for about 1 hour.

What happens: Droplets of water form and cling to the sides of the jar.

Why: The sun's heat warms up the jar's atmosphere and the movement of the water molecules in it speeds up. The water then evaporates into the air, but the moisture has nowhere to go, so it gathers into droplets, or condenses, on the cool glass sides. The lid on the jar acts as a greenhouse and produces the greenhouse effect. This is similar to the carbon dioxide gas that is produced by our own personal energy use and by the use of fossil fuels by industry which acts like a lid over the earth and prevents heat that is building up from escaping into space.

230 Greenhouse: An Open-and-Shut Case

Do the last experiment again, but this time don't put the lid on the jar. Try the experiment with different-size containers (with lids and without) and with different amounts of water. Does the heat buildup that causes steam through evaporation occur earlier or later?

What differences do you notice? How do the experiments show what's happening to the earth? Do the results suggest ways to prevent the greenhouse effect?

Warm Up

Measuring the heat energy trapped in a glass container shows us again how the greenhouse effect works and can affect us. You will have to do this experiment on a sunny day

What to do: Make sure that the temperature readings of both thermometers are the same—normal, outdoor temperature. Then find a sunny location outside and place the jar on its side. Put a small rock against one or both sides of the jar to keep it from rolling over.

Take one piece of black construction paper and place a thermometer on top of it, then slide both the thermometer and the material together into the bottle. Screw the lid on tightly but carefully so the thermometer stays in place.

Put the other thermometer on a dark strip next to the bottle. Record both temperatures, wait 10 minutes, then record the temperatures again.

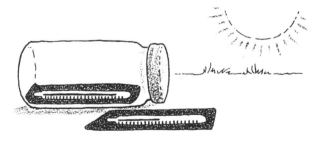

What happens: The thermometer in the closed bottle registers a higher temperature than the one outside.

Why: This closed-environment experiment demonstrates the effect of large amounts of carbon dioxide (CO_2) in the earth's atmosphere. CO_2 gas acts like the glass of the bottle, trapping heat. Although the sunlight falls equally on both sections of cloth, which absorb the light and produce the same amount of heat energy, the heat cannot easily radiate out through the glass barrier.

Carbon dioxide is produced on earth (given off as we breathe), but much more comes from the industrial burning of fossil fuels (smokestacks) and automobile engines, causing pollution and raising heat levels in the atmosphere. This "trapping" of heat by an increasing amount of CO_2 in the atmosphere is known as the greenhouse effect.

Cool Down

Try the same experiment again, but leave out the black strips. Is there a difference? Bring your bottle with the thermometer inside (don't open it) and leave the other thermometer indoors.

Write down the temperature as the thermometers cool down. Is there a difference in the cooling-off time of the thermometer inside the bottle compared to the one outside? Which cools faster, and at what rate?

Oh, Ozone!

233

YOU WILL NEED:
stick of chewing gum
short soda bottle
very hot tap water
magnifying glass

Make a model of the ozone layer, the thin layer of gas in the earth's upper atmosphere that protects us from the sun's damaging ultraviolet rays. Learn about CFCs, those chemicals that make life so much easier and better, but yet do so much damage (they destroy ozone molecules). Then, watch as your ozone–layer model produces holes, gradually tears apart, and finally disappears!

What to do: Chew the stick of gum thoroughly. When it is soft, take it out of your mouth. Flatten it into a small disk between your fingers because you need a thin flat cap to seal the top of the bottle. Now, fill the bottle right to the top with very hot tap water. Take the flat piece of gum and place it over the top of the bottle to seal it. Try to avoid making any holes, and make sure that the water slightly touches the gum cap. Observe what happens closely with the magnifying glass.

What happens: The gum cap, as it touches the hot water, loses its elasticity, or stretchability, and holes begin to form. Eventually the gum cap breaks apart.

Why: In your ozone model the bottle represents the earth while the gum cap represents the ozone layer. The hot water touching the gum cap stands for the CFCs (chlorofluorocarbons), the chemicals that can damage ozone molecules.

CFCs are found in coolants for air conditioners and refrigerators and in the foam–plastic packaging used by some fast–food restaurants. These chemicals are released into the atmosphere as chlorine gas, which eventually destroys ozone.

Stick to It

234

How can you reduce the amount of CFCs in the earth's atmosphere? Of course, you can't do it all alone, but you can do your part. Buy fewer products with CFCs in them, use less air conditioning, and remind others of our responsibilities to Mother Nature. Working together is the way to help save our Earth.

Now, do the same ozone experiment, but instead of filling the bottle to the top with hot water, stop when it is only half full. Does the gum cap still show signs of wearing away? Is there a difference? Now you can see how releasing fewer or no CFCs into the air can make a big difference to the earth's ozone layer.

235 It's a Solar System

YOU WILL NEED:

8 feet (265 cm) of aquarium air-line tubing (found in aquarium shops or pet stores at low cost)

rubber band

large, short wide-mouth jar

aluminum foil

baking pan

large soda bottle

water

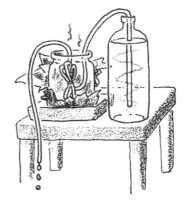

We're not talking about the sun, moon, and planets here, but rather about a solar water heater. In warmer parts of the world, a system of panels can be seen on the roofs of buildings and houses. These panels collect the sun's rays and use the energy to heat water.

Now it's time to make your own solar collector to heat water. It's fun, easy, and it won't take a lot of expensive equipment either. This experiment should be done outside in a warm place where the rays of the sun will fall directly on your solar collector. The best time for the experiment is between 1 and 2 P.M., when the sun is at its strongest. It is important to "preheat" the collector bottle by letting it sit in the sun 30 to 60 minutes before the experiment begins.

What to do: Coil the plastic tubing back and forth accordion style leaving about 1½ feet (48 cm) of tubing loose at each end. Place the rubber band around the middle of the tubing, then shove the bunched tubing into the jar. Cover it with the foil, sealing the open jar around the tubing. Place the wrapped bottle in the pan on a table outdoors to preheat for about 1 hour.

To complete the experiment, fill the large soda bottle with cool tap water, put it on the table next to your solar collector and place one end of the tubing into it. The other free tube should hang below the table.

Now, to get the water flowing through the collector bottle and out the free end, suck slightly on the end of the tubing as you would on a straw. This should start the water moving from the bottle through the collector and down the tube hanging below the table. The water will leave this tube in a slow, steady drip.

What happens: The water that drips slowly from the tube toward the ground will be slightly but noticeably warmer than the water in the bottle.

Why: Your solar heater is a miniature version of the large solar panels mounted on rooftops. Like the large collectors, your small model captures the sun's energy and heats the water traveling through the tubing. How much warmer the water will get, passing through your collector bottle, depends on a lot of things: the time of year, the time of day, the outside temperature, the location of the collector, how fast or slow the water passes through the system, and how long the collector is allowed to "preheat" before the water starts flowing.

Hot Under the Collar

236

YOU WILL NEED:

solar collector
large soda bottle
water

What's hot under this bottle's collar, or opening? Now's the time to find out. In "It's a Solar System" you really did two experiments. You built a solar collector, but you also made a siphon, a device used to draw off liquids from a higher to a lower place. A siphon works because of an important earth force—gravity!

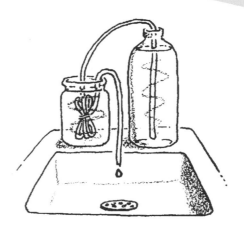

What to do: Remove the foil from the collector bottle. Leave the tubing as it is, and fill the jar with very hot tap water. Fill the soda bottle with very cool tap water.

Place the large soda bottle next to the collector bottle on the sink or on a small table outside. Insert one end of the free tubing into the bottle filled with cool water. The other end should hang down into the sink or toward the ground. Again, suck on the end of the lower tube to get your water moving.

What do you observe? Is the dripping water warmer than the water that came from your solar collector? What things, or variables, could have affected the temperature of the water coming through your collector?

Can you think of something you may have in your home that is similar to this device? How about a water heater?

Fossil Fuelish

Hundreds of millions of years ago great plants like mosses and ferns growing in swamps died and fell one on top of the other. These layers became peat, or decayed plant matter. This process continued through the centuries until great beds, or layers, of decaying plants were formed and were covered by mud, rock, and sediment. Pressed down by great weights, these layers were chemically changed by natural heat and pressure into beds of pure carbon, or coal, or became natural gas, mainly made up of a marsh or swamp gas called methane.

Crude oil was also formed in a similar way—chemically changed from the remains of small sea animals and plants by heat and great pressure. This compression, being tightly pressed together, turned the dead marine plant and animal matter into oil. Much of this chemical change took place under ancient seas—some of which no longer exist.

Spicy Test

You can do an acid-base test to measure pH. In this test liquids are applied to strips of test paper and the color change that results is compared to a pH strip to determine just how acid or alkaline (base) a substance really is.

The pH scale is a range of numbers and colors. Number 1 is extremely acid while 14 is extremely alkaline, or base, which neutralizes acids. Number 7 is considered a neutral number.

Now, make your own test paper by using a spice called turmeric. Since the turmeric solution stains, cover your work area with newspaper; then, in a small cup, make a turmeric-paste solution Add 1 tablespoon of turmeric to 5 tablespoons of hot tap water and stir until smooth.

Cut white construction paper (or thick paper towels) into small strips and dip them into the turmeric paste. Coat them well. The paste will stain your fingers, but it won't hurt you. Lay the golden, yellow-brown strips on newspaper to dry.

When the paper strips are thoroughly dried, test one in vinegar, one in soapy water, another in a baking soda solution, lemon juice, or water with detergent. If the solution is very acidic, the strip will turn yellow; if it is alkaline, it will turn a brownish-red. You can also use the turmeric test papers to test local tap water, the water in lakes and rivers, and soils.

After testing, let your test papers dry and label them, telling what substances they were dipped into.

Rainwear

Is acid rain responsible for a gradual destruction of the world's forests? Perhaps not directly, but most scientists agree that any conditions that affect trees and plants are important to their health and our survival.

Acid rain is made up of nitric and sulfuric acids and produces poisonous metals, like mercury, that can affect plants and animals. It contaminates the minerals in soil that plants need for food and destroys the plants we need for food.

The sulfur and nitrogen elements of acid rain and acid dust, called acid deposition, also affect buildings, cars, statues, and other nonliving objects, causing a lot of damage over the years.

These polluting acids can be found in rain, snow, fog, and the moisture available in the air in different strengths in all parts of the world. Did you know that some European cities have had rains that were as acid as lemon juice (2.3 on the pH scale)? How does the rain in your city compare? See the next experiment.

Papermaking: A Chip Off the Old Block

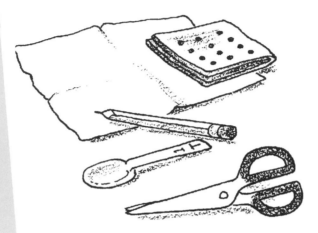

Paper is usually made of tiny slivers of wood and water and processed to produce a pulpy mush. This is spread over a screen, called a deckle, and left to dry. Now you can make your own paper simply and easily, and you won't even have to use a blender for chopping and mixing the glop or a deckle.

This "recipe" makes four 6 inch (15 cm) square note cards. It is a messy activity, however, so do the mixing on a kitchen counter and do the last part outside on a table that can be washed down. Also, be prepared! Paper making is a slow process. This experiment may take all day to complete.

What to do: Cut four pieces of aluminum foil and fold them over to make four 6 inch (15 cm) foil squares. They will be used to make a sieve, or simple deckle, to hold and drain the paper mixture. Punch holes with the pencil in each of the foil squares, about ½ inch (1 cm) apart and in vertical rows.

Next, cut sheets of newspaper into long, thin strips and then cut or tear them into smaller pieces. You'll need about 1½ packed cups of shredded paper.

Place the paper in the jar and fill it three-quarters full of hot tap water. Screw on the lid and let the mixture stand for about 3 hours, shak-

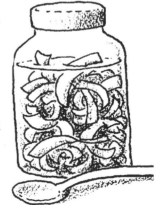

ing the jar from time to time and continuing to beat and stir the pieces with the wooden spoon to break them up. The more you stir and beat the pieces, the more the mixture will become pulpy, gloopy, creamier, and smoother. Add more hot water as the paper absorbs it.

When the mixture is pasty and creamy, pour it into the baking pan. Add a bit more water, if needed. Stir the mixture with the spoon again to be sure all the paper is broken up. Now, dissolve the 3 tablespoons of cornstarch in ½ cup of hot water. Pour the solution into the paper mixture and mix thoroughly.

It's best to do the last part of this activity out-

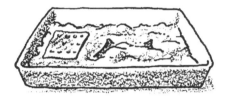

doors where the work area can be washed down. Place the tray with the mixture flat and put a foil square on top of it.

With the palms of your hands, press the foil downward until the mixture covers it. Bring the foil up and place it on the table. Press it flat with your hands to squeeze away the water. Repeat the process, using the other foil squares.

Lay a few sheets of newspaper in a sunny location and let your foil-backed paper dry. As the paper dries, continue to press it down to squeeze out water. While you are doing this, pinch together any holes you notice.

After 3 hours, carefully peel the paper from its

foil backing and trim it neatly into a square note card. With your crayons or paints, colored markers, pencils, or chalk, design a special, homemade recycled card for someone you know. A specially made card from a young, thoughtful conservationist like yourself is sure to be appreciated.

What now: Your recycled newspaper looks and feels much like a gray egg carton. But what would it look and feel like if you used different types of paper?

Collect scrap samples of used white writing paper and recycle it as you did the newspaper. What is the difference in the texture, or feel, and color of the paper?

Dear Aunt Nell, How do you like this paper? I made it myself! With love, Kim

WEATHER

Why is the North Pole colder than the equator? Why does the sun set? What causes thunder and lightning? From the experiments in the four chapters that follow, you will find out about these and many other mysteries of climate and weather. Climate is the average weather of a region over a long period. Weather has to do with daily changes in the lower part of the atmosphere—the ocean of air that surrounds the earth.

Both climate and weather are created by the interaction of the earth and the sun. Both climate and weather have to do with warmth, wind, and water. The experiments in these chapters all explore how and why.

You will discover why some places and some parts of the year are warmer than others. You may be surprised to know that closeness to the sun is not the reason! You will find out what creates wind and why it is sometimes so destructive. You will learn why cold air usually brings "high pressure" and good weather, while warm air often causes "low pressure," bad weather, and strong winds.

You will come to understand snow, sleet, and hail, lightning and thunder. You will be able to make your own weather station, putting together the instruments you need to keep track of temperature, air pressure, wind direction and speed, humidity and rainfall.

You can begin with any experiment in any chapter, but it is best if you take one chapter at a time and do most of the experiments in order.

In a few of the experiments, you will need to use a safety match or a stove, and these are labeled HOT! You can see them at a glance and get help, if that's the rule at your house.

Some of these experiments are great tricks that you can use to amaze yourself and your friends. But the best part is that they give you hands–on experiences that show the scientific principles behind weather, so that you can understand them—from the ground up.

Warming Up

What heats our earth? Why are some places warm and some cold? Why do we have tropical deserts near the equator and the frozen tundra at the poles? What causes the seasons? What is the "greenhouse effect"?

Perform the simple experiments in this chapter and discover the answers to these questions—and others!

Earth's Temperature Records

Highest temperature: 136° F (57.7° C)
Place: Azizia, Tripolitania, Libya
Date: September 13, 1922

Longest hot spell: 100° F (38° C)
for 162 consecutive days
Place: Martin Bar, Western Australia
Date: October 31, 1923—April 7, 1924

Highest annual mean temperature:
94° F (34.4° C)
Place: Dallol, Ethiopia
Date: 1960–1966

Hottest hot spell: 120° F (48.8° C) or more
for 43 consecutive days
Place: Death Valley, California
Date: July 6–August 17, 1917

Lowest temperature: –129° F (–89° C)
Place: Vostok, Antarctica
Date: July 21, 1983

Lowest temperature in an inhabited place: –90.4° F (–68° C)
Place: Oymyakon, Siberia, Russia
Date: Feb. 3, 1933

Lowest recorded annual mean temperature: –70 degrees F (–56.6degrees C)
Place: Pleasteau Station, Antarctica

What Warms Us?

YOU WILL NEED:
sunny window

Indoors, we use coal, oil, gas, or electricity to heat and light our homes and workplaces. But what provides the heat and light outdoors? What warms the earth and the objects on it?

What to do: On a sunny day, hold one hand up behind a shaded window. Lift the shade or blind. Now hold your hand up to the window again.

What happens: Instantly, your hand feels warmer.

Why: You didn't touch anything but you felt the heat. It came from the sun—a star 93 million miles away from the earth.

Like all stars, the sun is a great ball of hot gases that pours out huge amounts of heat and light and other energy. Only a tiny part of that energy reaches us. But it is enough to light and warm the earth.

About the Sun

The sun is a medium-sized star—a huge, hot ball of gas. It is one star among billions in the galaxy. Although the sun varies from 90 million miles (144 million km) away in winter to 96 million miles (153.6 million km) away in summer, it is still the closest star to earth.

The sun measures 864,000 miles (1,400,000 km) across—108 times more than the earth.

The sun makes its own light and heat—and provides the light and heat for the earth—by a process that is similar to what happens in the hydrogen bomb.

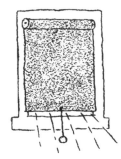

The sun's extreme heat (millions of degrees at the center) causes its hydrogen atoms to move at such super speeds that they smash together. The nuclei, or centers, of the atoms fuse together, in groups of four, forming a heavier atom called helium. The shock of the collision is so great that part of the atom is converted into energy. It is this energy that provides the light and heat for the earth. It is this energy that causes our weather.

240 Heat Wave

How does heat from the sun reach us?

What to do: Hold one end of the ribbon and shake it.

What happens: The movement you make travels the length of the ribbon, like a wave.

Why: Energy often moves from one place to another in waves. Short waves carry light and heat from the sun to the earth. Longer waves carry other forms of energy. When energy moves by waves it is called radiant energy.

241 Why is Spring Sometimes Late?

YOU WILL NEED:
Pyrex pie plate
unshaded lamp
cup of dark soil
cup of light sand
2 room thermometers
pencil
paper

Why does spring come later in some places? This experiment will explain.

What to do: Place the pie plate next to the lamp. Fill half the plate with dark soil and the other half with sand. Stick a thermometer into each half.

Write down the temperature of each side. Turn on the lamp and let the plate stand for 30 minutes. Then compare the new temperatures with the starting ones.

What happens: The dark soil gets hotter.

Why: The light sand bounces back the light energy before it can change to heat energy. The dark soil soaks up the light and converts it to heat.

This is what happens when the sun's rays reach the earth. The dark-colored areas absorb the sunlight and heat up quickly. Light-colored areas reflect the sunlight and remain cool.

The earth does not heat up evenly. The air around dark soil becomes warmer than it does around sand or snowcapped mountains. And so spring comes later in snow-covered countries.

Black, White, and Shiny

YOU WILL NEED:

3 clean, empty tin cans

white and black paint
(acrylic paint is fine)

warm water
room thermometer
paper
pencil
index cards
tray
cold water

Here is another way to find out how different colors and surfaces are affected by heat.

What to do: Paint one can white, inside and out. Paint the second can black. Leave the third can shiny.

Fill the three cans with warm water of the same temperature. Record the temperature

Cover each can with an index card, and set all three on a tray in a cool place. Record the temperature of the water in each can at 5 minute intervals, for 20 minutes.

Now empty the cans, dry them well, then fill each one with very cold water. Record the temperatures of the water in each can. Cover each can with an index card and place them in a warm place or in the sun. Record the temperature of the water in each can at 5 minute intervals, for 20 minutes.

What happens: In both cases, the water in the black can heats up the most, the water in the shiny can heats up the least.

Why: The dark can absorbs best and turns the light into heat. The others reflect or give back the light before it can turn to heat.

Let it Snow

Save this experiment for a snowy day.

What to do: After a snowstorm, when the sun is shining, put the square of aluminum foil and the square of black cloth on the snow. Leave them in the sun for 1 hour. Then see which has sunk the deepest.

What happens: The black cloth will be deeper in the snow than the foil because it has absorbed the most heat.

Why: The dark cloth absorbed the light, which turned into heat—and melted the snow. The foil reflected the light before it turned into heat.

244 Land versus Water

Which gets hotter—
land or water?

What to do: Pour the water into one plastic cup and the soil into the other. Put both cups into the refrigerator for 10 minutes. Then place both cups in sunlight for 15 minutes. Measure and record the temperature of the water and of the soil.

What happens: The soil gets warm, while the water remains cool.

Why: In sunlight, soil heats up faster than water. It's not only because land is darker than water that it retains the heat. In water, the heat can go farther down and spread out. Soil keeps the heat on the surface. If you dig down on a hot beach, you find that the sand underneath is cool. Sunlight can't pass through it. The surface, therefore, becomes very hot.

In addition, the specific heat of water is higher. This means it takes more heat to raise the temperature of water than it takes to raise the temperature of the same amount of soil.

These are the reasons why, on a sunny day, land feels warmer than water.

245 Water versus Air

Why is it warmer in summer and milder in winter near the ocean than it is inland?

What to do: Put the two glasses in the refrigerator for 15 minutes.

What happens: The water-filled glass feels warmer than the empty glass.

Why: The "empty" glass is, of course, filled with air. Both air and glass lose their heat much more rapidly than water. The glass filled with water does not let the cold air in and the water keeps the glass warmer longer.

That's the reason the world's oceans help to store up warmth from the sun. In winter, the oceans cool off more slowly than the land, so a city near an ocean stays warmer in winter than an inland city. Oceans also warm up more slowly in summer, so a seaside city has a milder summer, too.

246 Time in the Sun

Why is summer hotter than winter? This experiment will demonstrate one reason.

What to do: Place the black paper in the sun for 1 minute. Feel it. Then place it in the sun for 5 minutes. Feel it again.

What happens: The longer the paper is in the sun the hotter it feels.

Why: The amount of heat increases, because it is absorbed and retained.

One reason summer is hotter than winter is that the sun shines 15 hours a day in July, but only 9 hours a day in December—since every day the sun rises a little later and sets a little earlier. In the Southern Hemisphere, it is the reverse—the sun shines longest in December and least in July.

247 Why is Summer Hotter than Winter?

Here's proof that the direct rays of the sun are hotter than slanted rays.

What to do: Paint both sides of the tin can lids with black paint and let them dry.

Prop one lid up so the sun hits it directly. Place the other lid flat so the sunlight hits it at a slant.

Let both lids stand for 10 minutes and then touch them.

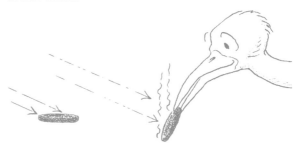

What happens: The lid facing the sun directly gets much hotter than the one the sun hits at a slant.

Why: In summer the sun's rays hit the earth more directly than in winter. That's why summer weather is hotter.

Why the Equator is Hotter than the North Pole

YOU WILL NEED:
flashlight
sheet of paper

Here's why the direct rays of the sun are hotter than slanted rays.

What to do: Shine the flashlight straight down on the sheet of paper. Then tilt the flashlight so its rays strike the paper at a slant, as in the illustration below.

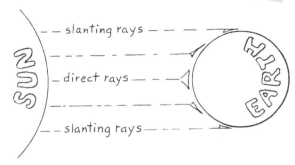

What happens:
When you point the flashlight straight down, it makes a small circle of light on the paper.

When you tilt the flashlight so its rays strike the paper at a slant, it makes a larger, dimmer, oval shape.

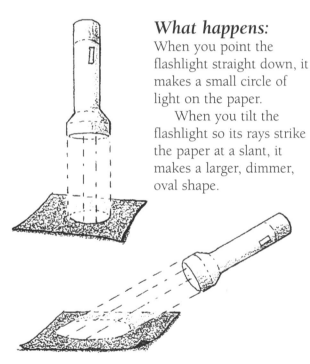

In the same way, a slanted ray of sunlight spreads out more thinly over the earth's surface than a ray that shines straight down. While both rays carry the same amount of heat from the sun, the heat carried by the slanted ray is spread out and less intense.

So, places at and near the equator—where the sun shines directly—get two-and-one-half times as much heat as the North and South Poles where the sun always shines indirectly.

Why: Both the oval and the circle were made by the same source of light (the flashlight). Therefore, the oval has the same amount of light as the circle. But since the oval is bigger, the light in it must be spread more thinly.

249 Make a Shadow Thermometer

YOU WILL NEED:

lamppost, fence post, or tree

tape measure

notebook

pencil

The higher the sun is in the sky, the more direct—and the hotter—are the sun's rays on the earth. A simple way to measure the position of the sun in the sky is to measure the length of the shadows it casts.

What to do: Choose a lamppost, a fence post, or a young tree to cast your shadow. Starting in the fall, observe and measure the length of the shadow at noon every week.

Make a chart in a notebook that records the length of the shadow, as in the illustration. Be sure to include the date.

What happens: The shadow gets longer each time you measure it.

Why: The higher the sun is in the sky at noon, the shorter the shadow it casts. The lower the sun is in the sky, the longer the shadow.

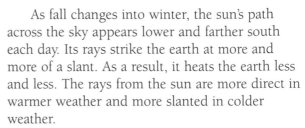

As fall changes into winter, the sun's path across the sky appears lower and farther south each day. Its rays strike the earth at more and more of a slant. As a result, it heats the earth less and less. The rays from the sun are more direct in warmer weather and more slanted in colder weather.

Of course, if you start this experiment in the winter or spring, instead of getting longer, the shadows will gradually get shorter as the sun rises higher in the sky and its rays strike the earth more directly.

 250 Length versus Height

Here is a simple way to see how the length of a shadow changes when the source of light changes position.

What to do: Stand one of the pencils in the center of the thread spool on the sheet of paper. Darken the room and hold the flashlight at different angles above the pencil. Record the length of each shadow.

What happens: When the flashlight is high and right above the pencil, the shadow is short. When the light is low and at a slant, the shadow is long.

 251 The House is Moving!

Step outside on a clear evening and watch the earth spin!

What to do: On a clear evening set out a chair or lie on the ground facing south with a corner of your house to your right. Pick a star close to the edge of the wall of the house and watch it steadily.

What happens: In a minute or two the star disappears behind the house.

Why: Though the sky seems to move, it is really the house that is moving—as part of the earth that is rotating on its axis.

252 Does the Sun Rise in the Morning?

What causes night and day? We know that despite what our eyes seem to tell us the sun does not rise in the morning and set in the evening. Here's one way to visualize what really happens.

What to do: Place the unshaded lamp near the center of a darkened room. The lamp represents the sun. Turn on the lamp. Push the knitting needle through the center of the orange. The orange represents the earth.

Holding the orange by the needle, turn it counter-clockwise as though it were a top, and walk around the lamp.

What happens: Different parts of the turning orange are lit and warmed by the lamp.

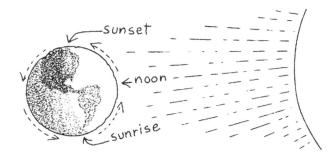

Why: Obviously, the lamp was not moving—the orange was turning. And the sun does not move up in the sky when it rises and down when it sets—it is the earth that is turning. Part of the earth's surface moves toward and then away from the sun as the earth spins toward the east on its axis.

When we are on the side of earth that is in shadow, it is night. When we come back into sunlight, it is day.

The earth spins around completely every 24 hours. Because the earth turns, the sun seems to "set" as we turn away from it and "rise" as we face it again.

253 Foucault's Pendulum

To show that the earth rotates, you can repeat an experiment performed in 1851 by the French physicist Jean Bernard Leon Foucault. He suspended a 200 foot (61 km) pendulum from the Pantheon, a huge public building in Paris. The weight traced the path of the earth on sand on the floor.

You can use your living room and trace the same path with a more modest pendulum. You don't need any sand.

Why: Its inertia keeps the pendulum swinging in the same plane. But it no longer swings over the chalk mark because the room has moved! It moved because of the earth's rotation.

A large pendulum demonstrating earth's rotation is kept swinging in the United Nations building in New York City.

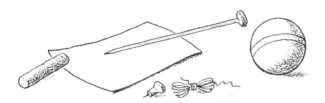

What to do: Push the knitting needle into the ball and attach the end of the knitting needle to the length of string or wire. Tape this "pendulum" to the ceiling so it can swing freely.

With the crayon draw a line on the index card and tape it to the floor directly under the knitting needle.

Start the pendulum swinging back and forth following the line on the index card. Note what happens after 2 hours.

What happens: Although the pendulum is still swinging in its original path, it is no longer swinging over the crayon line you made.

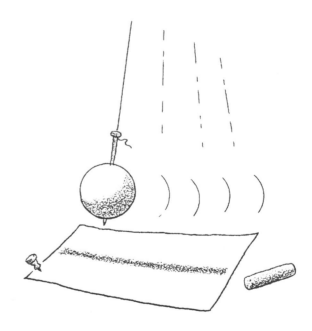

Why We See the Sun After it "Sets"

YOU WILL NEED:

tightly covered jar filled with water

books

unshaded lamp

We see the sun a couple of minutes before it comes up over the horizon at sunrise and after it has set! Here's how!

What to do: Place the jar on its side on a table next to a stack of books. Put the lamp on the opposite side of the table. Stack the books so high that you can't see the light from where you are standing. Then place the tightly covered jar filled with water in front of the stacked books, as in the illustration below.

What happens: You can see the light even though it is below the level of the top of the books.

Why: The rounded top of the jar is like the earth's atmosphere. It bends the rays of light and brings the image of the light into view. It creates a mirage, such as those sometimes seen in the desert, at sea, on hot pavement—and in the sky.

The light from the rising or setting sun passes through a greater thickness of the earth's atmosphere than noontime sunlight does. This bends the rays of the sun. So, at sunrise, when the sun seems to be moving up over the horizon, an image of the sun can be seen on the horizon before the sun actually reaches it. And at sunset, because of those bending rays, we continue to see an image of the sun briefly after the sun has actually set.

As the World Turns

Sun in Your Room

For many centuries, people believed that the sun circled around the earth. Now we know that not only does the earth rotate on its axis, but it also revolves around the sun. All you need for this experiment is a light chair.

What to do: Place a chair in the middle of the room. Move around the chair.

What happens: As you move around the chair, the chair lines up with different things in the room.

Why: The things in the room behind the chair seem to move, although you are actually doing the moving.

In the same way, the sun looks to us as if it is moving, but it is the earth going around the sun that makes it look that way.

The earth completes its journey of 598.3 million miles (965 million km) around the sun in a little more than 365 days, moving about 18½ miles (29.76km) per second. It revolves around the sun in an oval path—an ellipse. Therefore, it sometimes goes a bit faster and at other times a bit slower. The closer the earth is to the sun, the greater the speed.

Here's more proof that the earth changes position in a simple experiment that will keep you busy for months!

What to do: Mark a chalk line on the floor or wall where the sun shines in your room. Keep a record of the place and the exact hour, day, and month.

A week later, at the same time of day, make another line. Again, jot down the spot and the date.

Repeat this weekly throughout the year.

What happens: The sun shines at a different spot in the room each week.

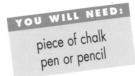

Why: The movement of the earth around the sun causes the change in position of the line from week to week and from month to month.

Why Do We Have Seasons?

Near the equator it remains hot all year round. At the North and South Poles it is always cold. But in most parts of the world there are four seasons every year. Why?

YOU WILL NEED:

orange
knitting needle
tall, unshaded lamp
piece of cardboard
marker

What to do: Push the knitting needle through the orange to represent the earth and its imaginary axis, as in the illustration.

With your marker draw an ellipse (see the next experiment) about 10 inches (25 cm) in diameter on a piece of cardboard to represent the earth's oval orbit. Mark the four quarter points north, south, east and west.

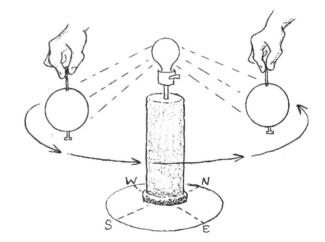

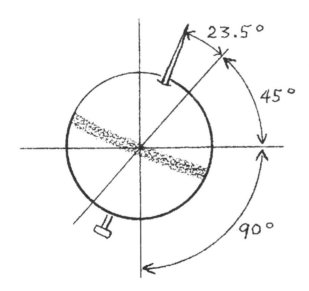

Place the lighted lamp in the center of the cardboard to stand in for the sun.

1. Holding the needle straight up and down, move the orange in turn to each of the four positions. Observe which part of the orange is lit up.

2. Now tilt the orange so that the axis is slanted about 23.5° away from the vertical. (See illustration). Place the orange in turn at each one of the four positions, keeping the needle tilted in the same

direction. Look at the lighted section of the orange. In each position observe which part receives the direct rays and which the slanting rays of light.

What happens:

1. When the needle is straight up and down, the same section is lit no matter where the orange is in relation to the light.

2. When the needle is at the 23.5° angle, the amount of light depends on whether the orange is tilted toward or away from the light.

Why: If the earth's axis were vertical, like the orange in the first experiment, there would be no seasons. But the axis of the earth points to the North Star at a 23.5° slant. (See illustration.) It is this slant that makes the seasons change as the earth revolves around the sun.

When the side of the earth we live on is tilted

toward the sun, we have summer because we receive the direct rays of the sun. Six months later our part of the earth is tilted away from the sun—it is winter because we receive the sun's rays at a slant and so get less of the sun's heat.

At the equator, the sun's rays are always direct. There are no seasons. At the poles, the rays always strike at a slant.

You can see, therefore, that seasons are not caused by the distance of the earth from the sun. Actually, in January in the Northern Hemisphere, the earth is closer to the sun than it is in June.

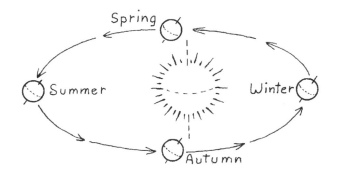

258 ◆ Making an Ellipse

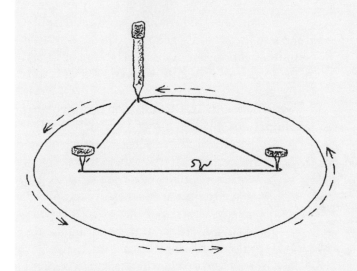

The earth's path around the sun is elliptical. Here's an easy way to make an ellipse.

Place a sheet of unlined paper on a piece of cardboard. Push two tacks (or pins) into the paper about 2 inches (5 cm) apart. Tie the two ends of a 6 inch (15 cm) length of string together and loop the string around the tacks. Insert a pencil in the loop and pull the string tight. Keeping the string tight, move the pencil around and you will draw an ellipse.

259 The Greenhouse Effect

The whole earth is warmed by the greenhouse effect. What is it? This experiment must be done on a sunny day.

What to do: Put a thermometer into the plastic bag. Close the bag and place it on a sunny windowsill. Place the second thermometer on the same windowsill.

After 10 minutes, read both thermometers.

What happens: The thermometer inside the bag reads several degrees higher than the other one.

Why: The sun's rays pass through the bag easily. Once inside, however, they convert into heat, which cannot get out as easily. Therefore, the temperature inside the plastic rises. The bag warms up like a greenhouse, in which gardeners grow plants.

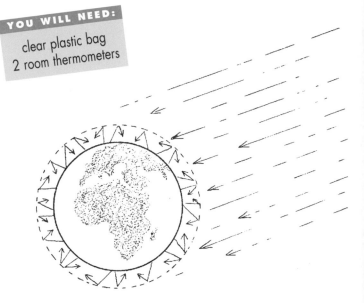

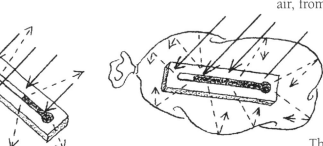

The sun's rays pass through earth's atmosphere in the same way. And when they convert into heat rays, they cannot get out easily. They are absorbed by the surface of the earth, warming it as if it were a large greenhouse.

Some scientists fear that carbon dioxide in the air, from our industrial use of such fuels as oil and coal, have increased the greenhouse effect. Carbon dioxide absorbs heat rays, and so they are radiated back to the earth instead of escaping into space. They believe that this will make the earth warmer, causing the ice at the North and South Poles to melt. They fear sea levels will rise and flood land areas, changing our climate altogether and creating many problems.

Other scientists predict a cooling trend, and suggest that air pollution will block out more of the sun's radiation and prevent the greenhouse effect from increasing.

WHIRLING WINDS AND GENTLE BREEZES

We live at the bottom of an ocean of air called "the atmosphere." Most of our weather changes take place in the lower 3 miles (5 km) of this atmosphere. And most of it is caused by the wind—as it spreads the heat of the sun from warm areas to colder ones.

Wind is simply air that moves. But what is air? What gets it moving? Why is it sometimes so destructive?

Earth's Wind Records

Fastest surface wind speed recorded:
231 miles (370 km) an hour
  Place: Mt. Washington, New Hampshire
  Date: April 12, 1934

Windiest place: gale winds reach 200 miles (320 km) an hour
  Place: Commonwealth Bay, Antarctica

Fastest tornado winds: 286 miles (457 km) an hour
  Place: Wichita Falls, Texas
  Date: April, 2, 1958

World's worst tornado: killed 792 people
  Place: South–central United States
  Date: March 18, 1925

Fastest hurricane winds near a storm center: more than 74 miles per hour (118 km per hour)

Hurricane with highest wind gusts:
175 to 180 miles per hour (280 to 288 km per hour)
  Place: Central Keys and lower southwest Florida coast
  Date: August 29 to September 13, 1960

World's worst hurricane (unleashed floods that killed one million):
  Place: Bangladesh
  Date: 1970

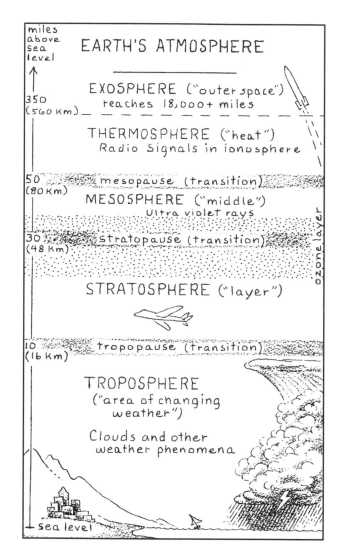

miles
above
sea
level

EARTH'S ATMOSPHERE

350
(560 km)

EXOSPHERE ("outer space")
reaches 18,000+ miles

THERMOSPHERE ("heat")
Radio Signals in ionosphere

50
(80 km)

mesopause (transition)

MESOSPHERE ("middle")
Ultra violet rays

30
(48 km)

stratopause (transition)

STRATOSPHERE ("layer")

ozone layer

10
(16 km)

tropopause (transition)

TROPOSPHERE
("area of changing weather")

Clouds and other weather phenomena

sea level

260 Air Takes Up Space

YOU WILL NEED:

funnel
empty soda bottle
wide masking tape
or clay
water

How do we know air is really there?

What to do: Put the funnel into the mouth of the soda bottle. Stretch the tape around the funnel and the bottle's mouth, or pack the clay around the neck of the bottle so there is no space between the bottle and the funnel.

Pour water into the funnel.

What happens: The water remains in the funnel. It does not flow into the bottle.

Why: The "empty" bottle is already full of air. It takes up space and prevents the water from entering.

If you remove the masking tape or the clay, the results will be very different because the air will be able to escape!

Air Has Weight

A Lot of
Hot Air

YOU WILL NEED:
balloon
soda bottle
pan of hot water

262

YOU WILL NEED:
ruler
clothes hanger
2 balloons
tape
string

Air is a real substance. It not only takes up space, but it has weight. Here's proof.

Why does warm air take up more space than cold

What to do: Suspend the ruler from the hanger by attaching a string to the middle of it. Then tape each balloon the same distance from the ends of the ruler. Make sure that the ruler is in balance.

Now remove one of the balloons and blow it up. Tie a knot to keep it closed. Replace it at the same place on the ruler.

What to do: Stretch the balloon slightly and pull it over the neck of the soda bottle.

Place the bottle in the pan of hot water and let it stand for 5 minutes.

What happens: The balloon begins to inflate.

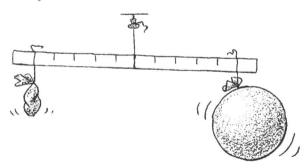

What happens: The balloon filled with air pulls the ruler down.

Why: The balloon filled with air is heavier than the other one. Air has weight. It is actually quite heavy. At sea level air weighs 14.7 pounds (6.6 kg) per square inch (2.5 cm). On a mountaintop, air is a little thinner and weighs less.

Why: The air in the balloon expands when it is heated. The molecules move faster and farther apart. That's what makes the balloon stretch.

And that's exactly how hot air works outside the balloon. Warm air is less dense than cold. It takes up more space than the same amount of cold air— and weighs less than the amount of cold air occupying the same space

263 Air Currents and Wind

264 How Much Oxygen is in the Air?

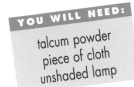

YOU WILL NEED:

talcum powder
piece of cloth
unshaded lamp

You can create an air current—and see what it does.

What to do: Sprinkle the powder on the cloth and shake a little of it near the unlit lamp. Notice what happens.

Then light the lamp. After a few minutes, when it is hot, shake some more powder off the cloth.

What happens: Before you turn the bulb on, the powder sinks slowly down through the air. After the bulb is hot, the powder rises.

Why: The air, warmed by the lighted bulb, rises—carrying the powder with it. The denser, cooler air sinks.

This is what happens in nature, too. Warmer air pushes upward because it is less dense, and cooler air flows in to take its place.

Air that moves up and down (vertically) is called an air current. Wind is air that moves on the same level (horizontally).

The speed of the air currents and the wind depends upon how much the temperature of one region differs from another. The direction of the wind depends on the location of these areas.

Air is a mixture of invisible, tasteless gases, including oxygen. How much oxygen is there in air?

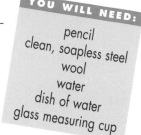

YOU WILL NEED:

pencil
clean, soapless steel wool
water
dish of water
glass measuring cup

What to do: Poke one end of the pencil into the piece of steel wool. Moisten the steel wool. Then prop up the pencil—with the steel wool on top—in the dish of water. Cover it with the measuring cup. Let it stand for 3 days.

What happens: The steel wool rusts—and the water rises until it fills about one-fifth of the cup.

Why: The rusting process uses up the oxygen from the air in the jar, creating an area of low pressure. Water rushes into the cup to take the place of the used-up oxygen. Since oxygen makes up approximately one-fifth of the composition of air, the air rises to the height of one-fifth of the cup.

The rest of the air is mostly nitrogen, with a few traces of several other gases, including carbon dioxide.

What Causes an Air Inversion?

HOT!

What happens during an air inversion? An adult must help you with this experiment.

YOU WILL NEED:
2 glass jars
hot water
cold water
index card
safety match
piece of twine

What to do: Rinse one jar with very cold water, and the other with hot water. Dry them thoroughly.

With the index card between them, place the jars mouth to mouth with the warm jar on the bottom.

Ask the adult to light the end of the twine so it smokes. Direct the smoke into the bottom jar, as you lift the index card. When the smoke fills the bottom jar, pull out the card.

Try the experiment with the cold jar on the bottom and the warm one on top. What happens this time?

What happens: When the warm jar is on the bottom, the smoke rises from the lower to the upper jar. When the cold air is on bottom, the smoke is trapped and cannot rise.

Why: The smoke rises as the warm air rises and the cold, denser air sinks. But when the warm air is trapped below the cold air, the smoke is also trapped.

This is what happens in the earth's atmosphere when a layer of warm air holds down the dust particles. This is an "air inversion." If the air is polluted, your eyes may smart, and you may cough or find it difficult to breathe.

The Air Pollution Control Laboratory records the air pollution index, which is computed based on the amount of sulphur dioxide, carbon monoxide, and smoke in the air. The average daily index is 12. An emergency level is placed at 50.

266 Is Your Air Polluted?

You don't need complicated instruments to find out whether the air around you is dirty!

What to do: Line the can with the white paper. Then place it outside the window for 1 week.

Take the can in and carefully remove the paper. Examine it the paper with the magnifying glass.

What happens: Dust and debris have discolored the paper.

Why: Impurities pass into the air from car exhausts and smokestacks and other sources. They pollute the air and remain there if no wind blows them away—or if a layer of warm air above them acts as a blanket as you learned in the previous experiment. Sometimes this dust in the air causes a haze, in which it is hard to see.

267 Whirling Winds

Why do winds whirl counterclockwise above the equator and clockwise below?

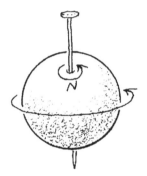

What to do: Push the knitting needle through the ball. Mark the top of the ball "N" for the North Pole and the bottom "S" for the South Pole.

Hold the ball so that the "N" is on top and whirl the ball from west to east. Look at the "N."

Now hold the ball high over your head and continue whirling it in the same direction.

What happens: At the North Pole the globe is whirling counterclockwise—but the area south of the equator is whirling clockwise!

Prevailing Winds

268

YOU WILL NEED:

1 marble
turntable (a lazy Susan
or stereo turntable)

The earth rotates—spins—from west to east. This affects the direction in which our winds blow. Here's a simple experiment that helps to explain why some winds blow from the same direction most of the time.

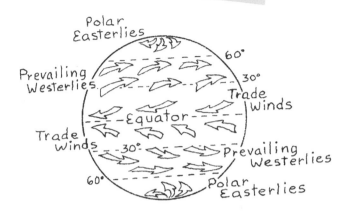

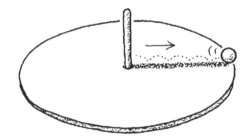

What to do: Roll the marble from the center of the turntable to the edge. Note what happens.

Then start the turntable spinning. Aim the marble at the center to the same point on the edge.

Finally, try rolling the marble from the edge to the center.

What happens: When the turntable isn't spinning the marble rolls in a straight line from the center to the edge. But when the turntable is moving, the marble seems to twist as it rolls from or toward the center.

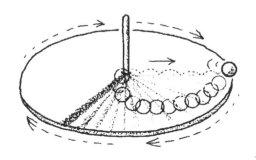

Why: When the turntable is still it is obvious that the marble moves in a straight line. But, even though it doesn't look that way, when the turntable moves, the marble continues to move in a straight line! The marble stops at different places on the moving turntable, and that's why it seems to twist and curve. But it reaches different places because the turntable is curving away from it. This phenomenon is known as the Coriolis effect.

In the same way, it is the spinning of the earth on its axis that makes the winds twist and turn in certain ways. This spin creates world-wide patterns of winds called "prevailing winds"—winds blowing from the same direction most of time. Much of world's weather depends on this great system of winds that blow in set directions.

Local Winds

Some winds are occasional, brief, and gentle. Other winds may last only a few minutes, but are strong enough to hurt people and property. Winds in some areas come regularly every year and last for months so that people must plan their lives around them.

Sea breezes are winds that blow from cooler high pressure areas over water to warmer low pressure areas over land.

Slope winds rush down mountain into valleys or rise up from the valleys. Winds that blow down the slopes of smaller hills are called helm winds.

Foehns are warm, dry winds that occasionally blow from a mountain ridge down the side of a mountain range away from the wind, the leeward side. In the Rockies, a foehn sometimes melts as much as two feet of snow overnight and is known as a *chinook*, the Indian word for snow eater. In South America, a westerly foehn blowing off the Andes is called a *zonda*, and an easterly foehn is called a *puelche*.

A squall blows strong gusts of cold air and lasts only a minute or two. It is usually accompanied by a wall of big black clouds and a short fierce shower. But a squall has been known to capsize hundreds of small boats in its brief life. In Alaska a squall is called a williwaw and in Australia it is called a Cockeyed Bob.

The mistrals blow cold dry air down from the western Alps across southern France in winter, sometimes for months. The monsoons, seasonal winds in the Indian Ocean and Asia, bring torrential rains in summer. Simoons, hot, dry winds in the Sahara and Arabian Deserts, blow up suffocating clouds of sand, sometimes for a few minutes and sometimes for days.

Jet streams are fast winds that start about four miles up in the atmosphere. Caused by the sharp difference in temperature between the air in the troposphere and the stratosphere, they can be thousands of miles long and several miles wide. Sometimes they rise higher into the atmosphere and sometimes they descend toward earth, forming storms.

Airplane pilots like to hitch a ride on these winds when they are going their way.

269 ◆ Air Masses and Fronts

An air mass is a body of air thousands of miles across that has about the same temperature and amount of moisture. How does it form? To find out all you need is a radiator or a heater and a refrigerator or air conditioner.

Short, hard rains → *Cold air* ← *Cold Front*

What to do: First stand in front of the radiator or heater for 2 minutes. Then stand in front of the opened refrigerator or an air conditioner for 2 minutes.

What happens: When you stand in front of the radiator or heater, you feel warm air. When you stand in front of the refrigerator or air conditioner, you feel cool air.

Why: The warm radiator heats the air around it. The refrigerator cools the air around it. Air masses work the same way. Air that lingers above a region without moving forms an air mass with the temperature and moisture of the area.

When an air mass moves on, it influences the weather of the area it passes over.

When cold and warm air masses meet, they don't mix. Instead, they form a zone that is generally hundreds of miles long. That zone is called a "front." It's called a "cold front" when a cold air mass replaces a warm air mass by forcing it to rise. It's called a "warm front" when a warm air mass pushes a cold air mass ahead of it. When neither mass moves, it is called a "stationary front."

Stationary Front

The arrival of a front indicates a change in the weather.

A cold front moves quickly. If the air is dry, it will become cloudy and the temperature will drop. If the air is moist, a cold front will bring thunderstorms and hail, but they won't last long.

A warm front moves in more slowly. If the air is dry, wispy clouds will form. But if the air is moist, the sky will become gray and the rain or snow that follows may last for many days.

After the front moves on, there will usually be fair weather—warm if the warm air mass remains, cold if the cold air mass remains.

Warm air → *Long, softer rains* ← *Warm Front*

Air Pressure and Weather Predictions

YOU WILL NEED:
piece of torn balloon
funnel
tape

Air pressure and the way it is changing helps you predict how the weather will change in the next few hours and days.

What to do: Cover the wide mouth of the funnel with the piece of balloon and tape it on tightly.

Suck some air from the narrow end of the funnel and notice what happens to the rubber.

Turn the funnel upside down and suck the air in again. Then turn the funnel sideways and suck in the air.

What happens: When you suck in the air, the rubber is pulled in, whatever the direction of the funnel.

Why: When you suck in the air, you are removing it from the inside of the funnel. When you do that, the push of air outside the funnel is greater than the push of the air from inside, even when you hold the funnel upside down or sideways. Air pushes—presses—equally in all directions.

Cool air, High pressure

Warm air, Low pressure

Rain

You already know that the air over each square inch of the earth's surface, pulled by the earth's gravity, weighs 14.7 pounds (6.6 kg). This weight is known as air pressure.

When cool, dense air presses down on the earth, the air pressure is usually high. Warm, less dense air rises away from the earth, and so, when it's warm, we generally have low air pressure.

High pressure usually brings clear weather while low pressure brings bad weather and strong winds. Changing pressure also brings winds.

When there are big differences in air pressure, air rushes out of the high pressure area to fill the low pressure area. Then there are strong, sometimes savage winds. If the difference in pressure is small, air gently drifts toward the low pressure area and we have gentle breezes.

A Trick Can

This experiment is best done over a sink or basin.

YOU WILL NEED:

empty can with a screw cap, like a floor wax can

hammer

nail

water

What to do: Using the hammer and nail, punch a small hole on one side of the can near the bottom. Fill the can with water and quickly screw on the cap. Then remove the cap.

What happens: The water does not flow out from the hole—until you remove the cap.

Why: Air is pressing up harder than the water is pressing down—until you remove the top of the can. Then the air pressing down on the opening in the can, added to the pressure of the water, makes the downward pressure greater than the upward pressure.

Ballot's Law

Using Ballot's Law we can find the location of high and low pressure areas.

Buys Ballot, a Dutch scientist, discovered in 1857 that there was a relationship between the direction of the wind and the locations of the high pressure and low pressure areas that were causing it.

In the Northern Hemisphere, if you stand with your back to the wind, the high pressure area will be on your right and the low pressure on your left. In the Southern Hemisphere, it is exactly the opposite.

A change in wind often brings a change in weather. In the Northern Hemisphere a south or west wind brings warm or mild, wet weather. A north or east wind brings colder, drier weather, especially in the winter. All winds are named after the direction from which they are blowing.

271

272

273

Tornado!

Although most of the destruction done by tornadoes is caused by the terrible speed of the whirling winds, lowered air pressure may also cause a great deal of damage.

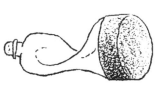

What to do: Remove the air from inside the bottle by sucking on it.

What happens: The bottle collapses.

Why: The air around the outside of the bottle pushes inward because you've removed some of the inside air. Normally, the air inside the bottle would balance the outer force.

The pressure inside the bottle drops, just as it does in the center of a tornado.

A tornado starts when cold dry air coming from the west catches up with unusually warm, moist air from the south. The result is a whirling wind with thick, black clouds and thunderstorms. Water vapor is swept upward as gusts of warm air rise in a spiraling motion. When the air cools, it forms the tornado's twisting, funnel-shaped cloud.

The funnel-shaped wind cloud whirls at enormous speeds and picks up dust, trees, animals, water, automobiles, houses—anything in its path—and whirls them upward. The rapidly rising column of air within the funnel lowers the pressure in the funnel's center as the tornado advances.

A house can be crushed in the midst of a tornado just as the bottle was crushed—because the air pressure in the center of the tornado is lower than the normal pressure inside the house.

The tornado spins, smashing and destroying, until all the heated air that was near land has been squeezed up by the cooler, heavier, inflowing air. Then the air stops flowing and the tornado dies.

More about Tornadoes

A tornado seldom lasts more than an hour and usually covers about two city blocks—less than one-tenth of a mile (158 m). Only 2 per cent of tornadoes are classified as "violent."

Tornadoes may last longer, however, with winds of up to 300 miles (480 km) an hour, and may cover a path of up to 26 miles (42 km) long and a mile wide (1.6 km). They can be the most destructive storms on earth. Most tornado injuries and deaths result from flying objects whirled about by the wind.

Tornadoes are sometimes called cyclones and twisters.

274 Bernoulli's Law

The air pressure of a tornado is so low that houses in its path may be destroyed. What causes this low air pressure?

What to do: Hang the apples 3 inches (7.5 cm) apart. Blow hard between them.

What happens: Instead of being pushed apart, the apples move toward each other.

Why: By blowing between the apples, you cause the air between the apples to move. This lessens the air pressure between them. Then the air on the

sides of the apples pushes them toward the area of lower pressure.

As the speed of air increases, the pressure of the air decreases. The faster air moves, the less pressure it has. This was discovered in 1738 by the Swiss physicist, Daniel Bernoulli.

This lessening of pressure caused by high-speed air movement is one of the reasons a tornado is so destructive. Objects are propelled into whirling air by the stronger pressure of air around them.

Eye of a Hurricane

YOU WILL NEED:
yo-yo

A hurricane is a violent storm that starts in tropical waters. In the middle of the swirling winds of a hurricane there is the calm "eye."

What to do: Whirl the yo-yo around your head.

What happens: The yo-yo seems to try to pull away from your hand holding its string. The faster you whirl it, the stronger the pull.

Why: The explanation is centrifugal force, the force that pulls an object outward when it is moving in a circle.

In the same way, the winds of a hurricane tend to pull away from the center as their speed increases. When the winds move fast enough, a hole develops in the center—the mark of a full-fledged hurricane.

The eye of a hurricane is a cloudless hole, usually about 10 miles (16 km) wide, within which all is calm and peaceful. But surrounding the eye, howling winds swirl at speeds up to 150 miles (240 km)an hour, with gusts up to 180 miles (288 km) an hour.

Hurricane winds may cover an area up to 60 miles (96 km) wide. They may rage for a week or more, and travel tens of thousands of miles over sea and land.

Hurricanes arise when warm moist air over tropical waters rises above 6,000 feet (1800 m). The water vapor condenses, turns to raindrops, releasing heat energy. This in turn forces columns of air to rise up quickly (updraft) to heights of 50,000 to 60,000 feet (80,000 m) and fluffy, cauliflower-like cumulus clouds become towering thunderheads. (See illustration.)

Then air from outside the storm area moves in to replace the rising air. It begins to swirl around the updraft because of the earth's spin. As it swirls over the surface of the sea, it soaks up more and more water vapor, which then gets pulled into the updraft, releasing still more energy as more of the water vapor condenses. The updraft then rises faster, pulling in larger amounts of air and water vapor from the edge of the storm, and the air swirls even faster around the "eye."

Hurricane winds circulate counterclockwise in the Northern Hemisphere and clockwise in the Southern Hemisphere.

They are called cyclones in the Indian Ocean, typhoons in the Pacific, and willy-willies in Australia.

Rain

Cross section through Eye of Hurricane

WATER, WATER, EVERYWHERE

How does water get into the air? Why does it come out of the air? Why does it snow? When does it rain? sleet? hail? In this chapter you'll find answers to these questions and more.

Earth's Precipitation Records

Greatest rainfall in one day:
73.62 inches (184 cm)
> *Place:* Le Reunion, island in the Indian Ocean
> *Date:* March 15, 1952

Greatest rainfall in one month:
366 inches (915 cm)
> Place: Assam, India
> Date: July, 1961

Greatest rainfall in one year:
1,041 inches (2,602 cm)
> *Place:* Assam, India
> *Date:* August, 1880 to August, 1881

Highest average annual rainfall:
460 inches (1,150 cm)
> *Place:* Mount Waialeale, Kauai, Hawaii

Greatest number of thunderstorms:
322 days a year
> *Place:* The island of Java, Indonesia

Lowest annual rainfall: 0.03 inches (0.08 cm)
> *Place:* Arica, Chile

Longest period without rain: 400 years
> *Place:* Desert of Atacama, Chile

Greatest snowfall in one day:
75.8 inches (189.5 cm)
> *Place:* Silver Lake, Colorado
> *Date:* April 14 to 15, 1921

Greatest snowfall in a single storm:
189 inches (472.5 cm)
> *Place:* Mt. Shasta, California
> *Date:* Feb. 13 to 19, 1959

276

Water Going into the Air

YOU WILL NEED:

2 jars (one with a lid)
water

Moisture in the air—humidity—is one part of a great water cycle. The main supply comes from the earth's five oceans and from many smaller bodies of water. How does the water get into the air?

What to do: Pour an equal amount of water into the jars. Put the lid on one of them. Place both jars on a table overnight. Check them in the morning.

What happens: There is less water in the open jar than in the covered jar.

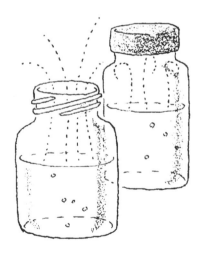

Why: Even at room temperature, the tiny particles, or molecules, of water in the uncovered jar move fast enough to fly out and escape into the air. The water turns into water vapor, an invisible gas. This process is known as evaporation.

If you've ever wondered what happens to puddles when the rain stops, that is the explanation. And that is how water gets back into the air.

Evaporation Race #1

277

YOU WILL NEED:

measuring cup
large flat dish
water
deep narrow jar

Which container of water will evaporate faster—the flat disk or the deep jar?

What to do: Pour an equal amount of water into the dish and the jar. Place both, uncovered, on a table to stand overnight. Check them in the morning.

What happens: Less water remains in the flat dish than in the narrow jar.

Why: The molecules of water can escape only from the surface. So water will evaporate faster when the surface is large.

A wide shallow puddle, therefore, will dry up more quickly than a deep narrow one.

278 Wind and Water

What effect does wind have on the water in the air? Why does fanning a washed blackboard make it dry more quickly?

YOU WILL NEED:
clothesline
piece of cardboard
2 wet handkerchiefs

What to do: Hang the two handkerchiefs to dry. Fan one with the cardboard.

What happens: The handkerchief that is fanned dries first.

Why: Fanning speeds up evaporation by replacing the moist air near the handkerchief with drier air. Blowing winds do the same thing with clouds in the sky.

279 Evaporation Race #2

YOU WILL NEED:
2 dishes
water

What role does the sun play in the evaporation of water in the air?

What to do: Half fill the dishes with water. Place one in the sun or on a radiator, and the other in the shade.

What happens: The dish in the sun dries first.

Why: The warmer the water, the faster the molecules move into the air and the faster they evaporate.

Most water vapor comes from lakes, rivers, oceans, leaves of plants, and wet ground. The heat from the sun causes the water to change from liquid to gas, which goes into the air. As its temperature increases, air can hold more and more water. As it gets colder, it holds less and less.

Evaporation Cools Air

280

Liquids require heat to evaporate—and so any place where evaporation takes place becomes cooler.

What to do: Place the thermometer where wind will strike it. Note the temperature after 30 minutes.

Using an eye dropper or a straw, dampen a small piece of cotton and wrap it around the bulb of the thermometer. Secure it with the rubber band. Leave the thermometer in the wind for 30 minutes and again note the temperature.

Why: In the process of evaporation, energy in the form of heat is removed from the thermometer. The hygrometer, one of the most important weather instruments, is based on this fact (see page 254).

What happens: The temperature of the thermometer with the wet cotton on it is several degrees lower than it was before.

Be a Rain Maker!

Make rain in your kitchen!

281

What to do: Boil water in the bottom section of the double boiler. Then pour cold water into the upper pot, add the ice cubes and place the pot over the boiling water. (If you don't have a double-boiler, you can make your own by stacking a small pot on top of a small can in a slightly larger pot.)

What happens: You see—rain!

HOT!

Why: The cold surfaces of the upper pot cool the steam from the boiling water. The steam changes back into water, collecting in drops. As the drops get bigger and heavier, it "rains."

The boiling water is like the water heated by the sun. The steam is like the water that evaporates into the air as water vapor. As the vapor rises, it cools. You see clouds when droplets form. As these droplets collect more moisture, they become heavy enough to fall to earth as rain.

Measuring the Size of a Raindrop

282

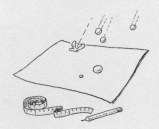

Hold a piece of cardboard outside your window when it first starts to rain, and you will be able to see the size of a raindrop.

Raindrops may measure from 1/100 of an inch across to ¼ inch (0.25 to 1 cm) across. Each is made up of millions of droplets of water.

Small raindrops—less than 2/100 of an inch (0.5 mm) across—often take an hour or more to reach the ground. Light rain like this is known as drizzle. It usually falls from a layered cloud less than 1.2 miles (2 km) thick.

A heavy, sudden shower of large raindrops or of hail falls from a heaped cumulo-nimbus cloud that might be 9 miles (15 km) or more deep.

283 Water Coming Out of the Air

YOU WILL NEED:
empty tin can
ice cubes
water
food coloring

You found out how water gets into the air. Let's look at how it gets out again.

What to do: Remove the label from the can, then fill the can with ice. Add water and a few drops of food coloring. Let the can stand on a table for 5 minutes.

What happens: The can seems to be "sweating." Drops of water form on the outside.

Why: The drops are not colored, so they couldn't be coming from the ice water leaking out of the can. The water must come from the air.

Water vapor—water in the form of gas—in the air around the can has been cooled by the ice.

Air molecules slow down when they become cold. They move closer together and change into liquid form. This is known as "condensation."

Great amounts of water are always evaporating into the air as the sun warms the earth's oceans, rivers, and lakes. On a day when humidity is high, as much as 5 percent of the air can be water vapor. The water vapor becomes part of the warmer air near the earth's surface. Because it is less dense than cold air, this warmer air tends to rise. It rises to colder and colder levels. When it reaches a cold enough level, the water vapor changes into droplets of water. Cold air can't hold as much water vapor as warm air.

Large numbers of these little drops of water collect on dust particles as the air cools. This forms clouds. The drops fall to earth as rain or snow when they become too heavy to be held up by the pressure of air.

The movement of water through evaporation and condensation is called the water cycle.

284 Indoor Cloud

You form a cloud in your kitchen every time you boil water in a tea kettle!

HOT!

What to do: Heat the water in the tea kettle. When it starts to boil, hold the pie plate in the steam.

What happens: When the water boils, a whitish "cloud" forms above the spout. When you hold the pie plate in the "cloud," drops of water form on it.

Why: The clouds in the sky form in the same way. Heated air containing invisible water vapor rises. As it rises, it cools. The water vapor condenses into millions of tiny water droplets, forming a cloud.

On a sunny summer day, the sun heats up the ground quickly. The ground heats the air next to it. Because warm air is less dense than cold air, it rises. As it moves away from the hot ground, it cools. When it rises high enough and becomes cool enough, the water vapor in the air condenses—turns into water droplets. Millions of these droplets together make up one of the fluffy clouds we see in the sky. These fluffy clouds are known as cumulus clouds.

Why Clouds Look White

The white light of the sun is really a mixture of all the colors. When sunlight enters a droplet of water, it is broken up into the different wavelengths that we see as red, orange, yellow, green, blue, indigo, and violet. Some of the colored light is reflected from the far side of the droplet back and out of the droplet.

The blue color of the sky results from the way tiny particles of dust and vapor in the air scatter light rays. The rays of shorter wavelengths (the blues and violets) are spread out more widely than the rays of longer wavelengths (the reds and yellows).

Too much dust, especially in large particles, causes the scattering of many rays—not only the blue ones. Then the sky becomes whitish or hazy. When a cloud forms, there isn't much difference in the scattering of the different wavelengths of sunlight. We see the mixture of all the colors of the spectrum and the clouds look white to us.

The sky appears red at sunset and sunrise when the longer wavelengths (the reds and yellows) are scattered more effectively. This happens because the sun is closer to the horizon, and so its light shines at an angle closer to the surface and through more atmosphere, dust, and water droplets.

285 What Causes Smog?

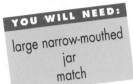

HOT!

Smog is a combination of fog—tiny droplets of water in the air—and smoke from pollutants in the air. Let's see how it happens. (You will need an adult's help with this experiment.)

What to do: Blow hard into a large narrow-mouthed jar and then remove your lips quickly. Ask an adult to light a match and you blow it out. While the match is still smoking, dip it into the jar so that smoke enters. Blow into the jar again and again remove your lips quickly.

What happens: Smog builds up in the jar.

Why: When you stopped blowing the first time, the sudden lessening of pressure produced a cooling effect. This caused a small amount of water vapor to condense—turn back into droplets of water in the jar. When you added the smoke of the match, the droplets combined with tiny particles of dust from the smoke to form smog.

On dry windy days, smoke and soot from factory chimneys and automobile exhaust systems are carried high into the air and blown away. But on cool damp days with no wind, the particles hang low in the moist air to form smog.

286 Refrigerator Weather

Raid your refrigerator and learn the difference between snow and sleet. If your refrigerator defrosts automatically, wait for a snowy day and collect your specimens outdoors.

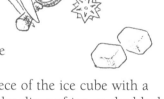

What to do:
Place the frost, or the snow, on the black paper or cloth and examine it with the magnifying glass.

Chip off a small piece of the ice cube with a large spoon and place the sliver of ice on the black cloth. Examine it under the magnifying glass.

What happens: In the frost, or the snow, you see a six-pointed star-shaped crystal. In the ice, you don't.

Why: The frost in the refrigerator and the snowflakes in the sky form in the same way. Water vapor in the clouds—and water vapor in the refrigerator—cools down so much that instead of turning into water, it freezes into snowflakes and frost.

The ice cube forms in the same way as sleet. Both start out as water—and later freeze. Sleet starts as raindrops. When it falls through very cold air, it freezes into little bits of ice.

Dissecting a Hailstone

If you've ever been in a hailstorm, you may know how violent they can be. In 1981, in Ohio, a hailstone was found that weighed thirty pounds! What causes hail? Like sleet, hail is made from raindrops that later freeze, but its formation is more complicated.

YOU WILL NEED:

hailstone
hammer
sheet of newspaper

What to do: Split open the hailstone on a newspaper. Count the number of rings you see.

What happens: You learn how many trips up in the cold air the hailstone made before it fell to earth.

Why: Strong winds pick up raindrops and fling them high up where the air is cold enough to freeze them into ice drops. If they fell to the earth at this point, they would be sleet. But instead of letting them fall all the way down, the winds blow them up again. In the very cold upper air, a new layer of ice freezes around the old. The ice drops fall and are blown up again and again. Finally, when they are too heavy for the up-blowing wind, they clatter to the ground as hail.

Hailstones sometimes get bigger than golf balls and they have been known to do damage to crops or buildings. The largest hailstone on record measured 17.5 inches (44 cm) and fell on Coffeyville, Kansas, on September 3, 1979.

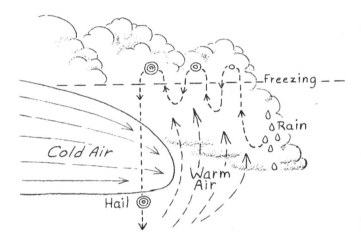

Ozone

Ozone, the main ingredient of smog, is an oxygen with three atoms. It forms when such chemicals as hydrocarbons and nitrogen compounds—released by factories and machines—react to heat and sunlight.

Ozone in the lower atmosphere can make people sick. When the air quality index for ozone climbs to over 200, people are advised to stay indoors, if possible.

In the stratosphere, from 10 to 30 miles (16 to 50 km) above the earth, a layer of ozone forms naturally, shielding the earth from the sun's harmful ultraviolet rays. But there is now evidence of an ozone hole above Antarctica. It has been traced to the use of carbofluorides and similar compounds. These are used in refrigerators and air conditioners, in cleaning electronic equipment, in the manufacture of plastic foam, and in pressurized spray cans. If the ozone layer continues to get holes in it—or the hole that exists gets larger—scientists warn that we can expect an increase in diseases that result from the sun's ultraviolet rays, like skin cancer.

288 What is Lightning?

YOU WILL NEED:
comb
piece of wool
metal doorknob

Make your own lightning! Don't worry—homemade lightning isn't dangerous. You've probably made it many times without realizing it.

What to do: Rub the comb with a piece of wool. Hold the comb near a metal doorknob.

What happens: You produce a small spark.

Why: By rubbing the comb with the wool, you charge it with electricity. The spark is made when the charge jumps to the uncharged, or neutral, doorknob. The spark is the passage of an electrical charge between two objects.

You may have seen a similar spark when you walked over a rug and then touched a doorknob. You may have heard a crackling sound while combing your hair or petting a cat. These are all examples of static electricity.

Lightning is a huge electric spark that results when charges jump from one cloud to another or to the ground. Though lightning may discharge an enormous amount of electricity, it lasts much too brief a time to be trapped into useful energy.

On a hot humid summer day, when hot air climbs quickly, moisture in the air condenses to form billions of water drops and ice crystals. These pick up tiny electric charges as they move through the air. The violent air currents in thunder clouds move different-sized drops and dust particles at different speeds. Those of the same size and with similar amounts of electricity get concentrated in the same part of the cloud. A very high positive electrical charge is often formed in the cold higher parts, while near the ground the thunder cloud is usually negatively charged. The big difference between the charges at the top and the bottom of the cloud creates a powerful voltage or electric pressure. This "push" sends a flash of lightning streaking through the cloud between those parts with opposite electric charges.

Does Lightning Ever Strike Twice in the Same Spot?

Despite sayings to the contrary, lightning may hit the same place or the same person several times. The United States Weather Bureau reports the case of a National Park Ranger who was hit seven times!

Storm Warnings

A summer thunderstorm clears the air and leaves us refreshed. The rumble and roar of thunder is all noise and no bite, and by the time you hear it all danger is usually past. But flashes of lightning may be dangerous. They can start fires, knock over trees, and injure or even kill people.

Lightning takes the shortest path. It hits the highest objects—a tall tree or house, a tower, a person standing alone in a flat field. Modern skyscrapers, however, are built so that lightning may strike them without doing any harm.

Here's what the weather service says to do, if a storm is close.

If You're Outdoors: Go indoors, if possible—inside a house or a large building. If you can't do that, get into an automobile. (Not a convertible!) Don't take refuge in a shed—metal or wood.

Don't stand next to a telephone pole. Keep away from a lone tree. Don't stand on a hilltop. Avoid being the tallest object. Seek shelter in low areas under small trees. If you're in a field, crouch on your knees and bend over.

Keep away from metal pipes, rails, metal fences, and wire clotheslines. Don't carry anything made of metal. Don't ride a bicycle or a scooter. If you're in a group, everyone should spread out. Keep several yards apart.

Keep away from water. If you are swimming, get out of the water. Don't stay out in a boat or stand under a beach umbrella.

If You're Inside: Keep away from windows and doors. Stay away from water taps, sinks, tubs, the stove—anything that could conduct electricity. Don't use electric appliances—the television, an irons, toaster, or mixer.

Don't use the telephone unless there is an emergency.

289 What Causes Thunder?

You hear a crackle when you raise a spark. What causes that sound and what causes the roar of thunder?

What to do: Blow up the balloon or the paper bag. Tie it closed with a rubber band or a piece of string. Then place one hand on the top and one hand on the bottom of the balloon or the bag and pop it.

What happens: You get a small clap of thunder.

Why: You created thunder by causing a small quantity of air to move fast. An object produces sound when it vibrates—moves back and forth or up and down. Humans only hear sound when an object vibrates at least 16 times a second—and not more than 20,000 times a second.

When a flash of lightning passes through the atmosphere, it heats the nearby air, and causes it to expand rapidly. It is this movement that causes the sound. A short crash of thunder results from a short flash of lightning. Rolling thunder occurs when lightning covers a large area, or when clouds, mountains, or other obstructions cause echoes.

290 How Far Away is the Storm?

When you see a flash of lightning, start counting seconds like this: "and one and, and two and, and three and"—and continue until you hear a roar of thunder. Divide the number you get by 5 (for miles) or by 3 (for kilometers). That will give you a rough estimate of how far away the center of the storm is.

Why: Lightning and thunder take place at the same time, but light and sound travel to us at different speeds, and so reach us at different times. Light travels at 186,000 miles (300,000 km) per second and takes only a fraction of a second to reach us. We see lightning the moment it flashes.

It takes about 5 seconds for sound to travel a mile (3 seconds for a kilometer).

When a thunderstorm is near, the thunderclap sound is loud and sharp. When it is far away, it is a low rumble. Ordinarily, you can't hear thunder more than 10 or 15 miles (16 or 24 km) away. If you see lightning and hear thunder at just about the same moment, the storm is right above you.

Make Your Own Rainbow

YOU WILL NEED:
glass of water
sheet of white paper

After the storm comes the rainbow. Here's one you can have on any sunny day.

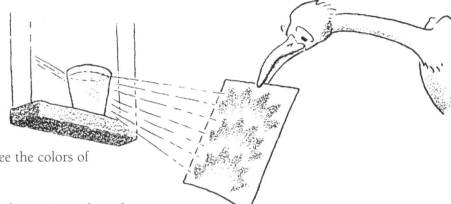

What to do: Stand the glass of water on a windowsill that is in bright sunlight. Place the sheet of paper on the floor.

What happens: You see the colors of the rainbow on the paper.

Why: You are separating the various colors, the spectrum, that make up white light. When light passes at a slant from the air through the glass of water, the rays change direction—they are "refracted." Each color bends differently: violet bends the most and red the least. So, when the light comes out of the glass of water, the different colors travel in slightly different directions and strike the sheet of paper at different places.

It is the same with a rainbow in the sky. It is simply a curved spectrum, made when sunlight shines through water drops in the air at an angle of between 40 degrees and 42 degrees with the horizon. The water drops bend the sun's rays.

The sun has to be behind you if you're going to see a rainbow in the sky. So you'll only see a rainbow early in the morning, when the sun is shining in the east and showers are falling in the west—or in the late afternoon, when the sun is shining in the west and showers are falling in the east.

The arc you see from the ground is just a part of the rainbow. Only if you happen to be flying in a plane will you see a rainbow's full circle.

BUILDING A WEATHER STATION

With everyday materials, you can make the instruments you need to keep track of temperature, air pressure, wind direction and wind speed, humidity and rainfall.

Don't feel too bad if your predictions are not always accurate. Meteorologists, the people who predict the weather, are not always right, either—even with the help of weather satellites circling the earth, radar, balloon-borne instruments, and super-speed computers to help them make their surface observations!

Keeping Records

Weather maps are based on information collected by hundreds of local weather stations. You may want to check the daily findings of your "station" with your local radio and television meteorologists—and with the information published in your local newspaper.

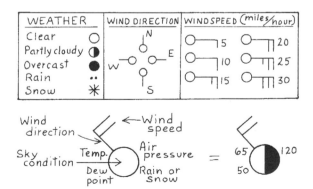

You can keep records and report your findings in several ways.

When you measure the various weather factors, using instruments and observations, make a chart of your findings, like the one on this page.

You may also want to make a station model. It's a handy way to show the same information. It uses a system of symbols that can easily fit on a map. You can adapt the symbols on the left so you can record and compare your daily findings. This sample model is reporting a partly cloudy day, northwest winds at 20 miles (32 km) an hour, temperature of 65 degrees F (18.3 degrees C), and a dew point of 50 degrees F (10 degrees C). Air pressure is reported in millibars (see page 247). You can substitute H (for high) and L (for low), and + for rising and − for falling pressure.

Straw Thermometer

How does a thermometer work? Make your own and find out.

YOU WILL NEED:
medicine bottle or small jar
cork to fit the bottle or jar
nail
glass straw or medicine dropper tube
water
food coloring
felt-tipped pen

What to do: Dig out a hole in the cork with the nail and fit the straw or tube through it.

Fill the bottle to the brim with water colored with a drop or two of food coloring and put the cork in securely. With the felt-tipped pen mark the line the water rises to in the straw or tube.

Note the height of the water in the straw at room temperature and also at different times and places—on a sunny windowsill, in the refrigerator, in a pot of hot water.

What happens: The water goes up the tube when the temperature is warm and goes down when it is cold.

Why: Temperature is measured by the changes made. Temperature is really a measure of whether one object absorbs heat from or loses heat to another object.

Liquids expand when heated and contract when cooled. The liquid of the thermometer absorbs heat. It expands when it contacts anything warmer than itself, and contracts when contacting something cooler. Mercury and colored alcohol are usually used as the liquid in thermometers because they react so quickly.

Makers of commercial weather thermometers use a sealed glass tube that has a little bulb blown out at one end. They mark the thermometer's scale by placing its bulb in contact with melting ice. The point at which the liquid contracts is 32 ° for

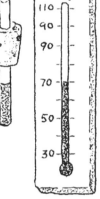

a Fahrenheit scale and 0° for a Centigrade scale. Then the bulb is placed in the steam from boiling water. The point at which it expands is marked 212° F or 100° C.

You can make a scale for your thermometer by comparing its levels with a commercial weather thermometer.

Gabriel Fahrenheit, a German physicist, devised the first commonly used scale in 1714. About thirty years later, a Swedish astronomer, Anders Celsius, established the centigrade scale, also known as the celsius scale.

The first thermometer was invented in 1593 by the Italian physicist Galileo.

293 Temperature Conversion

°Fahrenheit		°Centigrade
212	water boils	100
194		90
176		80
158		70
140		60
136	highest Earth temperature ever recorded	57.7
122		50
104		40
98.6	body temperature	37
86		30
68		20
50		10
32	water freezes	0
14		–10
–4		–20
–22		–30
–40		–40
–58		–50
–76		–60
–94		–70
–112		–80
–129	coldest Earth temperature ever recorded	–89
–130		–90

To convert from F° to C°:
Subtract 32° and then multiply by 5. Divide the result by 9.
For a quick estimate of Centigrade:
Deduct 30 and divide by 2.
To convert from C° to F°:
Multiply by 9. Divide the result by 5. Then add 32.
For a quick estimate of Fahrenheit:
Multiply by 2 and add 30.

294 Reading a Barometer

At sea level, in normal weather, the mercury in a barometer measures 29.92 inches (1013.2 millibars). In cool, dry weather the mercury level rises. In warm, wet weather, it drops, just the way the water does in the bottle barometer which you will find instructions to make in the next experiment.

The Weather Bureau prefers the mercury barometer to the aneroid (a barometer made without liquid) because it is more accurate. The Bureau finds it more convenient to measure air pressure in millibars. Millibar readings are shortened on weather maps by dropping the first two numbers and the decimal, so that normal pressure—1013.2—for example, is reported as 132.

The lowest barometric pressure ever recorded was 25.59 inches (870 mb) on October 12, 1979, about 300 miles west of Guam in the Pacific Ocean, during a typhoon. The highest barometric pressure recorded was 32 inches (1083.8 mb) in Agata, Siberia, in Russia, on December 31, 1968.

Air pressure is usually lower on stormy days than it is on clear, dry days. So, when air pressure falls, it often indicates that a storm is approaching. A change in pressure of one-tenth of an inch (2.5mm) or more in six hours means there is going to be a fast change in the weather.

To change inches to millibars, multiply the number of inches by 33.87.

Bottle Barometer

YOU WILL NEED:
saucer
water
plastic soda bottle
index card
tape

You already know that the layer of air surrounding the earth exerts a pressure of more than fourteen pounds on every square inch.

More than three hundred years ago Evangelista Torricelli, an Italian physicist, first figured out a way to measure this atmospheric pressure. He balanced a column of mercury with a column of air. You can make a barometer with ordinary tap water that will work like his.

What to do: Fill the saucer halfway with water. Pour water into the bottle until it is about three-quarters full. Keeping your thumb on the mouth of the bottle, turn the bottle upside down. Then remove your thumb and quickly put the mouth of the bottle into the saucer of water. Tape a strip of the index card on the outside of the bottle, as it is in the illustration.

What happens: The water doesn't pour out of the bottle. Instead, the water level drops slightly and comes to rest. Then, it moves up or down as the air pressure changes.

Why: Air pressing against the water prevents it from running out. The water stops moving downward when the water pressure is balanced by the pressure of the atmosphere.

Mark the index card at the point where the water settles, and you will be able to chart whether the water goes up or down in the bottle. An increase in air pressure sends the water up. When there is a decrease it drops down. When the water in the bottle drops down, you can expect warmer, wetter weather.

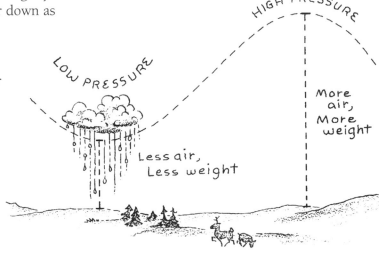

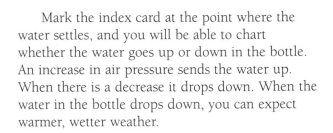

Balloon Barometer

This crude barometer will also show when there is a change in air pressure.

YOU WILL NEED:
balloon
narrow-mouthed jar
rubber band or
piece of string
glue
drinking straw
straight pin
index card

What to do: Stretch the balloon over the top of the jar. Fasten it with the rubber band or string. Then glue the straw horizontally, starting from the center of the rubber, so it extends beyond the edge of the top of the jar, as in the illustration. Attach the pin to the free end of the straw.

Prop up a marked index card so that you can follow the movement of the straw.

What happens: The unattached end of the straw (the pointer) sometimes moves up and sometimes moves down.

Why: When air pressure increases, the pressure inside the bottle is less than that of the outside air. Therefore the balloon rubber pushes down, and the pointer end of the straw moves up. When the air pressure goes down, the air inside the bottle presses harder than the outside air. The rubber pushes up and tightens, and the pointer moves down.

When your pointer moves down, bad weather is probably on the way. Air pressure usually falls when a storm is approaching. When air pressure rises, it is usually a sign that the weather is going to improve.

Your balloon barometer functions a lot like the aneroid barometer. A flexible top pushes in and out as air pressure changes, and moves the pointer around a scale on the face of the instrument.

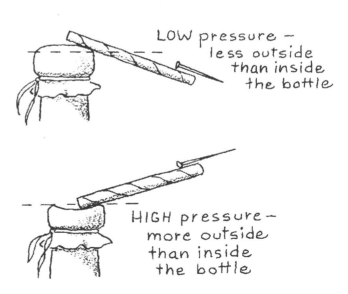

LOW pressure — less outside than inside the bottle

HIGH pressure — more outside than inside the bottle

Weather Vane

If we know the direction the wind is blowing, we can sometimes locate a low pressure system and forecast the bad weather that usually comes with it. A weather vane shows wind direction.

What to do: Make a 1 inch (2.5 cm) vertical slit in one end of the drinking straw. Using the index card or other piece of cardboard, cut out an arrow tail and glue it into the cut end of the straw, as in the illustration. Mark the other end of the straw with the red marker or crayon. Insert the straight pin through the straw about 2 inches (5 cm) from the arrow. Push the pin into the eraser end of the pencil. Be sure the straw can move freely.

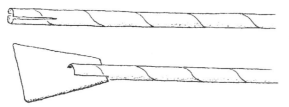

Form the letters N, S, E, and W from pieces of wire. Wind them around the pencil, 1 inch (2.5 cm) below the arrow. Prop the pencil up by its point in a lump of earth in a shallow flower pot or in a lump of clay.

Put the weather vane in a place where the wind is not blocked by buildings. Use a compass to make sure your letters are set up correctly.

What happens: As the wind blows, the weather vane moves.

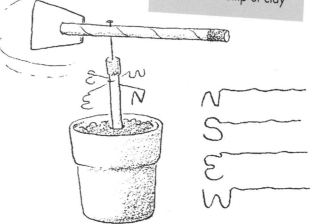

Why: When the wind blows, it pushes away the larger surface (the arrow). As a result, the other end points into the wind, in the direction from which the wind is blowing.

In the northern hemisphere, a wind that shifts in a counterclockwise direction usually brings a low pressure system and stormy weather along with it. East winds generally bring rain, west winds clearing. North winds mean cold weather, and south winds heat. In the southern hemisphere, it is exactly the opposite for every direction.

Cup Anemometer

How can you measure the speed of wind? One way is with a cup anemometer. This instrument has three or four small hollow metal hemispheres that revolve around a metal rod and catch the wind. How fast they move reveals the speed of the wind. Our anemometer looks almost like the real thing. But while real anemometers record the revolutions of the cups electrically, you will have to count them yourself.

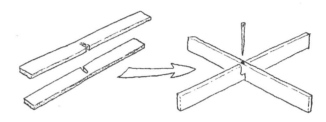

YOU WILL NEED:

2 pieces of heavy cardboard

scissors

staples or tacks

4 individual metal-foil muffin pans

paint

sharp, thin nail

large needle

pencil with eraser

spool of threed

clay or paper towels

glue or cord

block of wood or flat stone

What to do: Cut out two strips of heavy cardboard, approximately 2 inches x 18 inches (5 cm x 45 cm). Make a slit in the middle of each one so that they fit together to make a cross.

Staple or tack a small metal-foil pan to each end of the cross. If you don't have any old muffin pans around, you can make them by cutting out disks from heavy duty aluminum foil, or cutting down paper cups. Paint one of the pans a bright color. Make a hole through the center of the cross with the sharp thin nail or a large needle.

To make a base, stick the eye of the needle into the pencil eraser. Fit the pointed end of the pencil into the hole of a spool. (You may need the clay or paper towels to make it snug.) Glue or tie the spool to a block of wood or a flat stone.

Attach the cross to the base by placing it on the point of the needle. Blow on the cups. If the cross does not turn easily, make the hole in the crossed strips larger.

Place the base outdoors on a box about 3 feet (1 m) above the ground. Keep a record of the number of revolutions it makes per minute. You can do this easily by counting how many times the colored pan passes you.

What happens: The anemometer sometimes whirls around quickly. At other times it barely moves.

Why: The inward curve of the cups receives most of the force of the wind. That's what makes the cups move. The more revolutions per minute, the greater the wind velocity. A rapid increase in speed can mean approaching rain or snow or thunderstorms.

The Beaufort Scale

The Beaufort scale was originally designed by Francis Beaufort, a British admiral, in the early 1800s to help guide ships. It calculated wind speed at sea, but it has since been adapted for use on land. The Weather Bureau, though it uses an anemometer to measure wind speed, still reports winds to us using the Beaufort Scale.

It gives you a great way to judge the speed of wind—anywhere, any time—by watching the things that the wind moves. Memorize it and you'll be able to amaze people with your accurate readings.

0: Calm
Smoke goes straight up
Wind Speed: Less than 1mph

1: Light air
Smoke drifts in direction of wind
Wind Speed: 1–3mph

2: Light breeze
Wind felt on face; leaves rustle; flags stir; weather vanes turn
Wind Speed: 4–7mph

3: Gentle breeze
Leaves and twigs move constantly; light flags blow out
Wind Speed: 8–12mph

4: Moderate breeze
Dust, loose papers, and small branches move; flags flap
Wind Speed: 13–18mph

5: Fresh breeze
Small trees in leaf begin to sway; Flags ripple
Wind Speed: 19–24mph

6: Strong breeze
Large branches in motion; flags beat; umbrellas turn inside out
Wind Speed: 25–31mph

7: Moderate gale
Whole trees in motion; flags are extended
Wind Speed: 32–38mph

8: Fresh gale
Twigs break off trees; walking is hard
Wind Speed: 32–38mph

9: Strong gale
Slight damage to houses—TV antennas may blow off, awnings rip
Wind Speed: 47–54mph

10: Whole gale
Trees uprooted; much damage to houses
Wind Speed: 55–63mph

11: Storm
Widespread damage
Wind Speed: 64–75mph

12: Hurricane
Excessive damage
Wind Speed: more than 75mph

How Cold Do You Feel?

The speed of wind affects how cold you feel. The wind-chill factor is the relationship between the speed of wind and the temperature of the air. A wind chill table tells us the still-air temperature that would feel the same as the temperature and wind speed combined. For example, a temperature of 20° F (–6° C) and a wind of 20 miles (32 km) an hour makes us feel as though it were –10° F (–23° C).

Air Temperature (F°)

Wind Speed (miles per hour)	35	30	25	20	15	10	5	0	–5	–10	–15	–20	–25	–30	–35	–40	–45
0–4	35	30	25	20	15	10	5	0	–5	–10	–15	–20	–25	–30	–35	–40	–45
5	32	27	22	16	11	6	0	–5	–10	–15	–21	–26	–31	–36	–42	–47	–52
10	22	16	10	3	–3	–9	–15	–22	–27	–34	–40	–46	–52	–58	–64	–71	–77
15	16	9	2	–5	–11	–18	–25	–31	–38	–45	–51	–58	–65	–72	–78	–85	–92
20	12	4	–3	–10	–17	–24	–31	–39	–46	–53	–60	–67	–74	–81	–88	–95	–103
25	8	1	–7	–15	–22	–29	–36	–44	–51	–59	–66	–74	–81	–88	–96	–103	–110
30	6	–2	–10	–18	–25	–33	–41	–49	–56	–64	–71	–79	–86	–93	–101	–109	–116
35	4	–4	–12	–20	–27	–35	–43	–52	–58	–67	–74	–82	–89	–97	–105	–113	–120
40	3	–5	–13	–21	–29	–37	–45	–53	–60	–69	–76	–84	–92	–100	–107	–115	–123
45	2	–6	–14	–22	–30	–38	–46	–54	–62	–70	–78	–85	–93	–102	–109	–117	–125

How Hot Do You Feel?

If it is 85°F (29.4° C) how hot do you feel?

Well, if the humidity is 95 per cent—it feels like 105°F (40.5°C). The Heat Index prepared by the weather service shows what the temperature feels like as the humidity changes.

At 110° F (43° C), you only need relative humidity of 50 per cent to feel as if the temperature is 150° F (65° C)!

With a hygrometer, the relative humidity chart, and this index, you can figure out how hot it feels any day.

Relative Humidity (%)

Air Temperature (°F)	25	30	35	40	45	50	55	60	65	70	75	80	85	90	95	100
140																
135																
130																
125																
120	139	148														
115	127	135	143	151												
110	117	123	130	137	143	150										
105	109	113	118	123	129	135	142	149								
100	101	104	107	110	115	120	126	132	138	144						
95	94	96	98	101	104	107	110	114	119	124	130	136				
90	88	90	91	93	95	96	98	100	102	106	109	113	117	122		
85	83	84	85	86	87	88	89	90	91	93	95	97	99	102	105	108
80	77	78	79	79	80	81	81	82	83	85	86	86	87	88	89	91
75	72	73	73	74	74	75	75	76	76	77	77	78	78	79	79	80
70	66	67	67	68	68	69	69	70	70	70	70	71	71	71	71	72

Milk Carton Hygrometer

Humidity is the amount of water vapor, or moisture, in the air. Meteorologists usually report what is called "relative humidity," rather than actual humidity. Relative humidity is a figure they come to by comparing the moisture in the air to the amount of moisture the air can hold. And that amount will change according to the temperature of the air. High humidity combined with high temperatures makes most people uncomfortable.

You can figure out relative humidity with a homemade hygrometer.

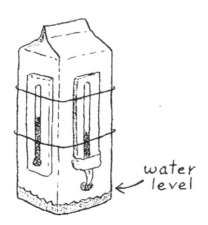

YOU WILL NEED:
2 room thermometers
small piece of cotton material
thread
quart milk carton
rubber bands
scissors
water

water level

What to do: Check the two thermometers to make sure they register the same temperature.

Cover the bulb of one of the thermometers with a 2 inch (5 cm) scrap of cotton material (an old handkerchief will do fine). Tie it on with thread and leave a "tail" on one end, as in the illustration.

Using rubber bands, attach the thermometers to two sides of the milk carton. Cut a small hole in the carton just below the thermometer with the covered bulb. Push the tail of cotton through the hole. Fill the carton with water up to the level of the hole so the cotton can be kept wet.

Read the dry bulb and wet bulb thermometers.

What happens: The temperature of the wet-bulb thermometer is always lower.

Why: Water evaporating from the thermometer with the moist cloth uses up heat. Therefore, the temperature drops.

The water in the cloth around the wet-bulb thermometer will keep on evaporating as long as the air can hold more water vapor. Dry air can take on more water vapor than air that is already filled with moisture.

The drier the air (the lower the humidity), the further apart the two temperature readings will be. When the temperatures are exactly the same, the humidity is 100 percent.

The higher the temperature, the more water vapor the air can hold at a particular temperature, the relative humidity is 100 percent. And it is foggy or raining or snowing.

Check the readings of the two thermometers and see the humidity table (below) to find the relative percentage of humidity.

Relative Humidity Table

Difference between dry-bulb and wet-bulb temperatures

Dry-bulb temperature (F°)	1	2	3	4	5	6	7	8	9	10	11	12	14	16	18	20	22	24
10	78	56	34	13														
15	82	64	46	29	11													
20	85	70	55	40	26	12												
25	87	74	62	49	37	25	13	1										
30	89	78	67	56	46	36	26	16	6									
35	91	81	72	63	54	45	36	27	19	10	2							
40	92	83	75	68	60	52	45	37	29	22	15	7						
45	93	86	78	71	64	57	51	44	38	31	25	18	6					
50	93	87	80	74	67	61	55	49	43	38	32	27	16	5				
55	94	88	82	76	70	65	59	54	49	43	38	33	23	14	5			
60	94	89	83	78	73	68	63	58	53	48	43	39	30	21	13	5		
65	95	90	85	80	75	70	66	61	56	52	48	44	35	27	20	12	5	
70	95	90	86	81	77	72	68	64	59	55	51	48	40	33	25	19	12	6
75	96	91	86	82	78	74	70	66	62	58	54	51	44	37	30	24	18	12
80	96	91	87	83	79	75	72	68	64	61	57	54	47	41	35	29	23	18
90	96	92	89	85	81	78	74	71	68	65	61	58	52	47	41	36	31	26
100	96	93	89	86	83	80	77	73	70	68	65	62	56	51	46	41	37	33

303 How Uncomfortable Do You Feel?

The Temperature Humidity Index (THI) shows how heat and humidity combined make us feel.

If you know the temperature and the relative humidity, you can use the chart below and tell just how uncomfortable you are. For example, if the temperature is 81 degrees F (27.2 degrees C) with the humidity at 55 per cent, the THI is 75, and about half the people are uncomfortable. At that same temperature and a humidity of 100 per cent, the THI is 80 and most people are uncomfortable.

If you love math, you can figure out the THI for yourself by using the following steps:

1. Add the wet bulb and dry bulb temperatures.
2. Multiply the sum by 0.4.
3. Add 15.

If you don't have the wet bulb temperature, but you know the temperature and the humidity, you can find the wet bulb temperature by using the relative humidity table on page 255. All you have to do is subtract the "difference" from the dry bulb temperature.

Temperature Humidity Index

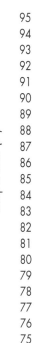

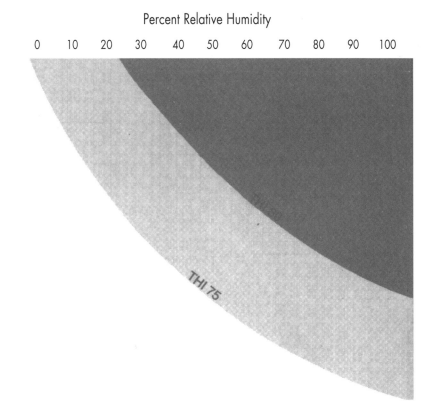

Dew Point

The dew point is the temperature at which the air cannot hold any more water vapor. That's when the moisture in the air begins to condense—to turn back from water vapor to droplets. This temperature will change from day to day depending on the temperature of the air and the amount of moisture in it. The closer the dew point temperature is to the air temperature, the more likely we are to have fog or rain or snow.

You can use simple equipment to determine the day's dew point, but you must set it up outdoors.

What to do: Write down the temperature of the air.

Remove the label from the can. Fill the can with water, and then make sure the outside is dry. Place the thermometer in the can.

Add ice to the water, a cube at a time. Carefully stir the water with the thermometer. Watch both the outside of the can and the thermometer closely.

What happens: Liquid begins to form on the outside of the can—and the temperature goes down.

Why: The temperature—at the point when liquid begins to form—is at or near the dew point—the temperature at which the relative humidity is 100 percent.

When water cools off and condenses on an object, the droplets are called dew. Dew forms when damp air touches anything that cools it to below its dew point—the point at which it cannot hold any more water.

When air currents are rising rapidly, cooling takes place high in the air and clouds form. When gentler air currents mix cool air into warmer air, fog forms.

Dew usually forms on grass or on plants that have cooled off. The temperature at which this happens depends on the amount of water vapor in the air. If it's small, dew may not form until the temperature drops to 32 degrees F (0 degrees C) or even below freezing. When it's that cold frost forms. If the air contains a great deal of water vapor, dew will form at 68 degrees F (20° C).

Rain Gauge

Measure the amount of rain that falls during a period of a week or month, and compare your results with the official statistics.

 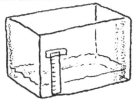

What to do: Using the ruler, measure off inches or centimeters on strips of masking or adhesive tape. Attach the tapes to the various containers.

Put the containers on a flat, level suface outside. It may be wise to place the containers in a box to make sure they remain upright.

Each time it rains, measure the amount of rain in the containers. The levels should be the same whatever the size of the container, provided that its sides are parallel. Record the amount and date.

Compare measurements from one rainfall to the next. And compare your measurements with those announced on television or radio. They may not always agree. Sometimes, the amount of rain varies from one side of the street to the other!

306 Reading the Clouds

When the air is heavy with moisture and it gets cool, the water vapor in it turns back into droplets and combines with tiny dust particles in the air to form fog. When fog is high in the sky, we see clouds. The type of cloud depends on how the air is cooled and the way the air is moving.

Cirrus clouds are high, feathery clouds.

Stratus clouds hang low in layers or sheets in the sky, causing overcast and fog.

Cumulus clouds look like cauliflowers with flat bases. They usually mean fair weather.

Nimbus clouds are dark gray rain clouds.

Most clouds change shape continually. Parts of them evaporate when touched by warmer air and when winds blow.

Weather is called cloudless when there are no clouds at all, and "clear" when clouds cover less than three-tenths of the sky. It is "partly sunny" when the sky is three-tenths to seven-tenths clouded, and "cloudy," or overcast, when the sky is more clouded than that.

Weather forecasters study clouds carefully. With the help of the Cloud Chart, you, too, can read the clouds!

CLOUD CHART

40,000 ft.
(12,000 m)

CIRRUS

CIRRO-
STRATUS

CIRRO-
CUMULUS

20,000 ft.
(6,000 m)

ALTO-STRATUS

ALTO-
CUMULUS

CUMULO-
NIMBUS

STRATO-
CUMULUS

CUMULUS

NIMBO-
STRATUS

5,000 ft.
(1,500 m)

3,000 ft.
(900 m)

STRATUS

1,500 ft.
(450 m)

pH Scale

The pH scale, developed by S.P.L. Sorensen, a Danish biochemist, is used to indicate how alkaline or acid a solution is.

All acids contain hydrogen. The stronger the acid, the more hydrogen the solution contains—and the less hydrogen the solution can accept when it combines with another substance. When it can't accept any more hydrogen its ph is 0. The stronger the acid, the lower its pH.

A solution with a pH above 7 is alkaline. A solution with a pH below 7 is acid.

alkaline

14.0 drain cleaner
13.0 lye/ammonia
12.4 lime
11.0
10.5 milk of magnesia
8.5 baking soda
8.3 seawater
8.0
7.4 blood
7.0 distilled water
6.6 milk
6.0
5.6 unpolluted rain
5.0 tomato juice
4.2 coffee
3.0 apple juice
2.2 vinegar
2.0 lemon juice
1.5
1.0 battery acid
0.0

acidic

Acid Rain

You can test whether the rain that falls in your area is polluted by using pH paper or litmus paper, both of which you can buy from chemistry laboratories or hobby shops. Or you can make your own indicator with juice from a jar of red cabbage.

YOU WILL NEED:

6 to 10 tablespoons of red cabbage juice

5 small glasses or paper cups

rain water
apple juice
lemon juice
clean jar
cooled boiled water
milk

What to do: Collect rain water in a clean jar.

Line up and number or label the paper cups. Put a tablespoon of red cabbage juice in each. Add rain water to the first, an equal amount of cooled boiled water to the second, milk to the third, apple juice to the next, then lemon juice to the last.

Compare the color of the cup with the rain water with the colors of others. When you find the one that comes closest in color to the rain water, refer to the pH chart on page 259 and estimate the pH of the rain water you are testing.

What happens: If the solution changes color only slightly, your rain water is normal. If it becomes as pink as the lemon solution, it has a very high acid content.

Why: Rain is normally slightly acidic because of the oxides in the air that form weak acids. Unpolluted rain water measures about 5.6 on the pH scale.

If your rain water has a lower pH level, the rain falling in your area is polluted with acids. When the pH of water in lakes and streams drops below 5 on the scale, most fish die.

When the waste from the fuel burned to run our factories—and our cars, trains, and planes—combines with the water in the air, it forms acids that fall to the ground—either in the form of rain or as dry particles.

This new man-made pollution has been called a slow poison from the sky. It harms trees and food crops, and poses a threat to life in lakes and streams, as well on land. It can even cause buildings to crumble.

AIR, H$_2$O, AND OTHER THINGS

Everything in this world takes up space and has weight: you, and even air, as this chapter will show!

The three states of matter are solid, liquid, and gas. This refers to how a thing feels, how hard it is, or how it moves or looks, even if it's invisible, like air. A table is a solid object, water is a liquid, and air is a gas, and these three things are made up of small parts called molecules and even smaller parts called atoms. It is these parts of things that chemists study, and rearrange to create new products that make our lives that much better.

Be Smart/Be Safe

You can be smart and do these experiments safely by following these general rules:

• Always wash thoroughly any kitchen containers, bowls, or tools you use before you put them back.

• Don't leave old chemical solutions lying around the house. Dispose of them carefully.

• Be especially careful using the stove or microwave, or handling boiling water or hot foods. Find a parent or an adult to help you use any appliances needed, or to do experiments you are unsure of.

• Be sure to label the contents of any bottles, jars, and containers you want to keep, and store them in a safe place, away from young children.

• Read through the What to do instructions completely before you start, to make sure you have everything you need and the time to complete the experiment.

• If an experiment may be messy, do it outside or in the sink, or cover your work area with a protective covering or old newspapers.

Atomic Brew: The Molecule and I

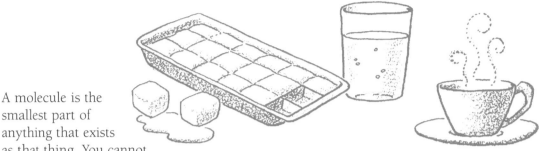

A molecule is the smallest part of anything that exists as that thing. You cannot see molecules, but everything in the world is made up of them. The best way to understand this is to imagine yourself shrinking way, way down until you become one. If you were a molecule of something on a tabletop, a salt crystal (one grain of salt) on the table would look like a mountain to you. If you were a molecule of water, you would be the last, littlest part of a drop. The last part of that water drop to evaporate would be you. Now you have a good idea of how small molecules really are. But, while molecules are small, the parts that make them up are even smaller. These very small parts that form molecules are called atoms.

If you were a molecule of oxygen, you would be made up of two of these very small parts, or atoms. You would need two atoms of oxygen, because one atom of oxygen does not behave like oxygen.

A substance with only one kind of atom is called an element. Oxygen, hydrogen, nitrogen, and carbon are all elements. (See The Periodic Table of the Elements on pages 264 and 265.) If you were an element of nitrogen, you would be made up of only nitrogen atoms. If you were an element of carbon, you would be made up of only carbon atoms. You could not be anything else.

Atoms of different elements come together to make different molecules. A molecule of water is made up of three atoms. If you were one atom of oxygen, you would have to be joined by two friends representing hydrogen atoms to make a molecule of water, because water has two atoms of hydrogen and one atom of oxygen. You would now be a substance, made up of two (or more) different elements, called a compound. Water, carbon dioxide, and sugar are all examples of compounds. As a molecule, or small bit of matter, you could exist in three possible forms. Chemists would identify you as one of the three states of matter: solid, liquid, or gas.

If necessary, a scientist, or chemist, could again split you apart, using electricity, into your original parts or atoms. Now you would no longer be water but three separate atoms, two hydrogen atoms and one oxygen atom. The very smallest part of you that could ever exist as water would be a molecule.

Atom Up!

Everything on the earth is made up of atoms. They are the smallest part of any element, and the atoms of each element are different. If you were to take all the electrons in each element and add 'em up, you would get different (atomic) numbers. Now, you know why we titled this section. "Atom Up!"

Each atom has a central point, or nucleus, made up of neutrons and protons. Some atomic parts contain electrical charges: the protons in the nucleus contain positive electrical charges, but the neutrons contain no charge (they are electrically neutral). Spinning around the nucleus, however, are even tinier parts called electrons. These have a negative electrical charge. These positive and negative electrical charges between electrons and protons are what keep the atom whole and together.

It helps to think of the nucleus of an atom as a ball, and the electrons as smaller balls circling it. Chemists sometimes call the paths the electrons take around the nucleus "shells." Better yet, think of the nucleus of the atom as the sun and the electrons as circling, or orbiting, it as its planets. The orbiting planets are attracted to, or pulled towards, the sun just as the electrons are to the nucleus of the atom.

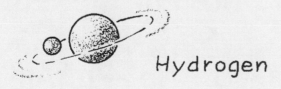

Hydrogen

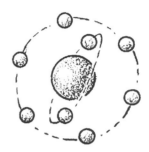

A special table known as the Periodic Table of the Elements can help you better understand atomic chemistry. Dmitri Ivanovich Mendeleyev, a Russian chemist, put together the first table of the elements in 1869. He left some spaces in it so that, when new elements were discovered, they could be placed on the chart. In a modern version (see The Periodic Table of the Elements chart) the seven rows numbered at the left and running across the table, called periods, tell the number of orbits the electrons take in each of the elements.

Period-one elements have only one orbit, period-two have two orbits, period-three have three orbits, etc.

Each element on the chart has a number (atomic number) and a letter symbol as well as an atomic weight. Find oxygen on the chart (period 2, column 16/6A). The atomic number of oxygen is eight. This shows that there are eight protons in the nucleus of the atom. Notice the numbers two and six on the right side of the box. They add up to eight. The two numbers, one on top of the other, represent the number of electrons in the first orbit (2) and in the second orbit (6) of the element oxygen. The number of electrons orbiting the nucleus of an atom is the same as the number of protons in the nucleus.

PERIODIC TABLE

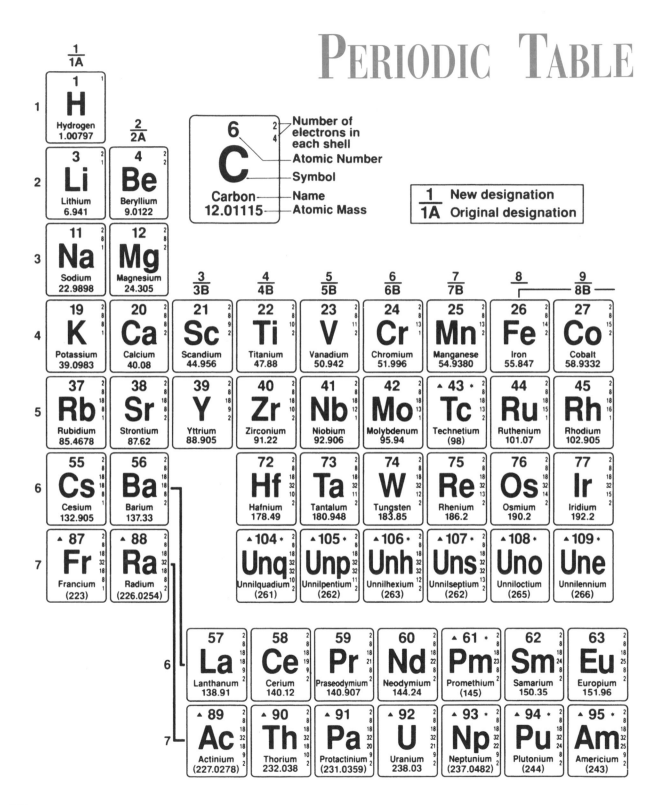

OF THE ELEMENTS

★ Synthetic

▲ Radioactive

( ) Indicates atomic weight of most stable isotope

	18 / 8A
	2 — **He** — Helium 4.0026

13 / 3A	14 / 4A	15 / 5A	16 / 6A	17 / 7A	
5 **B** Boron 10.811	6 **C** Carbon 12.01115	7 **N** Nitrogen 14.0067	8 **O** Oxygen 15.9994	9 **F** Fluorine 18.9984	10 **Ne** Neon 20.179
13 **Al** Aluminum 26.9815	14 **Si** Silicon 28.086	15 **P** Phosphorus 30.9738	16 **S** Sulfur 32.064	17 **Cl** Chlorine 35.453	18 **Ar** Argon 39.948

10	11 / 1B	12 / 2B					
28 **Ni** Nickel 58.69	29 **Cu** Copper 63.54	30 **Zn** Zinc 65.37	31 **Ga** Gallium 69.72	32 **Ge** Germanium 72.59	33 **As** Arsenic 74.9216	34 **Se** Selenium 78.96	35 **Br** Bromine 79.904	36 **Kr** Krypton 83.80
46 **Pd** Palladium 106.4	47 **Ag** Silver 107.868	48 **Cd** Cadmium 112.40	49 **In** Indium 114.82	50 **Sn** Tin 118.69	51 **Sb** Antimony 121.75	52 **Te** Tellurium 127.60	53 **I** Iodine 126.9044	54 **Xe** Xenon 131.29
78 **Pt** Platinum 195.09	79 **Au** Gold 196.967	80 **Hg** Mercury 200.59	81 **Tl** Thallium 204.383	82 **Pb** Lead 207.19	83 **Bi** Bismuth 208.980	▲ 84 **Po** Polonium (209)	▲ 85 **At** Astatine (210)	▲ 86 **Rn** Radon (222)

64 **Gd** Gadolinium 157.25	65 **Tb** Terbium 158.9254	66 **Dy** Dysprosium 162.50	67 **Ho** Holmium 164.930	68 **Er** Erbium 167.26	69 **Tm** Thulium 168.934	70 **Yb** Ytterbium 173.04	71 **Lu** Lutetium 174.97
▲ 96 ★ **Cm** Curium (247)	▲ 97 ★ **Bk** Berkelium (247)	▲ 98 ★ **Cf** Californium (251)	▲ 99 ★ **Es** Einsteinium (252)	▲ 100 ★ **Fm** Fermium (257)	▲ 101 ★ **Md** Mendelevium (258)	▲ 102 ★ **No** Nobelium (259)	▲ 103 ★ **Lr** Lawrencium (260)

© Ideal School Supply Company. Reprinted with permission.

265

Atomic Orbits

309

YOU WILL NEED:

4 colors of
modelling clay
newspaper (to cover
work area)
wide-mouth jar lid

An easy way to start learning about atoms is to make a model of one. Although electrons and protons are not clay balls (in fact, electrons are fast-moving, electrically charged particles that move faster than you can say "atom"), making a clay model will help you understand what can be a very difficult idea.

What to do: Spread some newspaper over your work area. Select any two colors of clay. We'll use red and blue. Now, make two red clay ropes and a blue rope, rolling them out with your hands. These will show the orbits, or shells, or paths the electrons will take around the nucleus. Make certain that you make the ropes long enough to make complete circles inside the jar lid. Press the first red rope against the inner rim of the lid. Follow it with the blue rope, pressed in next to the red. (When you finish your model, it will have a target pattern.) Now press another circle of red in next to the blue rope; then place a blue "bull's-eye" piece of clay in the middle. When you finish, flatten the clay with your fingers.

Next, make a "yellow" clay ball and stick it on the "bull's-eye." Make two smaller (green) balls and stick these to the outside of the blue bull's-eye, one on each side and in a straight line with the larger ball. Then place eight more green balls in four groups of two on the outer edge of the red ring.

What happens: You now have made a usable atomic model!

Why: Atoms can have no more than seven orbits, or paths, and only so many electrons can fit into each orbit. The larger ball in the "bull's-eye" represents the nucleus of the atom. The two smaller balls on the outer edge of the blue circle show that there are only two electrons in the first orbit. The second orbit, the edge of the red ring, has eight green balls around it, showing that only eight electrons can be in its orbit.

The third orbit of the model (outer edge of the blue clay circle, not filled) can have up to eight more green balls, or electrons, if it is the last orbit, but up to eighteen, if it is not the last. An important thing to remember is that, after the first orbit, each orbit in turn must have eight electrons before another orbit is started.

310

Identify the Model

Look at the Periodic Table of the Elements and identify the model you just made; then add balls, or electrons, to your atomic model to make other elements.

ISO What?

Isomers are essentially compounds, or atoms of two or more elements that chemically unite. Although they have the same number and kinds of atoms as other compounds, they are arranged differently. Scientists have taken compounds and chemically rearranged their molecules to form isomers and make new products. Detergent, paint, gasoline, and aspirin, products we use every day, are but a few examples of products made by this process.

Isomer Patterns

311

Now challenge your brain power. See how many isomer models you can make. Try this with friends. It makes a great brainteaser!

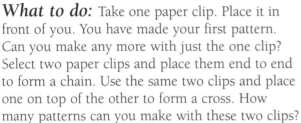

What to do: Take one paper clip. Place it in front of you. You have made your first pattern. Can you make any more with just the one clip? Select two paper clips and place them end to end to form a chain. Use the same two clips and place one on top of the other to form a cross. How many patterns can you make with these two clips?

Add another clip to the two to make three. How many patterns can you make now, using the added clip? Now add another clip to make four, then five, then six. How does increasing the clips by one increase your chances for making new patterns? Hypothesize, or guess, how many patterns you can make before each activity. Write down your estimate, or guessed number, and draw each pattern you are able to make.

What happens: Every time you add one more paper clip, you are able to make more new patterns.

Why: This experiment is based on a study of probability; in this case, how many patterns you can make in each activity. The more paper clips, or elements, you have to work with, the greater the number of patterns you are able to make. The number of possible patterns increases faster than the number of clips you add.

Pencil Pusher

312

Most pencils have six flat sides. Number the sides by writing 1 through 6 on them. Place a book on a table and roll the pencil towards it until it stops. What are the possible chances that a certain number will come up?

By chance, each number will come up equally; in mathematics, we say the outcome is "equally likely." Are there any variables, or things that could affect how many times a certain number side on the pencil could come up?

313 Molecules in Motion

You can demonstrate the movement of molecules in solids, liquids, and gases in a simple way.

YOU WILL NEED:

small box lid (or flat box with short sides)

marbles (or any other small spheres or balls)

scissors

What to do: Place a layer of marbles, or balls, in the lid so that they are jammed close together. Move the lid back and forth slowly. Now, take some of the marbles out of the lid and move the lid back and forth again, faster than you did when more marbles were in it.

Take more marbles out of the lid and move it at an even greater speed than before.

Finally, cut a hole in each side of the lid and shake the lid again, and again.

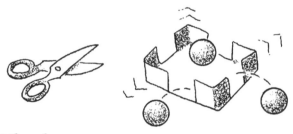

What happens: As the marbles get fewer and fewer, they spread out more easily. Some leave through the holes in the lid.

Why: The "packed marbles" at the start show molecules in a solid substance. This explains why these substances are hard. They move, but they don't move much.

A number of marbles taken out shows molecules in a liquid. They are farther apart and they move more easily.

Finally, the few marbles in the lid demonstrate molecules even farther apart and moving quite rapidly. This represents a gas.

The holes in the sides of the box show what happens when substances break away from substances: water boiling on the stove will turn to water vapor, or steam, and leave the pot. A drop of water left in a dish will evaporate. If one of its molecules is moving fast enough, it will move from the surface of the drop and into the air.

When an ice cube is heated, it changes from a solid form into a liquid state, and then into a gas. The molecules of water never change, but the forms the substance takes do change; for example, from ice to water to vapor.

The Spreading Molecules

314

Do water molecules really move? If so, how fast and how slowly?

What to do: Fill one glass with cool tap water. Fill the other glass with hot tap water. Now, quickly, place one drop of food coloring in each glass. (Make certain that all the variables are the same. This means that the glasses should have the same amount of water in them and that the same number of food coloring drops are added. Controlling variables is important to make the experiment scientifically correct.)

What happens: The food coloring spreads throughout the water in both glasses, but at different rates.

Why: The cold water eventually becomes completely colored because the water molecules are moving throughout the glass. But when the water is warmer (the hot tap water), the heat energy in it causes the water molecules to move much faster. This makes the food coloring spread out more rapidly.

You might want to chart, or keep a record of, how much time it takes for the food coloring to spread evenly throughout each glass of water.

Chemists in History

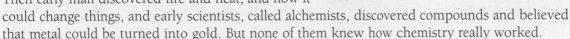

In prehistoric times, people believed nature and changes in nature were caused by spirits and magic. Then early man discovered fire and heat, and how it could change things, and early scientists, called alchemists, discovered compounds and believed that metal could be turned into gold. But none of them knew how chemistry really worked.

The chemistry we know (organic chemistry is the study of carbon compounds, while inorganic chemistry deals with all the other elements and compounds) began in the 1600s, when Robert Boyle started charting the list of elements still in use today. Chemists Joseph Priestley and Karl Scheele separately discovered oxygen in the late 1700s. It was then, too, that French chemist Antoine Lavoisier discovered combustion, or what chemical changes happened when things were burned. John Dalton thought elements were made of atoms (1803), while Jons J. Berzelius, a Swedish scientist, believed all atoms were negatively and positively charged (1812). He also gave atomic weights to elements, while Henry Moseley gave them atomic numbers. Finally, the French chemists Marie Curie and her husband, Pierre, discovered radium (1898), an element that is radioactive.

A Matter of Change

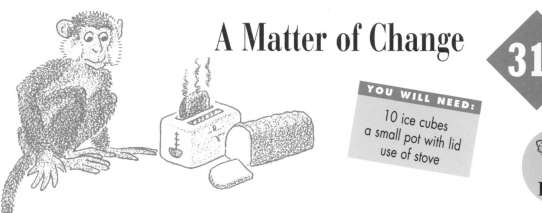

YOU WILL NEED:
10 ice cubes
a small pot with lid
use of stove

HOT!

Sometimes things change. When toast burns it is no longer the same substance. Its molecules have been rearranged by heat. What is left is carbon, an entirely new substance. This is called a chemical change. However, when ice turns to water and then to a gas, the molecules of water do not change. The forms which the substance takes change but the substance, water, does not. This is called a natural change. Let's see how this works.

What to do: Put the ice cubes in the pot and melt them on the stove. Once the cubes turn to water and the water starts to boil, place the lid on the pot. Let it boil for a few minutes, and then turn the heat off and let the pot cool. Then, as you lift the lid, observe the water drops on the underside.

What happens: The ice turns to water, the water to steam, a gas which we sometimes call water vapor, and the steam back into water.

Why: Ice is a solid. Its molecules move slowly but they do move. When you heat the ice cubes, the molecules move faster. The ice gets warmer and melts. When you continue to heat the water further, the molecules move even faster, bump into each other, and escape, leaving the liquid. The water drops that collect on the inside of the lid are a result of water vapor (gas). As the pot cools, the vapor turns back into water (liquid). This process is known as condensation. Chemists identify what happens in this experiment as demonstrating the three states of matter: solid, liquid, and gas.

The Water Factory

316

HOT!

In this experiment, you'll become a wizard of chemistry. You'll distill water, or take salt out of it, and you won't need a lot of expensive chemistry equipment to do it. Impossible, you say! Try it and find out. Adult help is recommended

What to do: Drop a few grains of salt into the jar of water. Stir it with a spoon and take a taste. The water should taste salty; if not, add a few more grains of salt. Put the jar of salt solution in the microwwave (without lid) for about 90 seconds, or until the water comes to a boil.

Do not touch or remove the jar from the microwave! The water is scalding hot!

Carefully reach in with a mitt or folded dish towel and hold the jar while you screw on the lid. (Better yet, get an adult to do it for you.) After the jar has thoroughly cooled, unscrew the lid and taste the water drops under it or on the sides of the jar.

What happens: The water drops on the sides of the jar or under the lid do not taste salty.

Why: The boiling water in the closed jar makes steam (water vapor) that collects as condensation (water drops) that forms on the sides of the jar or under the lid. Salt is a compound that will not leave the water (in steam) when boiled, so the salt is removed from the steam. This is a good way to purify water.

What's the Solution?

Chemists study suspensions and solutions—what are they all about? Try this simple experiment and find out.

What to do: Add the soil to one jar of water, the salt to the other. Stir both. Look through your hand lens at both jars.

What happens: The particles of soil appear to be hanging in the water. Because of their weight, the larger soil particles settle to the bottom of the jar first, followed by the medium particles, and then the smaller ones. The particles of salt in the other jar have disappeared, or dissolved.

Why: The soil did not dissolve, or mix and disappear, into the water, because soil and water are composed of molecules of different types. These different molecules cannot chemically combine. The soil and water are what chemists call a "suspension" because the soil particles spread, or become suspended, throughout the water and then later settle to the bottom of the jar, or come out of suspension. But water and salt do combine. The salt dissolves, or seems to disappear, in the water. Its particles (crystals) do not fall to the bottom of the jar. This is an example of a solution. Chemists call the solid molecules that become part of a solution, such as salt, a "solute," and the liquid molecules, such as water, a "solvent."

Act I:
All Mixed Up!

Chemists often talk about solutions and suspensions, and also emulsions and mixtures. In a solution, one substance is thoroughly dissolved in another (salt and water). In a suspension, one substance is mixed throughout the other, but is not dissolved (soil and water).

In an emulsion, one liquid "floats" in another, but is not dissolved. The spread mayonnaise is a perfect example of an emulsion. But a mixture, unlike the above, is made up of different substances that do not dissolve into one another or stay together. Salt and flour may be really mixed up, but don't you be! Try this experiment and find out what's going on.

What to do: Stir flour and salt together in the glass (do not add the water yet). Is it thoroughly mixed? Add the hot water to fill the glass. Stir well and wait about 30 minutes; then reach in with your finger and taste the water.

What happens: The water at the top tastes salty, and white covers the bottom of the glass.

Why: Salt and flour is a perfect mixture. These substances are so different that they cannot dissolve or chemically mix in any way. They also react differently to water. While the flour floats and then sinks to the bottom of the glass, the salt dissolves into the water to form a salt solution above the flour.

Save the mixture for the next experiment, "Act II: Bring Back the Substance."

Act II:
Bring Back the Substance

YOU WILL NEED:

wide-mouth jar
coffee filter
salt and flour mixture
(from last experiment)
rubber band
hot tap water
shallow container

Since salt and flour were so good in "Act I: All Mixed Up!" let's bring them back. So, here they are again, folks—salt and flour!

What to do: Place the filter over the top of the jar and put the rubber band around it to keep it in place. Let the filter droop or sag a little in the middle so that it will hold the water more easily. Pour the salty water and flour mixture from the last experiment slowly onto the filter. Very slowly, add a little bit of hot water to help the salt solution break through the flour. Be patient! It will take some time to recover, or get back, a good amount of salt solution. Save as much as you want, and then take the filter off the jar. Pour the salt solution out of the jar into the shallow container. Let it stand in a warm place for 24 hours.

What happens: The flour stays on the top of the filter while the salt in the water passes through it. When the water eventually evaporates from the shallow container, it leaves salt crystals behind.

Why: The molecules of solid salt crystals (called a solute by chemists) that had dissolved in the water (solvent) could pass freely through the filter, while the flour grains, which are much too large and do not dissolve, remained on top.

Because water evaporates but salt cannot, the salt molecules left behind as the water disappeared reformed into crystals.

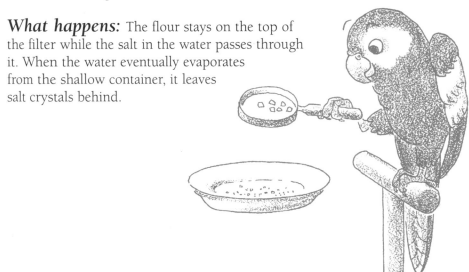

Drop Out!

320

Water and oil act differently as this experiment will show.

What to do: Place the oil into one shallow container and the water into the other. Cut two small strips from the construction paper. Dip one paper strip into the oil and the other into the water; then place them on the paper towels or napkins. Drop a drop of food coloring on each.

What happens: The drop of food coloring on the oiled paper sits on the surface while the drop on the water-dipped paper spreads out.

Why: The food coloring, which is water–based, sits as a drop on the oiled paper because its water molecules will not combine with the oil. A substance is called "immiscible" with another when it does not combine to become one substance. The food coloring on the water-dipped paper is said to be "miscible" with it. It dissolves on the paper strip and spreads out, even beyond the paper. Its molecules combine as do the molecules in a solution.

321

Chromatography: Watercolor

Chemists needed a way to separate substances such as dyes and chemical mixtures into their separate parts. In this experiment, we'll mix two different food colors and see if we can bring them back. This is a simple version of what chemists call "chromatography."

What to do: Mix 2 to 3 drops each of red and blue food coloring in the same small container. Put the two napkins together and place them on top of the newspaper. Pour the colored mixture in the center of the napkins. With the medicine dropper, squirt water on the food coloring and try to separate the colors.

What happens: The colored mixture separates into purple (red-blue) and light blue areas.

Why: The water acts as a solvent, dissolving the food coloring solution. Because the colors dissolve at different rates, they separate into circular colored areas as the solvent travels through the absorbent, spongelike napkins.

Fluttering Flatworm Marathon

Enter these fantastic paper flatworms in a marathon, or race, and see which one wins. It's all based on molecules, too!

What to do: Fold the strips back and forth, accordion-style. Line them up evenly on the kitchen counter. Load the medicine dropper(s) with water. Let a few drops of water fall on the ends and middle of the paper strips and try to extend, or stretch, the worms across an imaginary finish line.

What happens: The paper worms seem to flutter and turn.

Why: The thousands of open holes in the paper fill with water. This "capillary action" expands, or makes larger, those parts of the paper. As the paper expands, it moves, and so do your flatworms!

How to Make a Hydrometer

A hydrometer is an instrument that measures the density, or heaviness, of water compared to other solutions. You can make your own with just a few simple materials, but be patient, as it may take a few trials before you get your instrument to float properly.

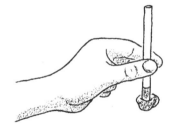 

What to do: Cut the straw in half. Close one end of the halved straw with the clay and form it into a small ball. Pour a small amount of salt into the top of the straw to weight it. The salt should rise about a ½ inch (1 cm) in the straw. Hold the straw up to the light to see the level.

Now, gently and carefully, lower the hydrometer into the water. It should float freely and straight up, and should not touch the bottom of the glass. If the straw does not float correctly, straight in the water, adjust the salt in the straw or the water in the glass until it does.

Hydrometer Holdup

324

YOU WILL NEED:

your homemade hydrometer
glass half-filled with tap water
2 rubber bands
2 tablespoons of salt

This hydrometer experiment is designed to make a real chemist out of you. In the experiments in this book, but particularly this one, you will need to control all the variables. This means that all the materials and measurements will need to be the same. You will need to be patient here, too. It may take a little time to get your hydrometer and measurements adjusted, but you will succeed!

What to do: Put one rubber band around the bottom of the glass of water and the other around the top. Carefully place the hydrometer in the water. Again, it should float freely straight up and should not touch the bottom of the glass. Push the hydrometer close to the side of the glass, being careful not to push the open end of it under the water, and let it float freely. Adjust the bottom rubber band around the glass so that it marks the bottom of the clay ball on the hydrometer. This will measure how far your instrument drops in the water. Move the top rubber band to mark the level of the water in the glass. Now, keep your same position and watch the rubber band

markers as you slowly and carefully add the first tablespoon of salt to the water, followed by the second. Make certain that the hydrometer is above the level of the water at all times and that the top of the straw does not fill with water or salt.

What happens: In the salty water, the hydrometer floats higher and rises above the bottom rubber band. The water level of the salty water also rises above the top rubber band.

Why: Salt water is denser, or heavier, than tap water, so fewer water molecules are displaced, or forced out of position, by the weight of the hydrometer. So the straw sinks less in the salty water and rises above the rubber band.

Sí, C!

No, you won't learn Spanish from this experiment, but you will learn how long it takes for vitamin C tablets to dissolve in hot or cool tap water (solubility).

What to do: Drop one vitamin C tablet in the cool tap water and one in the hot water.

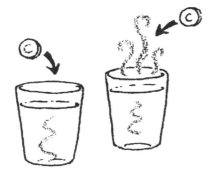

What happens: The vitamin C tablet in the hot water dissolves faster than the vitamin C tablet in cool water.

Why: The solid molecules of vitamin C tablet (solute) in the hot water (solvent) dissolve faster, or are more soluble, because heat energy from the water causes the molecules in the vitamin C tablet to vibrate and move farther apart. Without heat energy, no such sudden change can occur.

Tip of the Iceberg

If all the icebergs in the seas were to melt, would the sea level rise? This very simple experiment will give us the answer, and it's based on a very important compound chemists study—water!

What to do: Place as many ice cubes as you can into a glass; then fill the glass to the brim with warm water. Wait.

What happens: When the ice cubes melt, the water does not overflow.

Why: The ice cubes simply displaced the water in the glass, or the amount of ice that melted was exactly equal to the mass of the ice cubes below the water. Like the ice cubes in the glass, the main part of an iceberg is under water. If all the icebergs were to melt, as did the ice cubes in our experiment, the sea level would remain the same.

Air is Real

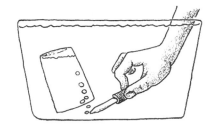

327

How do you know air is real? Since it is invisible, you certainly can't see it. Can you prove it really exists? The following experiment will give you the answer. Roll up your sleeves for this one!

What to do: Fill the glass with water. Put the water proof pad over the mouth of the glass. Hold it in place with your hand. Now, carefully turn the glass upside down and place it under the water in the pot or basin until it is completely under the surface. Do not remove the pad until the glass is completely under the water and touching the bottom of the pot.

Observe the water level in the glass. Tilt the glass to one side and carefully place the empty medicine dropper under it. Squeeze the dropper. Remove the dropper from the pot and squeeze the water out of it. Repeat what you did before (squeezing the empty dropper under the glass). Do this several times. You'll know you're doing this experiment correctly when, after squeezing the dropper, you see bubbles entering the glass of water.

What happens: Air bubbles move up the inside of the glass, and the water level in the glass gets lower.

Why: Air was in the medicine dropper when you squeezed it. The bubbles on the side of the glass were the air forced out of the dropper. As you "pumped" air into the glass with the dropper over and over, you saw the water level in the glass go down. Since the air had to go somewhere, it displaced some of the water, forcing it out of the glass. Now you know that air is real. It takes up space.

328 Pop Top

When its air is warmed, will a pop bottle pop its top?

What to do: Wet the cap of the soda bottle and place it upside down on the top of the container. Gently place your hands around the bottle. Hold it, but do not squeeze it.

What happens: The cap jumps or pops off the bottle.

Why: When you place your hands around the bottle, you warm the air inside it and the molecules of warm air expand and try to escape. The wet cap at first acts as a seal and keeps the air in place, but eventually some of it manages to escape and pushes the lid to the side or off the top of the bottle. If the cap doesn't fall and you keep your hands placed around the bottle, you can continue to make it jump.

Banana Split

Can you place a banana in a bottle without using your hands? Amaze your friends with this party–trick science experiment. Watch carefully, because the banana is quicker than the eye in this split–second surprise. Moreover, it all has to do with molecules and air.

Careful—boiling water involved! Also, it's best to do this in the sink.

YOU WILL NEED:

½ banana, peeled
teakettle with boiling water
clean, long, narrow bottle
(with banana-size mouth)
funnel
dish towel

What to do: Put the funnel into the bottle neck and carefully fill the bottle almost to the top with boiling water (adult help recommended). Remove the funnel. Wrap a dish towel around the bottle and gently swirl the water around; then pour it out. Quickly, fit the pointed end of the half-banana downwards into the bottle neck so that it makes an airtight plug. (Watch the variables—the size of the banana and bottle neck, the amount of hot water, the time it takes—and be patient! You may have to do this experiment several times to get it right, but you will succeed!)

What happens: The banana is sucked down into the bottom of the bottle.

Why: The heat from the boiling water causes the air inside the bottle to expand, forcing some of it out. When the banana is placed into the mouth of the bottle and the cooling air inside the bottle shrinks again, the air pressure inside is reduced, and the greater air pressure outside shoves the banana ahead of it into the bottle. This gives you an idea of what happens when air is removed from a space and nothing takes its place (partial vacuum). Just small differences in air pressure can cause things to move.

What now: You want to recycle the bottle, but the banana is inside it! What can you do?

Just wait a few days. Let the bacteria in the banana do their chemistry work. Bacteria give off enzymes that break down proteins and starches. The banana will eventually change chemically (ferment) and soften enough to be removed easily.

330 Air Force

YOU WILL NEED:
funnel
small, narrow-neck bottle
small piece of clay
glass of water

Molecules of air not only take up space, they can even stop water from entering a bottle.

What to do: Place the funnel in the bottle. Roll a small clay rope and fit it around the funnel in the bottle neck. Press the clay rope in firmly around the funnel to seal it completely, making the bottle airtight. Now, slowly pour a small amount of water into the bottle, a little at a time. Continue to do this until you've completely emptied the glass.

What happens: At first, water will enter the bottle, but as you continue to pour the water, less will enter. Finally, the funnel will fill up with water and none will enter the bottle.

Why: The molecules of air in the closed bottle will eventually press together and take up all the space there is, and so will stop any more water from entering.

331 Dry Goods

YOU WILL NEED:
small glass
napkin or
paper towel
glass bowl
water

Molecules of air can even stop paper from getting wet in a glass of water.

What to do:
Crumple the paper and place it in the bottom of the glass. Make certain it is tight so that the paper will not fall out. Fill the bowl with water. Now, turn the glass upside down over the bowl and lower it until it touches the bottom of the bowl. Lift the glass straight up out of the bowl. Continue to keep it upside down as you dry around and inside the rim of it. Now, take the paper out of the glass.

What happens: The paper inside the glass remains dry.

Why: When the glass is pushed into the water, the molecules of air do not escape but instead are pressed together and act as a shield between the water and the paper. Some water enters the glass but not enough to wet the paper. The molecules of air take up enough space to block it.

Soft-Touch Soapsuds

332

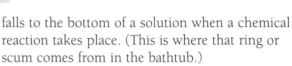

Did you know that water can be hard or soft? What effect does that have on soapsuds? (You'll use two chemical compounds again, Epsom salts and washing soda, or sodium carbonate.)

YOU WILL NEED:

spoon
warm tap water
3 jars or glasses of equal size
1 tablespoon Epsom salts
(found in supermarket
or pharmacy)
1 tablespoon of washing soda
3 teaspoons of dishwashing liquid

What to do: Fill all three containers with warm water. Pour the Epsom salts in one container. Stir the solution thoroughly. Do the same with the washing soda in the second container. Add a teaspoon of dishwashing liquid to each container, including the one with plain tap water. Stir each of the solutions and try to make suds.

What happens: Suds form in the water with the washing soda, but few form in the water with the Epsom salts.

Why: Washing soda "softens" water, while Epsom salts is a mineral that makes water "hard."

Tap water often contains calcium salts, which stops soap from making suds. If water has a lot of salts, it is called "hard." Washing soda "softens" or neutralizes the calcium salts in the water and forms a solid substance, called a precipitate, that falls to the bottom of a solution when a chemical reaction takes place. (This is where that ring or scum comes from in the bathtub.)

Epsom salts is a mineral that makes water hard. That is why you couldn't get soapsuds to form. Did your plain tap water make suds? Is your tap water hard or soft, or in between? Now empty the solutions in each glass. What do you see on the sides of the Epsom salts and washing soda containers?

HERE'S SUPERMAN, BUT WHERE'S CLARK?

When Clark Kent changes into Superman, he is no longer the same person. Clark is nowhere to be seen when Superman flies through the air.

In some ways, chemical reactions or changes are like Clark and Superman. After a chemical change or reaction, the molecules of a substance are no longer the same. The substance has changed completely.

Chemical changes occur every day everywhere—even our bodies are chemical factories. The food we eat combines with oxygen and causes a chemical change which releases heat and energy. Other chemical changes include the burning of coal, oil, gasoline, and wood. Chemists also produce chemical changes that make new products such as clothing, plastics, cleaners, paints, and foods.

In this chapter, we'll take oxygen from a compound, produce carbon dioxide from other substances, and even take two substances and make a new chemical compound called a precipitate.

These are just a few of the many exciting experiments which involve atoms being rearranged to make new substances.

333 Very Berry Litmus Paper

Here is your chance to make your own litmus paper to test for acids and alkalis, called bases. It's done with berries and it's very berry easy!

½ cup of berries (blackberries, blueberries, or strawberries)
small strips cut from white construction paper
small bowl
fork
water
teaspoon
paper towels

What to do: Remove any stems and place the berries in a bowl. Crush the berries with the fork until they look like jam. Add a little water to thin the juice. Dip the paper strips in the juice and spoon the juice over them until they are well coated. Slide the strips between your thumb and finger to remove the pulp. Place the strips on paper towels to dry. When they are dry, pick off any big pieces of pulp or berry skins you missed and your Very Berry litmus paper is ready for use.

What Do the Color Changes Mean?

Purple blackberry litmus turns pinkish-red in acids and deep purple in alkali compounds, or bases. These strips work best for litmus testing, for they show the most change.

Purple blueberry litmus turns reddish-purple in acids and light bluish-purple in bases.

Pink strawberry (although not as noticeable as the other two) turns bright pink in acids and light pinkish-blue in bases.

Thoroughly confused? Not to worry! We can tell you how to remember this easily: the paper that has more red in it is reacting to acids, while the paper that has more blue in it is reacting to bases.

334 Litmus Lotto

Why: Vinegar is acetic acid but soapy water is an alkali compound, or base. The berry-colored litmus papers are positive tests to determine which substances are acids or bases.

Note: Keep containers, litmus paper, pencil, and paper for the next experiment.

Are you ready to test your homemade Very Berry litmus paper? By dipping the paper into different solutions, you can find out if the substance is acid or alkali (a substance that can dissolve in water and weaken acids). When we test how much acid or alkali a substance has, we say we are testing for the pH of that substance.

YOU WILL NEED:

2 homemade Very Berry litmus strips
2 small containers, one with a lid
3 tablespoons of dishwashing liquid
½ cup of water
¼ cup of vinegar
paper and pencil
newspaper

What to do: First read "What do the color changes mean?" before continuing. Put the water and dishwashing liquid into the container with a lid, close it up and shake to mix well. Put the vinegar into the other container. Dip strips of litmus paper into the solutions. Hypothesize, or guess, if the color change will show whether that solution is acid or alkali. Write down the name of the solution (dishwashing liquid and vinegar), and record your answers. Now dry the strips of litmus on the paper towels (about five minutes) and label them as to what solutions they were dipped into and what color changes were noticed. Was your hypothesis, or guess, correct?

What happens: The litmus dipped into the vinegar has more red in it. The litmus dipped into the soapy water has more blue in it.

335 More Litmus Lotto

Are you ready to do some more testing with litmus paper? Basically, you'll be doing the same thing as you did in "Litmus Lotto" but with different substances.

YOU WILL NEED:

2 homemade Very Berry litmus strips
½ cup of water, with 2 or 3 squirts of window cleaner with ammonia (Be careful! This solution can be harmful! Dispose of it carefully when finished!)
¼ cup of lemon juice

What to do: Dip the litmus strips and record your guesses and the results of the test as you did under "Litmus Lotto."

What happens: The litmus that was dipped into the lemon juice will have more red in it, but the one that was dipped into the window-cleaner ammonia will show more blue.

Why: Lemon juice is another acid, called citric acid, but the ammonia solution is an alkali compound. Can you guess what other fruits may have citric acid, and test your hypothesis?

336

pH Power

Use your Very Berry litmus paper again to test your tap water, soil, swimming pool or pond water, even your saliva (spit)!

What to do: Dip the strips of litmus paper into the samples. (See "What to do" under "Litmus Lotto.")

What happens: The strips will change color depending on whether the samples are more acid or alkali.

Why: The litmus papers are positive tests for the acids or bases in substances. (See "What do the color changes mean?")

337 Starch Search

How do you know if certain substances contain starch? Starch, a substance found in plants, gives us energy (sugars and fats do, too!). Chemists are especially interested in starch because it is a compound made up of carbon, hydrogen, and oxygen. This experiment will help us find out if a solution has starch.

What to do: Spoon the cornstarch into the bottle of water. Add the drops of iodine to the water. Swirl the contents around and then let the solution "rest" for a few minutes.

What happens: The water turns dark blue or purple.

Why: Iodine is a good test for starch. It combines chemically with starch, in this case cornstarch, to produce the dark blue color. Chemists regularly use iodine for this purpose.

Look up iodine on the Periodic Table of Elements chart. What does it tell you about the iodine atom?

Note: Iodine is a poisonous chemical. Get adult help, if needed, and dispose of this chemical experiment carefully when finished! Wash thoroughly any utensils you wish to keep!

Plant Power

Plants don't eat. They make their own food from the energy of the sun (a process called photosynthesis). They change water and carbon dioxide into glucose, a kind of sugar, and oxygen. The sugar is then turned into starch. Both the sugar and the starch help plants live.

338   The Great Oxygen Escape

If you can add an atom, can you subtract one—or release an element from a compound? Watch carefully! Oxygen will actually escape before your very own eyes in this electric and thrilling experiment.

YOU WILL NEED:

small amount of rust (scraped from old iron object)

1 tablespoon of hydrogen peroxide

small bottle or jar (to hold hydrogen peroxide)

small, deep container or bowl filled with hot tap water (to submerge small bottle)

modelling clay

magnifying glass

What to do: Stick a small piece of modelling clay on the bottom of the bottle. (This will anchor the bottle down and keep it steady under the water.) Put the hydrogen peroxide into the bottle and then drop in the iron rust. Lower the container into the bowl of hot water and press it against the bottom. Watch the bottle closely through the magnifying hand lens.

What happens: Many small bubbles come from the bottle of hydrogen peroxide.

Why: A molecule of hydrogen peroxide (H_2O_2) contains one more atom of oxygen than a molecule of water (H_2O). When you drop the iron rust into the peroxide and place the container into the hot water, a chemical change takes place. The bubbles you see in the peroxide solution are really groupings of those "extra" oxygen atoms being released from the hydrogen peroxide compound.

Flour Power

YOU WILL NEED:

slice of rye bread
paper
pencil

Chemists know proteins as chemical compounds. Protein called gluten is found in grains, especially wheat. Now let's see how we can put the gluten in bread to work as a chemical.

What to do: With the pencil, scribble two or three dark areas on the paper. Tear off a piece of rye bread and rub it hard across the dark scribbled areas.

What happens: The bread works like an eraser and cleans the paper.

Why: The gluten protein in the rye bread is sticky. When you rub the bread across the dark pencilled areas, you lift the marks from the paper using the sticky protein.

340 Rye Clean

You know now why scientists use gluten in substances to clean things. But what things? The sticky protein in bread will erase pencil marks, but will it remove other spots? Soil your fingers with dirt, oil, or jam. Rub your fingers on the paper to make soiled areas on it. Now test how well the rye bread cleans these.

Color Me Gone

What happens to tea when you put lemon into it?

What to do: Squeeze a little of the first piece of lemon into the tea. Continue to increase the amount of lemon in the tea until all of the quarters are fully squeezed and used up.

What happens: The lemon causes the color of the tea to completely fade.

Why: The citric acid in lemon is a bleaching agent that reacts chemically with the dye in the tea to lighten it.

Detergent Derby

How do laundry detergents work?

What to do: Add the detergent to one of the jars. Screw the lid on, shake the jar, and remove the lid. The other jar will contain only plain water. Now drop three or four pieces of string into each jar and watch what happens to the strings.

What happens: The strings in the jar of plain water float on the surface, while the strings in the detergent water soon sink to the bottom.

Why: The strings that dropped to the bottom of the glass of detergent water had become water-soaked. The water and detergent mixture is an emulsion, or liquids floating in one another. This emulsion caused the strings to get wetter faster. The simple idea of using detergent as a "wetting agent" helps to remove dirt from clothes.

Keep materials for the next experiment, "Clean as a Whistle."

343 Clean as a Whistle

Now let's really challenge agent detergent, using newly soiled strings.

YOU WILL NEED:

jars with water and detergent-water solution from last experiment

more short strings

substances to soil strings: like grease, oil, dirt, jam, and juice

spoon

What to do: Soil pairs of strings in juice, grease, dirt, oil, ketchup, mustard, or whatever you have, and drop one of each pair into each jar or glass. Stir the contents of each container. After ten minutes, remove the strings from the jars.

What happens: The strings in the detergent-water solution appear cleaner, while the strings in the glass of plain water do not.

Why: Again, the emulsifying effect of the detergent in the water thoroughly soaks the strings and easily lifts the dirt from them. This is seen by the now discolored water in the detergent-water solution.

344 Take it to the Cleaners

Chemists are always working with new chemicals and trying to find out which ones clean best. Some everyday foods found around the kitchen make good cleaners, too, but which ones?

YOU WILL NEED:

piece of white cotton cloth

margarine, oil, or butter (to stain cloth)

paper towels
¼ lemon
¼ onion
vinegar
½ cup of whole milk
marking pen

What to do: With the margarine, oil, or butter, make several grease marks, or stains, on the cloth. Make certain they are not too close together. Take the cloth and spread it out on a hard kitchen surface. Squeeze some lemon juice onto a paper towel and, while holding the cloth against the hard surface, rub the juice on the towel against one of the marks. Rub hard and try to remove the stain. Crush the onion in another paper towel to make some juice and try to remove a second stain with it in the same way. Do the same with the other two substances. Make certain you record on the cloth which substances you used to clean the different grease stains.

What happens: The lemon, onion, and vinegar remove stains a little, but not as well as the milk does.

Why: The milk does a better job of neutralizing, or canceling out, the stains. This is a case of "Like will dissolve like." The butterfat in whole milk will dissolve grease stains such as that caused by fat in butter or margarine. Substances that have similar fat content will dissolve one another.

345 Put Out the Fire

YOU WILL NEED:

large, wide-mouth jar with lid

2 cups of water

3 tablespoons of baking soda

½ cup of vinegar

large nail

hammer

spoon

small jar

Make your own fire extinguisher with a few materials you can find around your house.

What to do: First, on a rock outside or on an old workbench or board, turn the lid of the large jar over, and with the hammer and nail pound a large hole through it. (Get adult help, if needed!)

Pour the water into the large jar. Add and mix in the baking soda. Fill the small jar with vinegar and gently place it, without a lid, into the large jar, making certain that the vinegar jar does not spill its contents. Screw the punctured lid onto the large jar. Turn the lid away from your face and tip the jar towards the sink.

What happens: A foamy liquid spurts out of the hole in the lid.

Why: Baking soda (sodium bicarbonate) puts out fires when used in soda-acid fire extinguishers. In your homemade version, the vinegar (acetic acid) mixes with the baking soda to produce the carbon-dioxide gas (CO_2) that smothers fires.

346 Eggs-tra Bounce: What Did You Eggs-pect?

Can an egg be changed chemically by placing it in different compounds?

YOU WILL NEED:

2 whole raw eggs (in shell)

glass of water

glass of vinegar

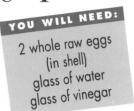

What to do: Put one egg in a glass of water and let it stand for a full 24 hours. Place the other egg in the vinegar and let it stand for the same length of time.

What happens: The egg in the water remains the same, while the egg in the vinegar compound now feels and looks like a rubber ball, and no longer has a shell! If you drop it a short distance into the sink, it will actually bounce. Now you know how this experiment got its name.

Why: In the vinegar, a chemical change took place in the egg. The acetic acid (vinegar) reacted with the calcium carbonate of the eggshell. The change caused the shell to soften and disappear, while the egg in the glass of water did not chemically change. Chemists would say that the shell of the egg in the vinegar becomes "decalcified."

No Bones about It!

347

Can you make chicken bones soft and even bend them? Try this experiment and see.

What to do: Place the vinegar in the jar and put the clean bones in it. Make certain the bones are completely covered by the vinegar. Leave the bones to set for two days.

What happens: The chicken bones are no longer hard, but soft.

Why: Bones are chiefly made up of the minerals calcium and phosphorus. When you soak the chicken bones in vinegar (acetic acid), a chemical change takes place and the mineral (stiffening) matter in them dissolves.

Water Softener

348

How would you like to make your own bath solution? This solution will make your water softer, and soft water makes more suds to clean you better. It's fun and easy, and it's real chemistry.

What to do: Pour some of the washing soda into the saucer. With the back of the spoon, crush the crystals of washing soda into a fine powder. Spoon the washing soda powder into the jar of water a little at a time until no more will dissolve. (If needed, crush more washing soda powder and add it to the jar of water.) You now have a "saturated solution." Store the solution in the jar and add a small amount to the water when you take your bath.

What happens: The washing soda dissolves in the water and creates a natural bathwater softener.

Why: Sodium carbonate, or washing soda, neutralizes, or softens, water by removing hard bath salts, such as calcium. When this happens, chemists call it precipitation, but unlike weather forecasters, they don't mean rain, the soft water that falls from the sky. Here, precipitation is the chemical splitting of the two compounds calcium salts and washing soda into simpler molecules which form a solid substance called a precipitate. (See also "Presto-Perfect Precipitate")

349 Designer Bath Solution

Add special cologne, scents, or other ingredients, such as coloring, to make your solution look and smell good. Put your special bath softener in fancy-shaped bottles or jars, and tie on some colorful ribbons. It makes a great and inexpensive homemade gift, and a little simple chemistry makes it all possible!

350 Shiny Silver Coins

HOT!

Why not make your own silver cleaner? It's cheaper and may be better than cleaner from the store.

YOU WILL NEED:
small container with water
1 teaspoon of baking soda
1 teaspoon of salt
aluminum foil
small enamel or glass pot
silver coins
water
use of stove
soft cloth

What to do: In the small container, dissolve the salt and soda in a small amount of water. Place the coins in the water so that it covers them. Fill the small glass or enamel pot with water. Tear the aluminum foil into pieces and add them to the pot. Bring the water in the pot to a boil on the stove (you may want to ask a parent to assist you), then turn off the heat and let the water stand and cool. Remove the coins from the salt and soda solution. Rinse the coins in the cooled aluminum water, and dry them with a soft cloth.

What happpens: You are now the proud owner of many shiny, sparkling-clean coins.

Why: Chemical reactions take place among the salt and soda (loosens tarnish) and the aluminum-foil solution. The heat turns the water and aluminum foil into an electrolyte solution, which carries a mild electric current that takes the tarnish off the coins.

Oxidation: Rust Race

When one substance gives oxygen to another, chemists say it is "reduced," and the substance that receives the oxygen is said to be "oxidized." Confused? Think of it this way: You have ten balls that stand for oxygen and a friend takes seven of them. Your friend would be oxidized, because he received extra oxygen from you, but you would be reduced because you lost some of your oxygen. Now you can produce this chemical change, oxidation, and see how it works.

What to do: Place a selection of metal objects into the various jars. Add two tablespoons of one of the liquids to each jar. Screw lids tightly on some jars; leave the other jars without lids. Place some of your experiments in shady, cool places, others in warm, sunny places. Set the experiments aside for one to three weeks. Keep good records: dates and times you started the experiments, substances used, and what happens.

What happens: A reddish-brown or brownish-yellow substance forms on some of the metal objets, but maybe not on all.

Why: Moisture, an oxidizing agent, causes oxygen from the air to attach to certain metals, like iron and steel, to form rust. This chemical change, called oxidation, corrodes, or rots, metals. That is why bridges and fire escapes, which often get wet, must be painted to protect them from being rotted and weakened by oxidation.

352

Why Rust?

In the last experiment did some objects rust while others didn't? Try to figure out why. Perhaps the oxidation takes a longer time, or the object is protected by a coating of non-rusting material. Redo the experiments exactly, or change one of the variables, and see what happens then. Compare the results.

Copperhead

353

Can you see whose head is on the penny or other dark, copper coins? If they are very dark and dull, it may be hard to tell. But it only takes a few minutes and a little simple chemistry to turn that dirty, dull copper into bright, shiny coins.

What to do: Place the coins in the container. In one cup, make a solution with the salt and water. Pour the vinegar into the other cup. With the medicine dropper, drop the salt solution on the pennies, followed by the vinegar. Repeat these steps and keep the pennies in the solution for five minutes. Clean the pennies by wiping them off with a damp paper towel.

What happens: The pennies turn shiny-bright and the dark and dull film is removed.

Why: The vinegar (acetic acid) when combined with the salt (sodium chloride) chemically changes into a weak solution of hydrochloric acid. Hydrochloric acid cleans metals like copper. After a while, the pennies will oxidize, or become dull and dark, again because of the water and oxygen molecules that they come in contact with in the air.

The Gas Guzzler

YOU WILL NEED:

piece of coffee filter, about 4 inches (10 cm) square

3 teaspoons of baking soda (sodium bicarbonate)

shallow bowl of water

rubber band

tall, narrow jar filled with water

permanent marker pen

magnifying glass

A car is called a gas guzzler when it wastes gas. In this experiment, gas wastes water. Try it and see!

What to do: Place the baking soda in the middle of the square of the filter. Gather the filter together to make a pouch and fasten the top with a rubber band. Place the baking soda pouch in the tall jar of water and place your hand over the opening. With your hands in place on the bottom and the top of the jar, turn the jar upside down and place its opening in the bowl of water. Remove your hands. Mark the water line on the jar. Watch the glass jar with the hand lens. Be patient; you must wait at least an hour for results.

Why: As the baking soda in the pouch is dissolved by the water, it produces carbon dioxide gas (CO_2). This gas needs room in the jar, so it displaces the water, or forces some of it out of the jar, lowering the water level.

What happens: Bubbles rise from the pouch in the bottom of the jar to the top of it. Some bubbles cling to the sides of the jar. Within an hour, the water drops slightly, but noticeably, below the marked water line.

355 King Kong's Hand

YOU WILL NEED:

disposable latex glove
(available in packages of ten)
¼ cup of baking soda
½ cup of vinegar
brown or black
permanent marker pen
(optional)

King Kong's hand must have been very big to hold a lady in it. Now, you can make your own big hand with just a few simple materials. Without the marker lines, the hand becomes a cow's udder, the bag under the cow that holds its milk—an udderly fantastic trick! Anyway you look at it, it's pure chemistry and it will teach you about an important gas that all chemists know.

What to do: A friend or assistant would be helpful for this experiment, and it's best done over a sink or basin (or outside) as it can be messy!

For a King Kong hand, make short vertical lines with the marker pen on each side of the glove to represent King Kong's hairy hand. If you're making a cow's udder, leave the glove plain.

Have your helper hold the glove over the sink or basin while you pour the baking soda, followed by the vinegar, into the glove. Now, very quickly, close the opening of the glove with your hand to make an airtight seal. Hold it tightly for several minutes.

What happens: The glove blows up like a balloon, then after several minutes goes back to its normal size.

Why: When you mixed the baking soda and vinegar together, you made a very popular gas called carbon dioxide (CO_2). This is why the solution started to fizz and foam up and spill out over the top of the glove before you closed it up. Once the gas is trapped in the glove, it has no place to go, so it blows the glove up. Eventually, the reaction grows less, the gas succeeds in escaping, and the glove returns to its normal size.

What a Gas

Baking soda (sodium bicarbonate) is a compound made up of the elements hydrogen, sodium, oxygen, and carbon. When vinegar is added (water and acetic acid), a chemical reaction takes place; the elements carbon and oxygen link together to make a new gaseous compound called carbon dioxide.

Exothermic Exercise

YOU WILL NEED:

thermometer
small bowl
1 tablespoon of
quick-rising dry yeast
¼ cup of hydrogen peroxide
spoon
pencil and paper

What kind of chemical change takes place when yeast mixes with hydrogen peroxide? This extremely exciting experiment is bound to warm you up.

What to do: Record the temperature showing on the thermometer, and then place it in the bowl. Pour in the hydrogen peroxide, add the yeast, and stir the solution. As you watch what happens, feel the lower sides and bottom of the bowl. Wait a minute or two; then spoon out the thermometer and record the temperature again.

What happens: The solution foams up and bubbles, and the bottom and sides of the bowl feel very warm. Steam can be seen coming from the solution. The higher thermometer reading shows that heat has been produced.

Why: When yeast and hydrogen peroxide mix chemically, the hydrogen peroxide changes into oxygen and water molecules. The bubbles are produced by the oxygen gas escaping during the chemical change. This change also produces heat. When heat is produced in a chemical change, we call the process exothermic.

Endothermic Cold Wave

YOU WILL NEED:

thermometer
1 tablespoon of Epsom salts
tap water, neither hot nor cold
spoon
medium-size jar
pencil and paper

If a chemical change can cause heat (exothermic), can another chemical change make something cold?

Caution: Epsom salts can be a harmful solution. Dispose of it carefully after use.

What to do: Fill the jar with tap water. Place the thermometer in the water. With your hand, feel the coolness of the jar while you wait until the thermometer registers the water's temperature. Write the temperature down. Now stir in the Epsom salts. Feel the jar again. Is there a change? After a couple of minutes, take out the thermometer and record the temperature again.

What happens: The jar feels slightly colder, and the temperature of the water after the chemical change is actually lower.

Why: In the previous experiment "Exothermic Exercise," a chemical change produced heat energy. But sometimes heat is instead used up in the chemical change. When Epsom salts, or magnesium sulfate, is added to water, it uses the water's natural heat energy to split apart ions of sulfate and magnesium. (Ions are positive or negative electrically charged atoms that occur when electrons are lost or gained.)

The chemical change in this experiment is called endothermic because more heat energy is being used up than is being produced. This is why the water gets colder, and why Epsom salts are used to soak a sprained ankle and draw the heat out of an injury.

358

It's Simply Marbelous!

YOU WILL NEED:

*colored chalk
*half sheets of white paper
*2 to 6 disposable cups

hammer or heavy stone
(for crushing chalk)

2 tablespoons of vinegar
paper towels or napkins

disposable plastic
spoon or fork

large bowl or basin
(plastic or rubber is best)

newspaper
water
cooking oil

*Quantities depend on how
many colors and how much
colored paper you want.

Wrap small presents up in your homemade marbly-colored gift wrap. When dried, this paper is like parchment, a crisp, crinkly, see-through kind of paper. It's crispy, it's streaky, it's simply marbelous!

What to do: Place some newspaper over the kitchen counter. Fill the bowl to the top with water and add two tablespoons of vinegar. Place the bowl in the middle of the newspaper. Lay extra newspaper down to hold drying papers. Place doubled paper towels down and add a small piece of different-colored chalk. Crush the chalk to a fine powder.

Carefully lifting the towels, pour the colored powdered chalk into as many disposable cups as you need colors. Place a tablespoon of oil into each cup, stirring thoroughly with the plastic fork or spoon. Pour the contents of each cup into the bowl of water. The chalky colored oil should form large colored circular pools on the surface of the water. Now, carefully lay each piece of paper on the surface of the water and lift away.

Dry the colored papers on newspaper over the next 24 hours. When they are fully dried, carefully wipe off any surface chalk grains with a paper towel.

What happens: The colored oil sticks to the paper and makes circles and streaky patterns.

Why: Negative- and positive-charged molecules are attracted to one another. The molecules of chalk (a type of calcium carbonate) and vinegar (acetic acid) and water and the surface of the paper all chemically combine to cause a chemical bond which causes the swirling colors to stick to the paper.

Presto-Perfect Precipitate

I bet you can't say that fast ten times! You can, though, make a preipitate in just seconds. If you remember, a precipitate is a substance that forms when a chemical reaction or change occurs. This substance, also, is insoluble. That means it does not dissolve or evenly mix as does a substance in a solution.

What to do: Dissolve the Epsom salts in the jar and add a few squirts of window cleaner.

What happens: The solution becomes milky white.

Why: When magnesium sulfate (Epsom salts) is mixed with ammonium hydroxide (ammonia solution), it forms a new chemical compound. The milky white liquid formed is a precipitate of magnesium hydroxide.

A New Precipitate

Repeat the Presto-Perfect Precipitate experiment, but this time use alum (found in the spice section of the supermarket) instead of the Epsom salts. You'll make a new precipitate called aluminum hydroxide. Compare the color change of the magnesium hydroxide with that of the aluminum hydroxide.

SALTY SOLUTIONS AND SWEET SUCCESS

Without salt and sugar, life would be very dull. Most important, we could not live without a proper balance of sugar and salt in our bodies. Now, we'll find out just what these chemical compounds are all about and what they can do.

Salt and Sugar

Salt ($NaCl$) is a mineral compound, which in this case means it is a combination of two elements and is a crystal substance. Each salt crystal is made up of millions of atoms that fasten on to one another. Salt is made up of the elements sodium and chlorine (a compound). Sodium is a metal solid and chlorine is a greenish gas. By themselves, these two chemicals are extremely dangerous but when they are combined into a compound, they become common table salt.

Sugar is a carbohydrate, or a chemical compound made up of carbon, hydrogen, and oxygen. Common table sugar is called sucrose. Other sugars are glucose, fructose, lactose, and maltose.

The Sugar Cube Race

YOU WILL NEED:

sugar cubes
clear glass of cold tap water
clear glass of very hot tap water
spoon
paper and pencil

Will more sugar cubes dissolve, or disappear, in cold water than in hot or warm tap water? Let's have a race and find out.

What to do: Put a cube of sugar in the cold water and stir until its crystals disappear, or dissolve, completely. Continue to put cubes of sugar into the water one at a time—count them—until no more sugar will dissolve. You'll know when this happens, because the crystal grains of sugar will begin to show in the solution and will start to gather on the bottom of the glass.

Now, repeat this activity using hot water. Make certain you count the number of cubes that dissolve in each glass of water. Record, or write, the number for each. Which can hold the most dissolved sugar cubes?

What happens: Fewer cubes should dissolve thoroughly in the cold tap water than in the hot.

Why: The first sugar cubes dissolve in each glass of water until no more sugar crystals can be seen. Then, as more cubes are added, the solutions reach a point where the crystals can no longer disappear and they can easily be seen. Scientists and chemists call this a saturated solution. More sugar dissolves in the hot water than in the cold because, when water is heated, its molecules move faster and farther apart. As a result, the spaces between the water molecules become larger, allowing room for more sugar molecules.

Sweet and Slow

362

Which dissolves faster, a whole sugar cube or a crushed one?

YOU WILL NEED:

2 sugar cubes
small disposable container
hammer or rock
(to crush one cube)
2 glasses half–filled with water

What to do: Crush one of the cubes in the container. Leave the other sugar cube whole, as is. Place each in its separate glass of water at the same time.

What happens: The crushed sugar cube dissolves faster.

Why: The water molecules must dissolve all of the outside parts of the solid sugar cube before they can reach and dissolve the inside. This takes longer. Because the water molecules come in contact with more outside surfaces when the sugar cube is crushed, the rate of solubility (or how fast a substance dissolves) is quicker.

Sweet Talk

YOU WILL NEED:
unsalted soda cracker

363

Our bodies are complicated chemical factories, as this simple experiment shows.

What to do: Chew the soda cracker slowly for a few minutes.

What happens: The cracker tastes sweet.

Why: Your saliva has a substance in it called an enzyme. The enzyme styalin breaks down starch or other carbohydrate molecules to a simple sugar called maltose. When you chew the cracker, the starch in it is changed to sugar, so it tastes sweet.

Carbohydrates

The organic compounds called carbohydrates are found in such foods as sugar, bread, potatoes, and crackers. They are made up of carbon, hydrogen, and oxygen atoms.

364 Sweet Tooth

Want to see how fast a tooth dissolves in a cola drink?

Don't pull out a tooth for this experiment, and don't use Grandma's dentures! But if you happen to have an extra tooth lying around the house, try it!

What to do: Place the tooth in the cola beverage. Leave it in the drink for at least a week.

What happens: The tooth starts to dissolve.

Why: Now you know why your parents and dentists warn you about drinking too many sugary drinks with a high acid content. Even though your teeth wouldn't be constantly sitting in a cola drink, the high sugar and acid content of these drinks can chemically affect your teeth over time. In this experiment, the sugar and acid eventually cause the tooth to dissolve, even right through its hard enamel surface coating.

Watercooler

365

Which is colder, regular ice water or salted ice water?

What to do: Mark each cup with the pen "Salt," "No salt." Place a thermometer in each cup. Pack the ice cubes around the thermometers, five cubes to each cup. Pour the salt over and between the ice cubes in one cup. Wait about 30 minutes for results. Read the temperature on each thermometer and write it down.

What happens: The temperature in the cup with the salted ice water is colder.

Why: Water freezes at 32 degrees Fahrenheit, or 0 degrees centigrade. In the unsalted water, the temperature is usually above freezing, while the salted water is much below. The salt draws heat from the ice and makes it much colder while lowering the freezing point on the thermometer.

What now: Do this same experiment again but this time substitute crushed ice for ice cubes. Does crushed ice make the water colder? Write down the temperature reading in each experiment and compare the differences if any.

INDEX

A

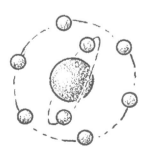

B

C

D

E

F

Fahrenheit, Gabriel, 246
Fat, 54
Faults, 142
Fibers, 57, 119
Finger lifting, 100
Finger tapping, 107
Fire extinguisher, 291
Fissures, 148
Foehn, 224
Force(s)
    of air, 66, 79, 103-104
    centrifugal, 64
    doing work, 62, 65, 66, 95,
        100-102
    gravity, 64, 83, 89, 180-
        183
    magnetism, 180, 183-188
    See also Air, pressure;
        Earthquakes; Erosion
Fossil fuels, 189-190, 191,
    196
Foucault, Jean Bernard Leon,
    211
Foucault's pendulum, 211
Fourdriniers, 24
Freezing point, 60, 305
Friction, 23, 80, 91, 96,
    157

Front, 225
Fruit, 38, 46
    See also Lemons
Fulcrum, 22
Funnel, 135

G

Galileo, 67, 246
Galvanometer, 42-43
Gases, 41, 73, 160, 202, 279-
    280
Geology, 141-151

    dissolving chalk and shells,
        149-150
    facts about, 141
    glacier, 150-151
    and pressure, 142-145,
        149, 151
    seismograph, 143
    types of faults, 142
    volcano, 148
    wave, 145
Germination, 166
Gift wrap, 300
Glacier, 150-151
Glasses, 102, 109, 138
Gluten, 288
Gnomon, 153, 154
Gravel, 171
Gravity
    definition of, 89
    facts, 180
    and inertia, 83, 86, 183
    scale, 181
    tricks using, 83, 86, 182-
        183, 195
    See also Center of gravity
Greenhouse effect, 169, 190-
    192, 216
Growth experiments, 45-46,
    164-169

H

I

J

K

L

Light bulb, 55
Lightning, 29, 241-242, 243
Limestone, 41, 149-150
Litmus paper, 39, 260, 284-286
Loam, 171

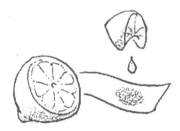

M

Magma, 148
Magnetic polar force, 180, 185-186, 188
Magnetism, 183-188
   compass, 184-186
   experiments, 31, 187-188
   facts, 180
Magnification, 56, 57, 124
Mantle, 141, 144
Matchbox, 85
Matter, 261-267
   atoms, 261, 262, 266

and chemists, 269
compounds, 261
elements, 263-265
isomers, 267
molecules, 261, 268-269
properties of, 270
states of, 261, 268, 270
Mechanical advantage, 101-102
Mendeleyev, Dmitri Ivanovich, 263
Metamorphic rocks, 149
Meteorologists, 245
Meteors, 157
Methane, 196
Milk, 47, 48
Miscible substance, 275
Mistral, 224
Mixtures, 273
Moebius strip, 32
Molds, 46
Molecules, 105, 125-126, 261-262, 268-270, 281, 283,300
Moraine, 151
Moseley, Henry, 269
Motion
   of earth, 153
   facts about, 95
   and gravity, 95-102
   and heat, 125-126
   laws of, 183
   of molecules, 125
Music, 20, 21, 109

N

Natural changes, 270
Neutrons, 263
Newspaper, 27
Newton, Sir Isaac, 180, 183
North Pole, 207
North Star (Polaris), 156, 214
Nuclei, of atom, 202, 263

O

Oboe, 20
Oil, 47, 53-56, 73, 120, 196, 275, 290, 300
Orbits, 158, 263, 266
Organic chemistry, 269
Oxidation, 294-295

Q

Quicksand, 174

R

Radiant energy, 203
Rain, 236
    gauge, 258
    See also Acid rain;
        Precipitation
Rainbows, 78, 122, 144, 160,
    244
Recycling, 189-190, 198
Red cabbage indicator, 39
Reduction, 294
Reflection, 56, 78, 121, 123,
    146, 203-204
Refraction. *See* Light, bending
    of rays
Relative humidity, 253-255
Resistance, 23
Respiration, 162
Robert, Nicholas, 24
Rock candy, 59
Rocket, 45

Rock(s)
    composition of, 149
    limestone, 41, 149
    metamorphic, 149
    and pressure, 141-142,
        144-145, 148-149
Rotation, of earth, 153, 155,
    209-211
Rust, 220, 294-295

S

Safety rules, 261
Salt, 59-60, 271, 273-275, 303,
    305
Saturated solution, 303
Scales, 22, 69, 115, 181
Scheele, Karl, 269
Sea breeze, 224

Seasons, 161, 206, 214-215
Sedimentary rocks, 41
Sedimentation, 172
Seeds, 45, 166
Seismograph, 143
Shadows, 153-154, 208-209
Shapes, 25
Shells, electron, 263
Simoons, 224
Siphon, 194-195
Slope wind, 224
Smog, 239
Snow, 204
Soap, 71-73, 85, 282
    bubbles, 73-80
    facts about, 70
    and surface tension, 71-73,
        112, 115
    See also Detergent
Soda, 44
Sodium carbonate, 282
Soil
    box, 179
    composition of, 173
    erosion, 178-179
    facts about, 170-171
    permeability, 175
    quicksand, 174
    sedimentation, 172
    types of, 170-172, 174
Solar collector, 194
Solubility, 304
Solutes, 272, 274, 278

T

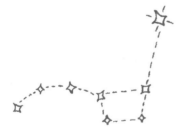

Y